UNDERSTANDING ORGANIZATIONAL COMMUNICATION

UNDERSTANDING ORGANIZATIONAL COMMUNICATION

Cases, Commentaries, and Conversations

PAMELA SHOCKLEY-ZALABAK

University of Colorado

Longman
New York & London

**Understanding Organizational
Communication: Cases, Commentaries,
and Conversations**

Longman, 10 Bank Street, White Plains, N.Y. 10606

Associated companies:
Longman Group Ltd., London
Longman Cheshire Pty., Melbourne
Longman Paul Pty., Auckland
Copp Clark Pitman, Toronto

Acquisitions editor: Kathleen Schurawich
Production editor: Linda Moser
Cover design: David Levy
Production supervisor: Anne Armeny

Library of Congress Cataloging-in-Publication Data

Shockley-Zalabak, Pamela.
    Understanding organizational communcation : cases, commentaries,
and conversations / Pamela Shockley-Zalabak.
        p.   cm.
    Includes index.
    ISBN 0-8013-0786-4
    1. Communication in organizations—Case studies. 2. Organization—
Case studies. I. Title.
    HD30.3.S552 1993
    302.2—dc20   93-9687
                                                          CIP

1 2 3 4 5 6 7 8 9 10-MA-9796959493

In memory of Tren Anderson
and my father, Jim Shockley,
and for Charles
and my mother, Leatha Shockley

Contents

Preface   *xiii*

Cross-Reference Guide   *xvii*

Case, Commentary, Conversation Guide   *xxvii*

**PART I: PERSPECTIVES FOR ORGANIZATIONAL
COMMUNICATION**   **1**

Commentary   1

Approaches to Organizational Communication   1
*The Construction of Shared Realities: Communicating and
Organizing 2, The Mechanistic Approach 3, The Human
Relations Approach 4, The Systems-Interaction Approach 5,
The Interpretive-Symbolic-Culture Approach 6, Emerging
Perspectives 6, Cases and Conversations 7*
References   8

**CHAPTER 1 UNDERSTANDING ORGANIZATIONAL
COMMUNICATION   9**

Granite City: Doing More with Less   *9*
The Acquisition of Abbott Hospital   *11*

Illinois Power and "60 Minutes": Communicating About the
    Communications   *Kim B Walker*   *21*
Organizational Communication: Italian Style   *31*
Jean Douglas—The Former Quality Assurance Manager   *34*

CHAPTER 2 **CULTURE AND COMMUNICATION**   **37**

Drake Computer Corporation—A Lesson in Designing an
    Organizational Culture   *37*
IBM and Apple: Contrasting Cultures Working Together   *40*
To Manage, Value, or Do What with Diversity?   *42*
Managing Cultural Diversity   *45*
Culture Shock: The Russian Entrepreneurial Revolution   *46*

CONVERSATIONS   **51**

Minorities in the Work Force: How Satisfied?
    Adelina M. Gomez   *51*
Moving toward the Year 2000—An Italian Perspective
    Ruggero Cesaria   *54*
Describing Our Changing Culture   *60*
Singapore: Impressions of Cultural Climate in a Distance Learning
    Program   *Barbara McCain*   *63*
Getting Beyond Monologues: A Cross-Cultural Meeting of
    Organizational Consultants   *Gaynelle Winograd*   *65*
Through Their Eyes: Russian Reflections on the U.S. Organizational
    Development Community   *Tantiana Kramtchenkova and Sergei
    Lebedev, with Gaynelle Winograd, English Editor*   *75*

PART II: ORGANIZATIONAL COMMUNICATION PROCESSES
    AND BEHAVIORS   81

Commentary   81

Leading, Managing, and Participating: Changing Organizational
    Imperatives   81
*New Leadership Imperatives 82, Managers in Transition 84,
    Changing Imperatives for Participants 85, The Ethic of
    Personal Advantage 86*

References   87

CHAPTER 3   **INDIVIDUALS IN ORGANIZATIONS**   89

My Style Is My Style: Like It or Leave Me Alone   *89*
The Coronado YERS Case   *93*
Ron Arnold's Job Crisis   *97*
Karen Rhodes—On Becoming a Manager   *98*
Managing Your Manager   *100*
My Japanese Counterparts   *101*

CHAPTER 4   **GROUPS AND PROBLEM-SOLVING
            COMMUNICATION   105**

Carson Products' Management Team Disaster   *105*
The R & D Lab: Teams Making "Go" or "No Go" Decisions   *108*
Decisions, No Decisions, More Decisions   *109*
The Wisdom of "The People"   *LaDonna Harris   113*
The Power of Empowerment: A Case History of Organizational
   Communications   *Larry Koperski, Linda Hertz, Jim Jost, and
   Arnie Berger   120*
Managing the Self-Managing Team   *133*

CHAPTER 5   **LEADERSHIP AND MANAGEMENT   135**

Mark Waite's Disappointed Staff   *135*
Dora Cartwright's Leadership Dilemma   *136*
Organizational Problems at a Community Nonprofit
   Organization   *Barbara McCain   138*
Managing at Dillard Electronics   *141*
Leadership: Margaret Thatcher, the Iron Lady   *148*
Leadership Takes on a Nonmanagement Look   *150*

CHAPTER 6   **CONFLICT AND COMMUNICATION   155**

Change Is Ruining Our Company   *155*
Severance Pay   *157*
The Revolution at Intex   *158*
The "What Do You Mean We Have to Retrain?" Case   *160*
The "Too Little, Too Late" Case   *163*
The "Don't Rock the Boat Around Here" Case   *165*

CHAPTER 7   VALUES, ETHICS, AND ORGANIZATIONAL COMMUNICATION   169

Lea Pearlman's Ethical Dilemma   *169*
U.S. Senator Williams and the Austin Manpower Administration   *173*
Can This Ethical Manager Survive, or Should She?   *176*
Fast-Track Executive   *179*
The "We Intended No Harm" Case   *181*
The "Do My Values Fit?" Case   *182*

CONVERSATIONS   185

Living and Learning: A Professor Goes Abroad
  Michael Hackman   *185*
There Is Life After Management   *187*
Fired for Bending the Rules   *189*
Entering the Profession: An Attorney Begins Her
  Career   *Evelyn Hernandez Sullivan*   *191*

PART III: ORGANIZATIONAL CHANGE, INNOVATION, AND EFFECTIVENESS   195

Commentary   195

Organizing, Innovating, and Communicating: Challenges and
  Changes   195
*Organizational Design 198, Technological Change 199,
  Jobs and Careers 200, Training 200, Organizational
  Communication 201*
References   202

CHAPTER 8   COMMUNICATION AND TECHNOLOGY   203

Tandem Industries: Managing by Electronic Adhocracy   *203*
The "Better Technology, More Complaints" Case   *205*
The "It Works So Well, Why Are We Falling Apart?" Case   *207*
The Fiber Management Team   *210*
Science Is Not All That Objective: The Mitchell Laboratories Case   *214*

CHAPTER 9 **CREATIVITY, EFFECTIVENESS, AND COMMUNICATION   217**

The National Aerospace Propulsion Agency Reorganization   *217*
The Individual Contributor   *220*
Overload or Innovation   *224*
Reengineering—A New Organization for Hockaday   *228*
Joint Organizational Development Visions and Ventures: Russian and
    U.S. Collaboration   *Gaynelle Winograd   234*

CHAPTER 10 **ORGANIZATIONAL COMMUNICATION IN THE TWENTY-FIRST CENTURY   243**

The Educational Revolution   *243*
Organizing and Communicating: Changing Processes   *245*
The New Communications Literacy   *247*
The New Organizational Control: Knowledge Masters   *248*
Individuals and Organizations in the Twenty-first Century: Changing
    Roles and Relationships   *251*

CONVERSATIONS   255

The Industrial Edge Lies in Telecommunications   *Neil
    Johnson   255*
The Educational Edge Lies in Telecommunications   *Shelly
    Weinstein   256*
Emergent Issues in Organizational Communication   *Gary L.
    Kreps   258*

Appendix—Researching and Reporting Case Studies   261

Bibliography   265

Index   279

Preface

We are in one of the most turbulent periods in human history—not a profound statement but real nevertheless. As we approach the twenty-first century our world is more complex, and the knowledge we bring to bear on our problems often adds to confusion and disagreement. We are in transition from an information to a knowledge age with rapid change in the institutions and organizations with which we are most familiar. We have unprecedented opportunities and unprecedented problems. And most of us seek a firm direction that is outmoded in the waning days of the twentieth century. We are unfamiliar with the concept of anticipatory direction; we have learned too well directions borne of past experiences. We need new thinking, new criticisms, new knowledge, new approaches, and new understandings.

This book was written to help readers experience organizational challenges within the context of learning about communication and organizations. Through cases, commentaries, and conversations, readers are encouraged to link theory to analysis and practice and to link individual action and organizational action. All of the cases represent real organizational situations; however, several companies and individuals have requested anonymity. Finally, the book is intended to raise many old questions—not because they have not been previously asked and answered, but because the answers are changing and need to change. We must learn to make new choices and provide new answers because the boundaries of knowledge have changed.

Part I, **Perspectives for Organizational Communication,** presents theoretical and context issues important for understanding organizations and organizational communication. Part II, **Organizational Communication Processes and Behaviors**, links individual and organizational actions. Part III, **Organizational Change, Innovation, and Effectiveness**, explores organizational challenges in the present and future.

PART I

This section includes an overview commentary to help us explore primary theories or concepts for understanding the processes of organizing and communicating. It also considers a variety of organizational environments and explores how organizing and communicating respond to perceived environmental uncertainty. The ten cases focus on macro-organizational issues and concepts of culture, which include work force diversity, organizational culture, and multinational issues. The conversations include responses from U.S. minorities, Russian and Italian professionals, workers experiencing organizational culture changes, and a professor teaching in Singapore.

PART II

The second section discusses leading, managing, and participating as changing organizational imperatives. The 30 cases focus on individuals in organizations, groups and problem-solving processes, leadership and management issues, conflict, and relationships of values and ethics to organizational communication. LaDonna Harris, president of Americans for Indian Opportunity, and members of a Hewlett-Packard project team provide special contributions. Conversations feature the experiences of a professor teaching in New Zealand, a person who has been fired for ethical abuses, and an individual leaving management after many years.

PART III

The final section identifies organizational communication challenges relating to technology, creativity, effectiveness, and organizational communication in the twenty-first century. Fifteen cases explore communication and technology relationships, describe communication issues for organizational creativity and effectiveness, and speculate about organizational communication in the next century. Of special importance is the description of a joint consulting venture between U.S. and Russian consultants, a pre- and post-August 1991 cooperation. The conversations that conclude the book feature an interview granted by the president of EdSat Institute and the comments of industry and academic leaders speculating about future issues for organizational communication.

This book is about rapid, dynamic change. It is about you and me as we communicate with each other and attempt to make sense of our lives and the organizations around us. It is about organizations—the inevitability of change, the need for change, and the turbulence of our times. This book is about humans innovating, communicating, and organizing. It is about understanding, experiencing, and planning for our organizational futures. This is not a book for passive reflection. This book challenges our assumptions and stimulates critical thinking.

ACKNOWLEDGMENTS

Acknowledgments are meant to thank those who assisted with and contributed to any creative effort. For me, however, this book has a special meaning. My first editor at Longman, Tren Anderson, died the month I began writing this book. He wanted me to develop it, he guided its initial formation, and, for his inspiration and support, I shall always be grateful.

I want to thank the many contributors to this effort—the individuals, organizations, friends, and colleagues—who have guided my thinking. In particular, I am indebted to students and clients who have taught me about the imperative for organizational change, a fundamental responsibility for communication professionals. I am also grateful to the following individuals who reviewed the manuscript and provided helpful suggestions:

Steven Corman, Arizona State University

Howard Greenbaum, Hofstra University

Gary Kreps, Northern Illinois University

Paul Krivonos, California State University, Northridge

Kathleen Krone, Ohio State University

Michael Mayer, Arizona State University

Michael Papa, Ohio University

Marshall Scott Poole, University of Minnesota

Robert Rosenthal, Suffolk University

W. Robert Sampson, University of Wisconsin, Eau Claire

On a personal note—words are not adequate. My husband, Charles, has served as research assistant, sounding board, friend, and advisor for this work. His love, support, and encouragement make all the difference.

I dedicate this book to students, clients, and my family (Charles, Jim, and Leatha Shockley; Yvonne; and my four-legged companions Dody and Buffy).

Cross-Reference Guide

The cross-reference guide categorizes cases, commentaries, and conversations into a variety of topical areas. The guide is useful for identifying material related to a specific topic and for comparing and contrasting a variety of issues and settings for each topic. Topics are listed in the left-hand column with cases, commentaries, and conversations (including page numbers) referenced in the right-hand column.

Topic	*Case/Commentary/Conversation*
Auditing (organizational, communication)	Managing at Dillard Electronics (141)
	Lea Pearlman's Ethical Dilemma (169)
Careers	Jean Douglas—The Former Quality Assurance Manager (34)
	Minorities in the Work Force: How Satisfied? (51)
	Leading, Managing, and Participating: Changing Organizational Imperatives (81)
	Ron Arnold's Job Crisis (97)
	The "What Do You Mean We Have to Retrain?" Case (160)
	Fast-Track Executive (179)
	The "Do My Values Fit?" Case (182)
	There Is Life After Management (187)
	Fired for Bending the Rules (189)
	Entering the Profession: An Attorney Begins Her Career (191)

Organizing, Innovating, and Communicating: Challenges and Changes (195)

The Individual Contributor (220)

Change

Granite City: Doing More with Less (9)

The Acquisition of Abbott Hospital (12)

Jean Douglas—The Former Quality Assurance Manager (34)

Leading, Managing, and Participating: Changing Organizational Imperatives (81)

Organizational Problems at a Community Nonprofit Organization (138)

Managing at Dillard Electronics (141)

Change Is Ruining Our Company (155)

The Revolution at Intex (158)

The "What Do You Mean We Have to Retrain?" Case (160)

The "We Intend No Harm" Case (181)

The "Don't Rock the Boat Around Here" Case (165)

Organizing, Innovating, and Communicating: Challenges and Changes (195)

Tandem Industries: Managing by Electronic Adhocracy (203)

The "It Works So Well, Why Are We Falling Apart?" Case (207)

Science Is Not All That Objective: The Mitchell Laboratories Case (214)

The National Aerospace Propulsion Agency Reorganization (217)

Overload or Innovation (224)

Reengineering—A New Organization for Hockaday (228)

Organizing and Communicating: Changing Processes (245)

Individuals and Organizations in the Twenty-first Century: Changing Roles and Relationships (251)

Communication perspectives, theory

Approaches to Organizational Communication (1)

Emergent Issues in Organizational Communication (258)

Communications literacy

The Educational Revolution (243)

The New Communications Literacy (247)

The Educational Edge Lies in Telecommunications (256)

Conflict

My Style Is My Style: Like It or Leave Me Alone (89)

The Coronado YERS Case (93)

Karen Rhodes—On Becoming a Manager (98)

Mark Waite's Disappointed Staff (135)

Organizational Problems at a Community Nonprofit Organization (138)

Change Is Ruining Our Company (155)

Severance Pay (157)

The Revolution at Intex (158)

The "What Do You Mean We Have to Retrain?" Case (160)

The "Too Little, Too Late" Case (163)

The "Don't Rock the Boat Around Here" Case (165)

Lea Pearlman's Ethical Dilemma (169)

Can This Ethical Manager Survive, or Should She? (176)

Consulting

Organizational Communication: Italian Style (31)

Getting Beyond Monologues: A Cross-Cultural Meeting of Organizational Consultants (65)

Through Their Eyes: Russian Reflections on the U.S. Organizational Development Community (75)

The Coronado YERS Case (93)

Managing at Dillard Electronics (141)

Lea Pearlman's Ethical Dilemma (169)

Joint Organizational Development Visions and Ventures: Russian and U.S. Collaboration (234)

Cross-cultural issues

Organizational Communication: Italian Style (31)

Minorities in the Work Force: How Satisfied? (51)

Singapore: Impressions of Cultural Climate in a Distance Learning Program (63)

Getting Beyond Monologues: A Cross-Cultural Meeting of Organizational Consultants (65)

My Japanese Counterparts (101)

Through Their Eyes: Russian Reflections on the U.S. Organizational Development Community (75)

Living and Learning: A Professor Goes Abroad (185)

Organizing, Innovating, and Communicating: Challenges and Changes (195)

Joint Organizational Development Visions and Ventures: Russian and U.S. Collaboration (234)

Cultural diversity   To Manage, Value, or Do What with Diversity? (42)

Managing Cultural Diversity (45)

Minorities in the Work Force: How Satisfied? (51)

My Japanese Counterparts (101)

The Wisdom of "The People" (113)

Customer satisfaction   The "Better Technology, More Complaints" Case (205)

Decision making   Granite City: Doing More with Less (9)

Carson Products' Management Team Disaster (105)

The R & D Lab: Teams Making "Go" or "No Go" Decisions (108)

Decisions, No Decisions, More Decisions (109)

The Wisdom of "The People" (113)

Leadership Takes on a Nonmanagement Look (150)

Organizing, Innovating, and Communicating: Challenges and Changes (195)

Downsizing   Jean Douglas—The Former Quality Assurance Manager (34)

Leading, Managing, and Participating: Changing Organizational Imperatives (81)

Change Is Ruining Our Company (155)

Effectiveness (creativity)

The Power of Empowerment: A Case History of Organizational Communications (120)

Organizing, Innovating, and Communicating: Challenges and Changes (195)

The National Aerospace Propulsion Agency Reorganization (217)

The Individual Contributor (220)

Overload or Innovation (224)

Reengineering—A New Organization for Hockaday (228)

Entrepreneurial culture

Culture Shock: The Russian Entrepreneurial Revolution (46)

Ethics

The Acquisition of Abbott Hospital (12)

Leading, Managing, and Participating: Changing Organizational Imperatives (81)

The Coronado YERS Case (93)

Lea Pearlman's Ethical Dilemma (169)

U.S. Senator Williams and the Austin Manpower Administration (173)

Can This Ethical Manager Survive, or Should She? (176)

Fast-Track Executive (179)

The "We Intended No Harm" Case (181)

The "Do My Values Fit?" Case (182)

Fired for Bending the Rules (189)

Future

Organizing, Innovating, and Communicating: Challenges and Changes (195)

The Educational Revolution (243)

Organizing and Communicating: Changing Processes (245)

The New Communications Literacy (247)

The New Organizational Control: Knowledge Masters (248)

Individuals and Organizations in the Twenty-first Century: Changing Roles and Relationships (251)

The Industrial Edge Lies in Telecommunications (255)

The Educational Edge Lies in Telecommunications (256)

Emergent Issues in Organizational Communication (258)

Group processes

Leading, Managing, and Participating: Changing Organizational Imperatives (81)

Decisions, No Decisions, More Decisions (109)

The Wisdom of "The People" (113)

The Power of Empowerment: A Case History of Organizational Communications (120)

Managing the Self-Managing Team (133)

Leadership Takes on a Nonmanagement Look (150)

Guides

Cross-Reference Guide (xvii)

Case/Commentary/Conversation Guide (xxvii)

Researching and Reporting Case Studies (261)

Bibliography (265)

Innovation

Organizing, Innovating, and Communicating: Challenges and Changes (195)

The "It Works So Well, Why Are We Falling Apart?" Case (207)

The Fiber Management Team (210)

Overload or Innovation (224)

Reengineering—A New Organization for Hockaday (228)

Joint Organizational Development Visions and Ventures: Russian and U.S. Collaboration (234)

International business

Organizational Communication: Italian Style (31)

Culture Shock: The Russian Entrepreneurial Revolution (46)

Moving toward the Year 2000—An Italian Perspective (54)

My Japanese Counterparts (101)

Living and Learning: A Professor Goes Abroad (185)

Organizing, Innovating, and Communicating: Challenges and Changes (195)

Joint Organizational Development Visions and Ventures: Russian and U.S. Collaboration (234)

Italy

Organizational Communication: Italian Style (31)

Moving toward the Year 2000—An Italian Perspective (54)

Getting Beyond Monologues: A Cross-Cultural Meeting of Organizational Consultants (65)

Joint ventures

IBM and Apple: Contrasting Cultures Working Together (40)

Through Their Eyes: Russian Reflections on the U.S. Organizational Development Community (75)

Joint Organizational Development Visions and Ventures: Russian and U.S. Collaboration (234)

Leadership

The Acquisition of Abbott Hospital (12)

Leading, Managing, and Participating: Changing Organizational Imperatives (81)

Ron Arnold's Job Crisis (97)

Karen Rhodes—On Becoming a Manager (98)

Carson Products' Management Team Disaster (105)

Mark Waite's Disappointed Staff (135)

Dora Cartwright's Leadership Dilemma (136)

Organizational Problems at a Community Nonprofit Organization (138)

Managing at Dillard Electronics (141)

Leadership: Margaret Thatcher, The Iron Lady (148)

The Revolution at Intex (158)

The "Too Little, Too Late" Case (163)

Can This Ethical Manager Survive, or Should She? (176)

There Is Life After Management (187)

Management (see Leadership)

Media relations   Illinois Power/"60 Minutes": Communi-
                                cating About the Communications (21)

                                U.S. Senator Williams and the Austin
                                Manpower Administration (173)

Mergers   The Acquisition of Abbott Hospital (12)

Motivation   Drake Computer Corporation—A Lesson
                                in Designing An Organizational Culture (37)

                                Change Is Ruining Our Company (155)

New Zealand   Living and Learning: A Professor
                                Goes Abroad (185)

Organizational culture   Organizational Communication: Italian
                                Style (31)

                                Jean Douglas—The Former Quality
                                Assurance Manager (34)

                                Drake Computer Corporation—A Lesson
                                in Designing An Organizational Culture
                                (37)

                                IBM and Apple: Contrasting Cultures
                                Working Together (40)

                                Moving toward the Year 2000—an Italian
                                Perspective (54)

                                Describing Our Changing Culture (60)

                                My Japanese Counterparts (101)

                                Managing at Dillard Electronics (141)

Organizational structures   Leading, Managing, and Participating:
(design)   Changing Organizational Imperatives (81)

                                The Power of Empowerment: A Case
                                History of Organizational Communica-
                                tions (120)

                                Managing the Self-Managing Team (131)

                                Organizing, Innovating, and Communi-
                                cating: Challenges and Changes (195)

                                The "It Works So Well, Why Are We
                                Falling Apart?" Case (207)

                                The National Aerospace Propulsion
                                Agency Reorganization (217)

                                Reengineering—A New Organization for
                                Hockaday (228)

                                The New Organizational Control:
                                Knowledge Masters (248)

Organizational perspectives, theory | Approaches to Organizational Communication (1)

Personnel decisions | Mark Waite's Disappointed Staff (135)
Science Is Not All That Objective: The Mitchell Laboratories Case (214)

Power | Managing Your Manager (100)
Can This Ethical Manager Survive, or Should She? (176)
Organizing, Innovating, and Communicating: Challenges and Changes (195)

Problem solving (see Decision making)

Project management | The R & D Lab: Teams Making "Go" or "No Go" Decisions (108)
Decisions, No Decisions, More Decisions (109)

Public administration | Granite City: Doing More with Less (9)
The Coronado YERS Case (93)

Public figures | Dora Cartwright's Leadership Dilemma (136)
Severance Pay (157)
U.S. Senator Williams and the Austin Manpower Administration (173)

Public relations | Illinois Power and "60 Minutes": Communicating About the Communications (21)

Russia | Culture Shock: The Russian Entrepreneurial Revolution (46)
Getting Beyond Monologues: A Cross-Cultural Meeting of Organizational Consultants (65)
Through Their Eyes: Russian Reflections on the U.S. Organization Development Community (75)
Joint Organizational Development Visions and Ventures: Russian and U.S. Collaboration (234)

Singapore | Singapore: Impressions of Cultural Climate in a Distance Learning Program (63)

Strategic planning | Carson Products' Management Team Disaster (105)
The Wisdom of "The People" (113)

Styles

My Style Is My Style: Like It or Leave Me Alone (89)

Karen Rhodes—On Becoming a Manager (98)

Managing Your Manager (100)

My Japanese Counterparts (101)

Leadership: Margaret Thatcher, the Iron Lady (148)

Technology

Organizing, Innovating, and Communicating: Challenges and Changes (195)

Tandem Industries: Managing by Electronic Adhocracy (203)

The "Better Technology, More Complaints" Case (205)

The "It Works So Well, Why Are We Falling Apart?" Case (207)

The Fiber Management Team (210)

Science Is Not All That Objective: The Mitchell Laboratories Case (214)

The New Communications Literacy (247)

Individuals and Organizations in the Twenty-first Century: Changing Roles and Relationships (251)

Training

Organizational Communication: Italian Style (31)

To Manage, Value, or Do What with Diversity? (42)

The "What Do You Mean We Have to Retrain?" Case (160)

Organizing, Innovating, and Communicating: Challenges and Changes (195)

Reengineering—A New Organization for Hockaday (228)

Values (see Ethics)

Video literacy

The Fiber Management Team (210)

The New Communications Literacy (247)

The Educational Edge Lies in Telecommunications (256)

Case, Commentary, Conversation Guide

Each of the three parts of *Understanding Organizational Communication* contains commentaries, cases, and conversations grouped to reflect the general issues and topics covered in each section. Commentaries introduce each of the three parts and are intended to raise theoretical and practical concerns illustrated in the cases and conversations that follow. Commentaries provide frameworks for analyzing cases and conversations and can be utilized in conjunction with the annotated bibliography and other sources to expand our understanding of relationships between theory and practice.

Cases in each part have been selected to reflect a variety of issues and ranges of complexity. Fifty-five cases have been developed from real organizational situations and eight of these cases are followed by "What Happened Next?" descriptions of events occurring after case conclusions. Discussion questions are provided with each case.

The conversations that follow the cases are interviews with individuals experiencing the issues being covered. Conversations are with unknown individuals and experts. They are most often reported in interview format and were developed from verbatim transcripts. They are intended to help us understand how people describe their experiences and advise others based on their organizational learning. Discussion questions follow most conversations.

Cases and conversations can be read and studied in any order. The Cross-Reference Guide helps readers select cases appropriate to subject matters of interest.

The commentaries, cases, and conversations deliberately leave unanswered questions and require readers to make assumptions and ask questions. They are designed to provide analysis opportunities that link theory to practice and guide our thinking about organizational communication. Cases are presented to encourage active learning while engaging critical thinking and problem-solving capabilities. The Appendix provides guidance for the development of case studies. It also can be useful in developing analysis frameworks for existing cases and conversations.

UNDERSTANDING ORGANIZATIONAL COMMUNICATION

Perspectives for Organizational Communication

Commentary

APPROACHES TO ORGANIZATIONAL COMMUNICATION

Embedded in any discussion of organizational communication perspectives are important notions of what we mean by communication, how we conceive of organizations, and how the processes of organizing and communicating relate to a variety of organizational environments. Part I helps us explore four primary theories or concepts for understanding organizing and communicating: the mechanistic approach, the human relations approach, the systems-interaction approach, and the interpretive-symbolic-culture approach. In addition, Part I asks us to consider a variety of organizational environments and how organizing and communicating respond to perceived environmental uncertainty. We will examine the notion of internal and external cultures as well as organizing and communicating from a cross-cultural and international perspective. The following commentary briefly reviews basic concepts of communicating and organizing and describes major and emerging perspectives for under-standing organizational communication. It is in no way intended as a comprehensive review of the field but is provided as a beginning for examination of our changing organizational environments.

The Construction of Shared Realities: Communicating and Organizing

Human communication is the process of constructing shared realities—creating shared meanings. It is our attempt to have others understand our world as we do and to assign meaning to the world of those around us. The process is culturally and contextually influenced, and, as such, is dynamic and ever-changing. Of particular interest, of course, is the issue of communication in organizations and how it influences organizational processes and events.

The term *organization* is applied to the results of the process of organizing. Organizing is an attempt to bring order out of chaos or establish organizations—entities where purposeful and ordered activity takes place. Organizing is accomplished through purposeful activities generated as a result of communication behaviors. In other words, the process we call organizing is accomplished through human communication as individuals seek to bring order out of chaos and establish entities for purposeful activities.

Organizations have been described as social units or groupings of people deliberately constructed and reconstructed to strive for specific goals. As such, they are characterized by divisions of labor for goal achievement. These efforts also are directed by relatively continuous patterns of authority and leadership. Interdependence exists both among organizational components and with the external environment. This complex interdependence requires coordination achieved through communication.

Organizations can be characterized as dynamic systems in which individuals engage in collective efforts for goal accomplishment. To remain dynamic, they must adapt to continually changing environments—both internally and externally. From this perspective of adaptation and change, organizations can be understood as active and dynamic mergers of human behaviors and technological operations. As such, they can be understood by looking at their structure and by studying how they continually create and change what they do. This occurs through communication behaviors. Put another way, understanding what an organization is and how it works requires an understanding of the process of organizational communication.

Organizational communication is both similar to and distinct from other types of communication. It has sources and receivers who are engaged in encoding and decoding messages. Messages are transmitted over channels distorted by noise. As with other forms of communication, organizational communication is related to the competencies of individuals, their fields of experience, the communicative context, and the effects or results of interactions. Yet it is more than the daily interactions of individuals within organizations. It is the process through which organizations create and shape events (Shockley-Zalabak, 1991).

Organizational communication is best understood as an ongoing process without distinct beginnings and endings. The process includes patterns of interactions that develop among organizational members and the way these interactions shape organizations. The process can be described as evolutionary and culturally dependent because it is ever-changing. In other words, the ongoing process of creating and transmitting organizational messages reflects the shared realities that result from previous message exchanges and evolves to generate new realities that create and shape events.

Individuals bring to organizations sets of characteristics that influence how information is processed. Organizational communication contributes to the creation of relationships and assists both individuals and organizations in achieving diverse purposes. It occurs between and among people who share both work and interpersonal relationships.

Organizational communication is also the creation and exchange of messages. It is the movement or transmission of verbal and nonverbal behaviors and the sharing of information throughout the organization. Communicators are linked together by channels, and messages are described with terms such as frequency, amount, and type. Concern is expressed for message fidelity, or the extent to which messages are similar or accurate at all links through the channels.

Finally, organizational communication is organizing, decision making, planning, controlling, and coordinating. It is people, messages, and meaning. It is the process through which individuals and organizations attempt goal-oriented behavior in dealing with their environments. As such, organizational communication can be understood as a combination of process, people, messages, meaning, and purpose.

The Mechanistic Approach

Sometimes referred to as classical theory, the mechanistic approach to communicating and organizing is based on the analogy of the well-tooled machine operating with quality precision. "The key organizational activities, according to this analogy, are planning, design, and maintenance of organizational structures and activities. The mechanistic model of organization stresses order, machinelike regularity, and rationality in organizational processes'' (Kreps, 1990, p. 63). The mechanistic approach asks questions about how organizations should be designed, how workers can be trained for maximum efficiency, how the chain of command works, and how division of labor should be determined.

Communication from the mechanistic approach is designed to facilitate task completion. Communication activities are specialized, as are tasks and jobs. Communication trains workers and gives daily instructions concerning job requirements. It is formal, and interpersonal communication of a social or personal nature is generally discouraged, especially among peers.

Based on the work of Fisher (1978), Krone, Jablin, and Putnam (1987) suggest four assumptions that provide the basis of the mechanistic approach to organizational communication: quasi-causality, transitivity of communication functions, conceptual materialism, and reductionism. Specifically,

> A mechanistic perspective views communication as a transmission process in which messages travel across a channel from one point to another. From this perspective, communication is best under-stood . . . [as] (1) the channel or vehicle for transmitting messages; (2) a linear, causal, and chainlike relationship between parts of the processes; (3) the effects of the source on the receiver; (4) the concrete or physical nature of messages; and (5) the role of noise and gatekeeping in preventing communication breakdowns and in achieving message fidelity. (p. 23)

The Human Relations Approach

The human relations approach shifts the emphasis from the structure of organizations, work design, and measurement to the interactions of individuals, their motivations, and influence on organizational events. The human relations approach assumes that work is accomplished through people and emphasizes cooperation, participation, satisfaction, and interpersonal skills. This viewpoint depicts organizational design and function as reflections of basic assumptions about human behavior.

Communication is a cornerstone of the human relations approach. Management is charged to trust employees, and employees are encouraged to discuss job-related concerns with their supervisors. Peer-group interaction is recognized and viewed as potentially positive for productivity. Formal and informal communication networks carry task and social support messages. Interactions at all levels are expected to be extensive with substantial support throughout the organization. Communication is important for use of human resources and effective organizational decision making.

Krone, Jablin, and Putnam (1987) refer to tenets of the human relations approach as the psychological perspective. They suggest,

> The psychological perspective locates communication in the conceptual filters that encode and decode information and stimuli from the environment. The materialism, transmission effects, and emphasis on channels that characterized the mechanistic view are subjugated to internal cognitive processes of senders and receivers. Components like encoding-decoding, barriers, gatekeeping, and noise stem from psychological processes in interpreting message stimuli rather than message transmission effects. Barriers and gatekeeping become forms of selective exposure rather than obstacles in the transmission process. . . . In summary, the psychological perspective of organizational communication concentrates on explaining the informational environments in which individuals are located and the range of stimuli to which they respond using a variety of conceptual filters. (p. 25)

The Systems-Interaction Approach

Both the mechanistic and human relations approaches have been criticized for their failure to integrate organizational structure, technology, and people with the larger environments in which organizations exist. The systems-interaction approach attempts to explore how people, technologies, and environments integrate to influence goal-directed behavior. Process and environmental approaches to organizational theory attempt to describe how complex processes, such as decision making, influence the internal operation of organizations and are influenced by external environments. Questions are asked about how human and technical systems interact with the broader environments in which organizations exist.

According to Kreps (1990),

> General systems theory represents the organization as a complex set of interdependent parts that interact to adapt to a constantly changing environment in order to achieve its goals. Some of the key components that make up organizations are individual organization members, structural and functional groups . . . and

organizational technologies and equipment. All the system parts are dependent on one another in the performance of organizational activities. Any change in or influence on one component inevitably affects other system components. (p. 94)

Sequences of communication behavior are part of the evolving system. The systems-interaction perspective emphasizes a communication system in continual adaptation to changing circumstances.

The Interpretive-Symbolic-Culture Approach

Interpretive-symbolic-culture approaches to organizational theory and communication describe how organizational members collectively interpret the organizational world around them in order to define the importance of organizational happenings. They explain organizational behavior in terms of the influence of cultures that exist both internally and externally to the organization. Questions are asked about how a unique sense of the place (interpretive, symbolic, culture descriptions) contributes to individual behavior and organizational functioning.

Krone, Jablin, and Putnam (1987) suggest that

The interpretive-symbolic perspective focuses on role-taking and shared meanings as forming organizations. Thus patterns of coordinated activities create, maintain, and dissolve organizations. Individuals respond to others based on role-taking and shared meanings for words and actions. These meanings are derived symbolically through the mutuality of experience and through negotiating consensual interpretations of organizational events and activities. Organizational culture develops from and in turn shapes consensual meanings, thus culture is what an organization is rather than what it has. (p. 29)

Emerging Perspectives

The growing number of multinational and multicultural organizations give emphasis to new questions, problems, and challenges. Issues arise for multinationals as to cultural differences in values, motives, and communication processes. Similar concerns apply to single-country organizations, which find their work forces increasingly diversified by ethnic, racial, age, and gender factors. The emerging challenges for communicating and organizing are based on understanding the interrelationships among cultural differences, communication behaviors, and organizational relationships. Much of our current thinking has been devoted to understanding emergence and maintenance of shared realities, that is, shared cultures. Emerging perspectives will focus on the fundamental need to reduce communication distortions based at least in part on dissimilar realities and complex cultural differences.

Evolving perspectives for communicating and organizing will increasingly describe organizational dependence on internal and external environments. Environments have come to be recognized as complex pools of scarce and vital resources, with organizations described as entities that adapt themselves in terms of behaviors and structures to acquire needed resources (Euske and Roberts, 1987). Organizational uncertainty and interdependence, therefore, become crucial to understanding organizational events and processes such as mergers, joint ventures, leveraged buyouts, international competition, ethics scandals, and internal and external cultural issues. As power distributions change, organizational communication processes routinely will extend beyond traditional organizational, national, political, and cultural boundaries.

Some argue that potent external influences (i.e., Russia in August 1991) determine organizational structures and processes, whereas others suggest that interactions between internal and external influences best predict organizational functioning. Regardless, questions arise concerning information load, complexity, and turbulence and how each contributes to perceived environmental uncertainty (Huber and Daft, 1987). And, from a communication perspective, it is uncertainty that becomes our challenge and opportunity. Certainty, although never a concrete observable, may come to mean the shared reality of only a fleeting point in time. Uncertainty will be the more common condition, and is, therefore, our future. Organizational communication processes will deal with uncertainty reduction and the strategic generation of uncertainty. Organizing and decision making will become more fluid processes and subject to more rapid change. In sum, we will be seeking new answers to old problems, and asking new questions to better inform our organizational futures.

Cases and Conversations

The cases and conversations in Part I provide an opportunity to examine organizing and communicating from traditional perspectives and to address emerging issues. You will examine change in organizations regulated by public constituencies and explore the agenda-setting functions of media to report organizational decisions, processes, and events. You will be exposed to international organizational communication issues and have the opportunity to consider the impact of work force diversity for a variety of organizational processes.

You will be asked to analyze, apply theory, extend theory, and examine reasonable alternatives for each case. Hopefully you will be stimulated to think about your role in the organizations of today and tomorrow. And hopefully you will be challenged to actively engage in generating new and improved approaches for organizing and communicating.

REFERENCES

Euske, N. A., and K. H. Roberts. 1987. Evolving perspectives in organization theory: Communication implications. In *Handbook of organizational communication,* eds. F. Jablin, L. Putnam, K. Roberts, and L. Porter, 41–69. Newbury Park, Calif.: Sage.

Fisher, B. A. 1978. *Perspectives on human communication.* New York: Macmillan.

Huber, G. P., and R. L. Daft. 1987. The information environments of organizations. In *Handbook of organizational communication,* eds. F. Jablin, L. Putnam, K. Roberts, and L. Porter, 130–164. Newbury Park, Calif.: Sage.

Kreps, G. 1990. *Organizational communication.* White Plains, N.Y.: Longman.

Krone, K. J., J. M. Jablin, and L. L. Putnam. 1987. Communication theory and organizational communication: Multiple perspectives. In *Handbook of organizational communication,* eds. F. Jablin, L. Putnam, K. Roberts, and L. Porter, 18–40. Newbury Park, Calif.: Sage.

Shockley-Zalabak, P. 1991. *Fundamentals of organizational communication: Knowledge, sensitivity, skills, values.* White Plains, N.Y.: Longman.

Understanding Organizational Communication

Granite City: Doing More with Less

It was not the typical morning after a general election in the office of Roger Peytons, the city manager. The results of the November elections in Granite City had been expected to bring new council members and possibly a new mayor but no one expected an entirely new council and the tax limitation amendments. As Roger Peytons reviewed the results in the morning paper he knew that his administration was going to be called on to do more with less and to do it quickly.

Granite City, with a population of 450,000, has experienced rapid growth during most of the last decade. Only in the last three years has an industrywide slump in electronics manufacturing slowed employment and growth opportunities. During the past ten years Granite City has been a haven for developers; the city council has frequently overridden city planner recommendations for modest development in favor of more aggressive plans. Although general property taxes are low, several special property improvement districts have defaulted on bonds, which has substantially raised taxes in some portions of the city. Granite City is the lowest-cost utilities market in the nation among cities of comparable size with a utilities monopoly run by city government. Roger Peytons was surprised that the citizens of Granite City did not have a more favorable picture of their city government.

The tax limitation amendments were Roger Peytons's real challenge at the meeting of his senior staff. Amendment 3 provided for no new taxes without voter approval. He could live with that and even saw some advantage to the amendment because it provided for extensive public debate concerning needed projects and improvements. Amendment 4 was the disaster for the city budget. It mandated a tax rollback over a two-year period. The impact in the coming fiscal year would be over $12 million from an annual operating budget of $112 million. The new council had run on a platform supporting the amendments and would certainly want rapid action from the city manager's office.

As Peytons began his meeting with senior staff he sensed the despair and concern around the table. His public relations director had four calls from media asking for his response to the elections and his plan to bring city spending and programs in compliance. Peytons described the challenges he saw ahead— reductions in services and programs that would affect the public; elimination of jobs to reduce overhead; and communication with members of a new council, most of whom had strong convictions about the types of services and programs the city should provide. Senior staff members were given two weeks to prepare budget reduction proposals for all departments except uniformed services, namely police and fire. Peytons decided to postpone a news conference until he had an opportunity to meet privately with the mayor and council.

Peytons's first meeting with the mayor and council convinced him that he had a difficult job ahead. He had to persuade the council of the need for balanced cuts across the budget rather than the elimination of specific programs, which might meet with the disapproval of particular council members. Peytons was relieved when the mayor seemed to side with his plan. At the end of the meeting the council voted to accept for consideration a budget reduction plan from the city manager's office before asking for staff support to devise a council-directed plan.

At the next meeting of his senior staff, Peytons listened to proposals for budget reductions in 12 program areas, with heavy emphasis on reductions in street improvements and repair and the development of parks and recreational facilities. The program reductions would, over a two-year period, eliminate approximately 400 jobs. Senior staff seemed unwilling to go to the public for hearings on the proposed changes much less take the proposal to the council. Peytons directed public hearings to be set for two weeks from the day of the meeting. Moreover, he asked the human resources director to work with him to notify all city employees of the types of program proposals that would soon appear in the local press. Peytons also set up a meeting with the mayor to review the proposals.

The human resources director recommended that all department heads have brief information meetings with their employees. No firm decisions would be reached for several months, so the goals of the meetings were to inform employees of the magnitude of the budget program and to communicate the commitment of management to minimize the number of jobs subject to lay-offs. The human resources director told Peytons he hoped to achieve at least one-third of the reduction through normal attrition. He did suggest that some employees would have to be moved laterally to fill positions where job needs required replacements.

The mayor approved the initial proposals and the establishment of public hearings to gather reaction to the reduction plans. He advised Peytons to wait until after the public hearings to take proposals to the council at large. Press coverage would keep the council generally informed and they, of course, could attend all hearings. Peytons was somewhat uncomfortable making public plans that the remainder of the council had not reviewed. He chose to take the mayor's advice because he knew the mayor was politically astute in such matters.

The public hearings were frustrating. The 12 areas of program reduction affected citizens in all sectors of the city and met the overall budget reduction goals. Citizens who had led the fight for the tax rollback called the proposals punitive and designed to exaggerate the impact of Amendment 4. They contended a significant reduction in payroll would minimize reductions in programs. Various public constituencies supported all 12 of the proposed programs or projects.

Council members attending the public hearings became concerned about the complexity of the overall problem. In addition to members of the public who wanted specific programs and projects, council members had received letters and telephone calls from over 300 city employees voicing concerns about their jobs and the overall perception of the quality of city services.

Media stories on the city's budget problems were daily front-page news. Two companies considering Granite City for plant locations expressed concern to the chamber of commerce economic development committee; they felt the political climate was less favorable than it was at the time they had put Granite City on their short selection lists.

The city manager's office had increasing inquiries from employees about their futures with the city and morale in general seemed low. Roger Peytons decided he needed to establish a comprehensive communication plan for the internal organization and, to a lesser extent, to deal with public inquiries. He called his staff together and suggested they design a communication program to address council issues, employee concerns, public inquiries, and the media in general. Although his staff members were concerned about their capability to do so, they agreed that many of their current problems may have resulted from the lack of a comprehensive information plan prior to the election.

YOUR ASSIGNMENT

1. What, if anything, should Roger Peytons and his staff have done to prevent the problems they are facing?
2. Describe the various communication issues in the case.
3. Should the city manager have separate communication plans for employees, the council, the public, and the media?
4. What is needed in each of the plans? What communication channels would you use? How would you monitor the effectiveness of your efforts?
5. How would you advise Roger Peytons to proceed?

The Acquisition of Abbott Hospital

The Acquisition of Abbott Hospital is a two-part case describing a
12-month span when Abbott Hospital was acquired and began operation
as a satellite facility to Mt. Mercy Hospital. Both parts of the case illustrate

major organizational change issues, describe communication dynamics within the Auston, Oklahoma, community, and examine the leadership decisions of Sister Mary Theresa, longtime head of Mt. Mercy Hospital. An earlier version of this case was distributed by the Harvard Business School.

PART ONE

The Setting

In late July 1990, the *Auston Transcript* reported that Sister Mary Theresa, on behalf of Mt. Mercy Hospital, had received notification of acceptance of her offer to purchase Abbott Hospital, a 108-bed nonsectarian short-term acute general care facility located in the rapidly growing northwest portion of Auston, Oklahoma. Mt. Mercy Hospital—headed by Sister Mary Theresa and run by the Sisters of the Sacred Heart—is a 372-bed short-term acute general care facility and is Auston's dominant medical force. News of the impending acquisition of Abbott by Mt. Mercy fueled a controversy that threatened to split much of the Auston medical community. One prominent doctor accused Sister Mary Theresa of attempting to have the Holy Roman Empire control the northwest portion of town.

Auston is a city of 200,000 people located 70 miles from Oklahoma City in Oklahoma's wheat and oil production belt. The latest census lists Auston as the fastest growing city in the state. The city's labor force has a high percentage of skilled white-collar and professional employees. Auston is also the home of Adams University, which has a student body of 20,000 and a new medical school scheduled to open in late 1993. The general economy is stable, primarily due to federal facilities. A national postal training center, Anderson Air Force Base, and the Center for Solar Design inject a half-billion dollars annually into the local economy. Major electronics firms form the base of private sector employment.

The eight civilian and military hospitals in Auston have a combined bed capacity of 1,500. There are approximately 338 physicians, surgeons, dentists, and dental surgeons operating from these hospitals. The chamber of commerce and the medical community predict that this level of care will not be adequate to service Auston's population expansion at its present growth rate.

Sister Mary Theresa, Chief Administrator
of Mt. Mercy Hospital

At the center of the Abbott–Mt. Mercy controversy is Sister Mary Theresa, chief administrator of Mt. Mercy Hospital. A member of the order of the Sacred Heart nuns, she is the eldest of six children in a devoutly religious Catholic family. She entered the convent at age 17 and initially trained as a teacher. After teaching for six years, she entered nurse's training and obtained both her B.S. in nursing and a graduate degree in hospital administration. She became the administrator of Mt. Mercy Hospital 16 years ago.

During her tenure as administrator of Mt. Mercy, Sister Mary Theresa has become a controversial figure in Auston. Her supporters describe her as a strong-willed, articulate, well-organized woman who deserves credit for developing Mt. Mercy into a regional force in both medical care and basic research. Her enemies in the lay and medical communities contend that she is a cold, calculating opportunist who works only for the interests and gains of Mt. Mercy Hospital, the Sisters of the Sacred Heart, and the Catholic church. Sister Mary Theresa describes herself as a hard worker with little patience for incompetence. Both supporters and detractors agree she is persuasive, intelligent, unafraid of confrontation, and a tough competitor.

Sister Mary Theresa has spent much of the past 16 years building a solid core of well-trained, capable physicians who admit primarily to Mt. Mercy Hospital. The restrictions for full staff privileges at Mt. Mercy are stringent in comparison with other hospitals in Auston. Many doctors who have practiced elsewhere in the country feel these rules are too strict and object to spending five years on courtesy staff privileges before they may become full staff members. As a result, some choose not to admit to Mt. Mercy.

Mt. Mercy and Abbott Hospitals

Mt. Mercy Hospital was opened by the Sisters of the Sacred Heart 22 years ago. The 372-bed facility is run as a not-for-profit hospital, as are the other six institutions located throughout the country and operated by the Sisters of the Sacred Heart based in Orange, New Jersey. Sister Mary Theresa credits the not-for-profit concept with generating the revenues to finance the expansion and development of Mt. Mercy.

In 1985, Mt. Mercy Hospital retained Kenner, Kenner, and Olson of Detroit to assist the hospital board of directors in the development of a long-range plan. This long-range plan was to address itself to the projected shortage of hospital beds in Auston. Whereas much of the plan called for the renovation of the existing facility located in the center of Auston, it also provided for the acquisition of property for construction of a satellite hospital in the northwest sector of the city.

Subsequent to the completion of Mt. Mercy's long-range plan and prior to any property acquisition by Mt. Mercy, Abbott Hospital was constructed and opened. Abbott Hospital was owned by MEDICO, a professional hospital management firm located in Los Angeles and operated as a not-for-profit corporation with no sectarian affiliations. Abbott is located in northwest Auston, which is in the heart of the city's growth pattern. In 1990, of the 30 new doctors in Auston, 27 located their offices near the Abbott facility.

During Abbott's first year of operation in 1988, MEDICO lost over $2 million. Late in the year, MEDICO management fired the administrative staff at Abbott and offered Dr. John Coletti the position of chief administrator. Dr. Coletti had been with MEDICO while completing his doctorate in hospital administration. His reputation in the company was based on his experience in several difficult administrative situations. MEDICO management viewed Coletti as a strong, decisive, and self-confident administrator.

Coletti spent much of his first months at Abbott staffing departments with people he characterized as strong leaders. Coletti revised the wage and benefits program for employees in order to stabilize what had become an excessive turnover rate. Coletti liked Abbott and the city of Auston. He was extremely pleased when, within 14 months, Abbott was operating at break-even. MEDICO management consequently viewed him as one of their most successful administrators.

The Acquisition Period

Early in 1990, Sister Mary Theresa, Sister Mary Joseph, director of nursing at Mt. Mercy, and Dr. John Cassler, Mt. Mercy medical chief of staff, began reviewing the long-range plan for Mt. Mercy. Both Sister Mary Joseph and Dr. Cassler are strong supporters of Sister Mary Theresa. The three mutually agreed that a contact with MEDICO with intent to purchase Abbott might be timely after MEDICO's initial financial losses. Sister Mary Theresa felt the acquisition of Abbott was the best way to pursue the satellite hospital concept outlined in Mt. Mercy's long-range plan. Sister Mary Theresa contacted only select members of the board of directors of Mt. Mercy regarding her decision to approach MEDICO.

Sister Mary Theresa was frustrated when MEDICO management refused to answer her telephone calls. Dr. Cassler and Sister Mary Joseph received no responses either. MEDICO seemingly would not communicate directly with anyone at Mt. Mercy. Sister Theresa, once again with only informal approval of selected board members, hired McGill Associates of Chicago to act as an intermediary for discussing the purchase of Abbott with MEDICO.

In late May 1990, a McGill representative notified Sister Mary Theresa that MEDICO would entertain an offer somewhere in the vicinity of $20 million. Sister Mary Theresa and Sister Mary Joseph met with financial advisors to the Sisters of the Sacred Heart and determined that an offer of $18 million was in order. It was the verbal acceptance of the offer by MEDICO that made headlines in the *Auston Transcript* in July 1990.

Sister Mary Theresa called a board of directors meeting immediately after the *Auston Transcript* article announced the tentative agreement between Mt. Mercy and MEDICO. At the meeting she obtained unanimous approval to proceed with the necessary steps to finalize the purchase. And although some members of the Mt. Mercy board felt she was again operating autocratically, they could not fault the results of her efforts.

In order to finalize the Abbott purchase, Sister Mary Theresa began the formal application process for a certificate of public necessity. Oklahoma state law requires that transfer of ownership of an acute care facility be preceded by obtaining a State Certificate of Public Necessity for Construction or Modification of Acute Care Facilities. The procedure to obtain state consent for transfer of ownership involves formal documentation of projected benefits to the community and clients within the service area of the facility. Part of this documentation includes public testimony from hearings held in the local community and at the state level. Timing of the hearings was important to Sister Mary Theresa because the purchase agreement between Mt. Mercy and MEDICO called for an additional $96,000 per month for the months of January, February, and March 1991 if closing and transfer of ownership did not occur prior to December 31, 1990.

The Public Response

The certificate of public necessity had to be presented to the Project Review Board of the Auston Council of Governments, the Northeastern Oklahoma Health Systems Agency, and the State of Oklahoma Health Services Agency. Mt. Mercy personnel were expected to present and defend their position with regard to the Abbott purchase. Any interested parties from the community or health service field were invited to present information relevant to the proposed transfer of ownership.

On September 19, 1990, at a meeting of the Northeastern Oklahoma Health Systems Agency, the certificate of public necessity was presented to the public and affected agencies. Sister Mary Theresa had developed a purchase rationale centered around the efficiencies of cost and service from a multihospital concept.

Sister Mary Theresa began her formal statement to the group by indicating the significance of changing from a single autonomous institution to a multi-hospital system. The multihospital system was defined as a combination of distinct operating institutions under the single ownership and operation of one manage-ment unit. Sister Mary Theresa proposed that a multihospital system would achieve economies that could possibly contain or even reduce cost of patient care. She proposed that economies of scale are possible through central management and judicious consolidation of services, equipment, and personnel. She further argued that the smaller institution (Abbott) could improve care by its linkage to the larger comprehensive institution with its greater technology and scope of resources and services. And the shifting population of Auston would be better served by the branch hospital concept; Sister Mary Theresa contended that competition among local hospitals had not benefited patients. The multihospital system would still be locally operated while effecting cost containments that could not be achieved by the duplication of services necessary for single unit care facilities. Her final argument centered around the advantages of a combined medical staff and administrative services. Sister Mary Theresa submitted in writing a detailed plan of proposed economies that would substantiate Mt. Mercy claims of debt service capability through combined operating revenues of Mt. Mercy and Abbott.

Sister Mary Theresa's written statement confirmed publicly the purchase price of $18 million. An initial $2 million was available from the operating reserves of Mt. Mercy Hospital. The hospital's operating budget would assume associated expenses for acquisition estimated at $300,000. The Monroe Foundation of St. Louis had made a $2 million donation to be applied directly to the purchase price. The balance of $14 million was to be obtained through the issuance of tax-exempt bonds.

Sister Mary Theresa estimated consolidation savings during the first year of acquisition at $373,000. These savings would result from the elimination of the Abbott management contract with MEDICO, the utilization of Mt. Mercy data-processing capabilities, and the combination of maintenance contracts with Mt. Mercy's existing suppliers. Additional revenue economies were projected to exist in laboratory services, purchasing, nursing administration, admitting, and electrocardiography.

Staff of the health systems agency did not take issue with Sister Mary Theresa's rationale of the multihospital concept. Instead their line of questioning centered around determination of a purchase price. They were concerned about the lack of formal assessment of the value of Abbott Hospital. Sister Mary Joseph responded that assessors qualified to evaluate the worth of a hospital were extremely rare, and in any case, MEDICO and Mt. Mercy had mutually agreed on the price. At this point, the staff recommended approval and Sister Mary Theresa's plans had cleared their first public test.

On October 1, 1990, a meeting of the Auston County Medical Society featured extensive discussion of the proposed acquisition of Abbott by Mt. Mercy. Many local doctors went on record opposing the purchase. Among the most vocal was Dr. Martin Leeham, a powerful member of the "old guard" of the medical society. Dr. Leeham, noted for having a hot temper and being very outspoken, is considered a fine doctor and surgeon by his colleagues. He was one of the first doctors in Auston to perform legalized abortions. During the past 16 years he has not exercised his admitting privileges at Mt. Mercy Hospital, even for cases not expected to run afoul of the Catholic Code of Ethics.

Six years ago Dr. Leeham organized a group of doctors and businesspersons in the community to approach the city council with a certificate of public necessity to build a 200-bed hospital in the northwest section of Auston. The hospital was to be doctor-owned and administered with no religious affiliation. Sister Mary Theresa and her board were very vocal in their opposition to such a plan and attended all public hearings to voice their objections. The plan for the doctor-owned hospital was defeated and left Dr. Leeham with a bitter attitude toward Sister Mary Theresa.

The morning following the county medical society meeting, the *Auston Transcript* carried excerpts of Dr. Leeham's remarks charging Mt. Mercy and Sister Mary Theresa with an attempt by the Holy Roman Empire to take over the northwest section of town. Upon reading the account, Sister Mary Theresa is credited with smiling and saying, "Oh, good, then I'll be the Holy Roman Empress."

The second public hearing for approval of the certificate of public necessity was scheduled for October 10, 1990, with the project review board of the Auston Council of Governments. Publicity from the county medical society meeting had aroused broad community interest. The Catholic Code of Ethics and the subject of legalized abortions and sterilizations received widespread press coverage.

Legalized abortions and sterilizations constituted 25 percent of the surgical revenues at Abbott. The Catholic Code of Ethics prohibits abortions or sterilizations in hospitals under Catholic ownership and operation. Opponents of the acquisition claimed that many of the new doctors locating their offices near Abbott intended to utilize the surgical facility at Abbott for abortions and sterilizations.

Sister Mary Theresa expected the project review board meeting to be emotional with strong opposition to approval of the certificate. During the meeting she refused to answer any questions relating to a description of the

Catholic Code of Ethics. She stated the code would be operational at Abbott and consistently confined her comments to advantages from the multihospital concept and cost economies. The public opposition from the lay and medical community was not well-organized and failed to mount any significant counterarguments. The project review board voted to approve the certificate of public necessity, thus clearing the way for a final hearing to be held in Oklahoma City with the State Department of Health Facilities Advisory Council of the Oklahoma Health Systems Agency.

The final public hearing was scheduled for December 5, 1990, just days short of the purchase penalty deadline. Sister Mary Theresa felt pressure to obtain immediate approval from the Oklahoma Health Systems Agency in order to avoid activating the price escalation clause. A delay through the holidays could cost Mt. Mercy $96,000 on January 1, 1991.

Sister Mary Theresa, Dr. John Cassler, Sister Mary Joseph, and Dwight Morris, attorney for Mt. Mercy, attended the meeting. Unlike the previous hearings, Mt. Mercy representatives expected the state staff of the health facilities advisory council to be well prepared. Sister Mary Theresa repeated her basic remarks about the multihospital concept. The health facilities advisory council staff immediately challenged the validity of her projected economies and raised the issue of closing emergency room services at Abbott. Sister Mary Theresa countered with a flat refusal to consider closing emergency room services without a thorough needs analysis. She supported her figures by asking council staff to specifically indicate areas of possible error in her projections. The council attorney, Jim Redden, launched into a lengthy statement about the power and influence of Mt. Mercy. He questioned community willingness to allow further expansion of that influence. He cited newspaper publicity following the county medical society meeting. The representatives from Mt. Mercy were somewhat alarmed at what they considered Redden's lack of objectivity. During a noon recess in the hearings, Sister Mary Theresa and her advisors gathered to consider their approach during the afternoon session.

YOUR ASSIGNMENT

1. Describe the organizational change issues in this case. Discuss the impact of the acquisition of Abbott from the perspective of the medical community, the management at Abbott, the public, and Mt. Mercy leadership.
2. Identify a variety of sources of potential conflict as leaders of Mt. Mercy acquire Abbott Hospital. Describe the differing values, interests, and influences in the medical community and at Mt. Mercy. Determine how past events have contributed to the present situation.
3. Describe the leadership approach of Sister Mary Theresa. How effective is she? Should members of her board support her actions without more information? Why? Why not?
4. What are the value and ethical issues in this case?

PART TWO

Mt. Mercy Acquires Abbott

On December 6, 1990, a certificate of public necessity was granted by the state of Oklahoma to Mt. Mercy Hospital for the acquisition of Abbott Hospital in Auston, Oklahoma. Sister Mary Theresa had won her battle over the opponents of Mt. Mercy's expanding influence in the medical community.

Upon receipt of the certificate, Mt. Mercy retained Kidder, Kidder and Company to handle a private placement of tax-exempt bonds to finalize the $18 million purchase. Bonds were quickly placed, and combined with operating reserve and foundation monies, the acquisition was completed.

Sister Mary Theresa planned for Mt. Mercy to begin operating Abbott on February 15, 1991. She contacted Dr. John Coletti, Abbott administrator under MEDICO, and asked him to remain. Coletti agreed feeling the progress he had made at Abbott could continue.

Early in January 1991, Sister Mary Theresa requested that the Mt. Mercy personnel department interview all Abbott staff members, who were asked to sign a letter of intent with regard to their continued services on the combined Mt. Mercy/Abbott staffs. Staff members were notified that signing the letter would insure them of continued employment for a three-month probationary period, at the end of which permanent placement would be discussed. Staff of both hospitals were to be informed they could be transferred between hospitals at administrative discretion. No seniority and accrued benefits from Abbott would transfer to Mt. Mercy/Abbott staff status. John Coletti was not consulted or notified of these actions by the Mt. Mercy personnel department. He complained directly to Sister Mary Theresa and expressed concern that these actions would seriously undermine morale.

Sister Mary Theresa nevertheless directed the personnel department to continue with the interviews. Sister Mary Joseph was instructed by Sister Mary Theresa to advise all Abbott department heads that they were to report directly to their counterparts at Mt. Mercy. Abbott department heads thus became assistant department heads. John Coletti was furious and threatened to resign his position immediately unless this policy was altered. Sister Mary Theresa held to her basic reorganization plan, and Coletti resigned on February 1, 1991. Five department heads from Abbott also resigned.

The First Six Months

Amidst turbulent conditions, Abbott Hospital became an operating satellite of Mt. Mercy Hospital on February 16, 1991. The Catholic Code of Ethics became the governing code at Abbott on the same day.

Within two weeks of the Mt. Mercy takeover, six doctors had resigned from the staff of Mt. Mercy at Abbott. They had transferred their staff privileges to Memorial, a local hospital permitting legalized abortions and sterilizations in its surgical facilities.

Sister Mary Theresa addressed herself to the task of replacing John Coletti. She was disturbed by reports that the management of Memorial had offered Coletti a position, and that he would join their staff on March 1. In late February 1991, Sister Mary Theresa hired Adam Sampson to become assistant administrator for Mt. Mercy at Abbott.

Adam Sampson is from a family of physicians. After an unsuccessful semester at medical school, Sampson turned to hospital administration and has met both success and failure during his career. At his last position, the hospital's financial problems were dramatically turned around. Sampson has taken the credit for the progress, although reliable sources consider the hospital staff to be the major change factor. Sampson considers himself an idea man who will work to avoid confrontation if possible. Observers generally describe him as a nice person who takes orders well. Adam Sampson assumed his duties at Mt. Mercy at Abbott on March 1, 1991. Sister Mary Theresa asked him for monthly reports summarizing the general operating and financial status of the new satellite.

During the same month, Sister Mary Theresa formed a Mt. Mercy at Abbott Operational Review Committee composed of Sister Mary Joseph, Dr. John Cassler, and Adam Sampson. The committee was to meet monthly to review all phases of the Abbott operation. Sister Mary Theresa had set a goal for Abbott to break even within 13 months. She intended to make whatever adjustments necessary to facilitate the goal.

The Early Results

During April, May, and June 1991, revenues for Abbott ran 15 to 20 percent below projected levels. Revenues from surgery and associated patient care days were the hardest hit, with a decline of 62 percent. The pediatrics occupancy rate was an unacceptably low 21 percent. Mt. Mercy staff doctors were not admitting patients to Abbott at a greater rate than before the purchase. Administrative costs were up 6 to 8 percent, within the anticipated range for the change to Mt. Mercy procedures.

In June 1991, a somewhat frustrated Adam Sampson indicated he was not getting cooperation from the Abbott staff. Sampson asked Sister Mary Theresa and the other committee members to consider transfer of Mt. Mercy personnel to Abbott to give him a staff that might be more responsive to his needs for operating information. Furthermore, he was finding it difficult to fill the administrative vacancies that had followed the Coletti resignation.

Sister Mary Theresa and Sister Mary Joseph both agreed Sampson was premature in requesting additional changes at Abbott. Sister Mary Theresa assured Sampson the staff discontent caused by the initial takeover would take some time to dissipate.

Sister Mary Theresa expressed concern about Abbott revenues to Dr. Cassler. She reminded him that cost economies from consolidation were meaningless if she could not keep her operating revenues at a level to service the acquisition debt.

The July Operational Review Committee Meeting

When the committee met in July, Abbott revenues were running 18 percent below projections. Surgery revenues had improved slightly but still registered a 58-percent decline. The pediatrics occupancy rate remained a dismal 21 percent. Administrative cost increases had leveled off at 6 percent. Sampson's specific analysis of doctor admissions confirmed Mt. Mercy staff doctors were not increasing their utilization of Abbott facilities. A somewhat surprising picture surfaced with emergency room revenues running ahead of projections for break-even.

Dr. Cassler confirmed John Coletti's appointment as director of planning for Memorial Hospital. He further reported Dr. Leeham's latest efforts to persuade several new doctors to move their practices to Memorial. Committee members were aware that Memorial had applied for a certificate of public necessity to add 26 additional beds. Sister Mary Theresa felt it prudent to support the application.

Sampson indicated he was impressed with the competency of the Abbott staff but did not feel he was getting helpful input to facilitate correcting the bleak revenue picture. Sister Mary Theresa and the committee agreed on corrective action. The committee discussed how to approach the various facets of the problem.

Sister Mary Theresa was opposed to transferring personnel between the two facilities. She proposed immediate reinstatement of accrued benefits from Abbott tenure to all Abbott staff members remaining on the combined staffs. Sister Mary Joseph strongly concurred, emphasizing the linkage between overall staff morale and the high quality of staff–patient relations for which Mt. Mercy and Abbott had been known. Sampson seemed hesitant about their proposal but did not challenge it. Dr. Cassler proposed initiation of formal conversations with a number of his colleagues to determine what types of services might attract both new doctors and increased admission to Abbott from doctors currently exercising staff privileges at Mt. Mercy. All committee members agreed a public response to Dr. Leeham was inappropriate.

Sister Mary Theresa asked Sister Mary Joseph to compile a detailed analysis of the Mt. Mercy pediatrics ward. Sister Mary Theresa instructed the Operational Review Committee to look for possible consolidation of services, which would revise the operating structure of Mt. Mercy as well as Abbott. She was clearly considering closing pediatrics at Mt. Mercy in order to strongly encourage Mt. Mercy staff doctors to utilize Abbott for all pediatrics and related cases. The beds vacated by pediatrics at Mt. Mercy could accommodate a planned surgical ward expansion. Sister Mary Theresa was curious about the emergency room revenue reports from Abbott. She asked the committee to consider what implications this might have for other services.

YOUR ASSIGNMENT

1. Evaluate the effectiveness of the first six months of Mt. Mercy's operation of Abbott Hospital. Specifically consider the events leading to John Coletti's resignation. Develop rationales supporting and opposing Sister Mary Theresa's approach to Abbott personnel status at the time of the merger with Mt. Mercy staff.

2. What are the major change issues in this case? Describe communication problems in merging two separate organizations.

3. How would you describe Sister Mary Theresa's leadership style during the merger period? Develop a rationale for her ignoring John Coletti's advice. Evaluate this decision.

4. What changes would you recommend in the approach management took at Abbott? What should remain the same? Describe the relative merits of autocratic approaches versus more participative ones.

5. What are the major organizational issues in this case? Describe in terms of organizational structure, leadership, climate, effectiveness, resistance or acceptance of change, and risk taking.

WHAT HAPPENED NEXT?

The End of the First Six Months

By the end of July 1991, accrued benefits had been reinstated for the original Abbott staff members. Sister Mary Theresa and Sister Mary Joseph had begun plans to relocate all pediatrics services from Mt. Mercy to Abbott. An *Auston Transcript* article outlining plans for the consolidation portrayed a favorable community reaction. Several staff doctors had expressed mild displeasure to Dr. Cassler but did not seem to be contemplating any serious opposition. Cassler also reported success in forming a group of staff doctors to study service needs that could be accommodated specifically at Abbott. No decision was made concerning emergency room service.

Sister Mary Theresa, without committee or board knowledge, began seeking additional foundation monies for debt service in the event revenues were not sufficient within 13 months to meet the debt service schedule. As she looked ahead, Sister Mary Theresa saw many difficulties but was exhilarated by the challenges of making a multihospital concept work.

Illinois Power and ''60 Minutes'': Communicating About the Communications

KIM B. WALKER, PH.D.

Kim Walker holds a Ph.D. from Southern Illinois University and is an associate professor of Communication at the University of Colorado at Colorado Springs. Dr. Walker has managed telecommunications facilities and taught media courses since 1980. His published research specializes in media effects and distance learning. He has consulted for private industry and local and state governments in the Midwest and West.

During the late 1970s there was something of a ''standing joke'' throughout the business world that a visit from the crew of ''60 Minutes'' was destined to ruin your day, if not your career. And the nuclear power industry seemed particularly vulnerable to such scrutiny after Three Mile Island and the release of a presidential commission report on hazards. The following case examines how one power company in the Midwest handled its treatment by the press—specifically, its coverage by one of the fifth estate's most important and ferocious "watch-dogs," "60 Minutes."

BACKGROUND

In the 1970s residents of the central Illinois communities of Clinton and Decatur had mixed opinions about building a local nuclear power plant. Unemployment was high, and Illinois Power Company provided local officials hope for an upturn in the economy. A new reservoir was built, the fishing was excellent, and, at the height of construction, the company and its contractors employed over 3,500 workers.

At the time of the "60 Minutes" visit, national media outlets had brought the issue of nuclear power into a world spotlight. On the local scene, reporters frequently covered the Illinois Power plant's detractors. Stories of rate increases and construction overruns were frequent media items.

In late September 1979, "60 Minutes'" producer Paul Loewenwarter wrote a short note to Illinois Power asking if the company would participate in interviews about the high costs of building nuclear generating facilities.

Corporate executives met to determine Illinois Power's (IP) "attitude" toward the dubious distinction of such coverage, and exactly how to handle it. IP officials believed "60 Minutes" was intent on covering the story. Refusing to participate could leave negative impressions in the minds of 24 million viewers. What had interested "60 Minutes'" producers was a briefing they had received from critics of the construction. Thus a refusal of coverage implied "guilt" by insinuation, and left no means to expose the company's position or to enable rebuttal. Interdepartmental memos cited the "less than unanimous" agreement among executives to cooperate, supported by the belief that CBS had demonstrated an "antinuclear" and "antibusiness" bias in the past. Nonetheless, IP officials decided to cooperate, and more than that, the company would make every effort to provide access and information for the story.

Illinois Power specified only one condition. The company would videotape everything shot by "60 Minutes" crews. For every minute of film shot, there would be corresponding video taped by IP in-house media staff. In return for IP's cooperation, producer Loewenwarter assured "fair and balanced" coverage of the issues involved.

The research and information-gathering phase of the story took place during September 1979. Harry Reasoner conducted a 90-minute interview with W. C. Gerstner, executive vice-president of Illinois Power, on October 9. The next day Reasoner filmed interviews with employees at the plant construction site. Then a number of phone calls between the CBS staff and IP representatives finalized the story. The 14-minute segment aired on the November 25, 1979, "60 Minutes."

Reasoner introduced the segment by stating:

The American Nuclear Power program is in trouble. And not only because of Three Mile Island and the presidential commission's report on hazards. It's in trouble because the cost of building the plants has gone crazy. A China Syndrome of cost.

Take Illinois Power, for example, which wants its customers to help pay for a nuclear power plant whose costs have gone up three times since the original estimates. If the customers don't pony up the company's financial rating, their ability to sell bonds and meet their customers' energy needs is in trouble. We went to Clinton, Illinois . . .

The story went on to describe proposed rate increases in order to cover costs estimated at $30 million per month. Interviews with former employees critical of the project provided examples of expenditures without incentives for cost controls. One former employee stated, "It's like Watergate. They've got themselves committed, they went into it and all of a sudden they've got a bear by the tail and they don't know how to let go." Comparisons with other nuclear projects were discussed, delays were cited, and the segment concluded with Reasoner stating:

Illinois Power was proud that it met one critical milestone in its schedule. Albeit, a revised, updated, two-and-a-half-year-behind-schedule schedule. It installed its nuclear reactor vessel right on the new timetable and called out the media to witness it one balmy day in October. But the work to come is far more complicated, the kind that has caused mistakes and delays at most other plants, forcing them to fall behind schedule.

Illinois Power insists that won't happen here. But if the charts are right, it will happen here. And costs will rise again. The thing is, someone has to pay for all that. That someone, of course, will be, one way or another, sooner or later, the customers of Illinois Power.

But what Illinois Power and its critics have learned about nuclear power, if they have, is important to us all because all energy is going to cost a lot more, so much more that anything extra from lessons not learned, is simply something we can't afford. From the standpoint of the utility company or its customers or a nation, there is no percentage in solving an energy crisis by going broke.

Illinois Power was appalled by the broadcast and received an immediate barrage of calls from employees, customers, and the press. According to one document on the aftereffects of the coverage, the response in the stock market was shocking. "By 10 A.M. on the Monday following the broadcast 10,000 shares had been traded and the price (was) beginning to slip. By the end of the day three times as many shares had been traded as ever before in a single day and the price had fallen something over a dollar. Our employee morale was suffering badly and the hate letters soon began to arrive from ex-stockholders and the public'' (H. Deakins, A Summary of a CBS Visit to Illinois Power Company, p. 3).

THE COMPANY RESPONSE

The broadcast occurred three days prior to a decision on Illinois Power's rate case before the Illinois Commerce Commission. The case before the commission was a request for money, part of which would be used to help complete the nuclear facility. A negative decision would seriously damage company plans.

By 10 A.M. on the Monday following the broadcast, IP decided to make a rebuttal videotape. It was produced by IP's own in-house media staff, under the direction of the public affairs department. The objective of the tape, and accompanying print efforts, was to "defuse" the impact of the broadcast and to "get the facts" to employees, press, the financial community, IP stockholders, and the general public.

Company officials viewed the CBS broadcast several times to decide which positions were, from their perspective, most erroneous and damaging. It was determined that the IP response should be relatively brief (45 minutes) and designed to correct as many of the "major inaccuracies" as possible. The response would compare the "60 Minutes" broadcast with the in-house video shot at the same time. The in-house video would feature a staff narrator to tie together segments and reinforce particular counterarguments. Completed one week after the original broadcast, the production also contained sworn testimony and exhibits from the ongoing rate case.

The program entitled, " '60 Minutes'/Our Reply," was narrated by Howard Rowe. Rowe began by asking:

> What happens when a major TV network comes to town to do a news feature on the power company? Plenty! And not much of it's very pleasant, as we learned when Illinois Power became the target on . . . "60 Minutes."
>
> On November 25th the CBS news program "60 Minutes" broadcast a feature on the construction costs of the Clinton nuclear power plant. The program was the result of interviews conducted by CBS early in October. They came to Clinton, and to Decatur, at the urging of one of the opponents to Illinois Power's rate case.
>
> In line with our policy of providing all news media with the facts about our operations, the company agreed to cooperate fully with the producer, Paul Loewenwarter. He assured us, in turn, that CBS was going to produce a balanced, factual presentation of the economics of building nuclear power plants. We told him that we were going to film anything that the "60 Minutes" crew chose to film on Illinois Power property. This turned out to be a good idea.

What we're going to show you is the complete presentation as it appeared on "60 Minutes." But what we're also going to do is to stop from time to time and expand on those areas that "60 Minutes" either edited out, presented incorrectly, or chose to ignore.

The video went on to refute, point for point, facts and conclusions presented by "60 Minutes."

Public and private release of the IP tape began immediately. Distribution included video set-ups at locations where local customers paid bills, presentations by field representatives to service and civic organizations, employee showings during work times, complimentary copies to securities analysts, and distribution to local media editors and publishers. Requests for the tape from utility groups and major corporations exceeded IP's expectations.

A copy of the rebuttal tape and an open letter to IP stockholders was sent to Robert Chandler, CBS vice-president and director of Public Affairs Broadcasts. In the letter to stockholders the chairperson and president of IP, Wendall Kelley, quoted an official of Standard and Poor's Corporation as saying in commerce commission testimony that Illinois Power's management of the power plant construction project was doing "a good job." Kelley's letter stated further that the "60 Minutes" telecast was "yet another example of sensationalism in journalism at the expense of the facts of the matter." He then provided five specific counterarguments to the broadcast.

1. Harry Reasoner stated that Illinois Power scheduled only two weeks to complete the full-system tests that on similar projects take an average of 14 months to make. He concluded by saying that we planned to accomplish in two weeks what no other nuclear builder had ever accomplished in that time period.

   In the complete interview with our Mr. Gerstner, Mr. Reasoner was told that the chart he was looking at was not a construction schedule; it was a milestone chart. Its purpose is to let the Nuclear Regulatory Commission know the approximate time during which the test is to be made. The particular test itself requires only three days to complete. In addition, the same chart Mr. Reasoner was using on camera shows that the testing of some seventeen sub-systems which precede the full-system test, are scheduled individually over a 25-month period prior to the full-system test. The fact is that our schedule is reasonable and attainable.

2. Mr. Reasoner stated that against other plans of similar design, Clinton cost overruns are well ahead of the pack.

   Mr. Gerstner showed Mr. Reasoner, on camera, a list of all seven one-unit boiling water reactor nuclear plants being built in the United States. On this list, Clinton has the lowest cost increase.

3. Mr. Reasoner made the flat statement that Clinton was the Company's first nuclear project and the first for our contractor, Baldwin Associates.

   During "60 Minutes' " visit to the Company, it was explained to them that Baldwin Associates was a consortium of four major construction companies: Power Systems, Inc; Fruin-Colnon; McCartin & McAuliffe; and Kelso-Burnett. It was pointed out to "60 Minutes" that two of these companies, prior to starting Clinton, had worked on 14 nuclear projects. It would be difficult, you would think, to refer to all of that as "no nuclear experience," but that's what "60 Minutes" did.

4. The major points of the "60 Minutes" program were based on the comments of three former employees of either the Company or its contractor. Two of these men were fired for cause and the third resigned because he was not satisfied with a seven per cent pay increase. All were associated with the Clinton project for short times only.

   The most vocal of these critics also appeared as an "expert" witness in opposition to our recent rate case before the Illinois Commerce Commission. After he was cross-examined in regard to his testimony, the hearing examiner ruled: "The witness has not demonstrated that he is qualified by educational experience or work experience concerning the subject matter of his testimony and should not be permitted to testify as an expert and provide opinions or arrive at all of the conclusions which are contained in his testimony." "60 Minutes" knew of this ruling, yet chose to present him on camera to recite those same opinions and conclusions.

5. Lastly, it was stated on "60 Minutes" that even the usual neutral staff of the Commerce Commission joined in asking that the rate increase be denied. This was not true. Just three days after the "60 Minutes" telecast, the Commission, at the recommendation of its staff, granted us the major portion of the rate increase we had requested, including additional revenues to cover part of the cost of capital we have already raised and spent on the Clinton plant. (Letter from Wendell J. Kelley, chairperson and president, to the stockholders of Illinois Power Company, December 14, 1979)

Chandler, responding on behalf of CBS in correspondence to Kelley dated January 21, 1980, stated simply that neither the tape nor letter to stockholders "persuades us that our story was unfair." His letter went on to state that "60 Minutes" found two inaccuracies in their story that would be corrected on "60 Minutes" on Sunday, January 27. Specifically Chandler stated:

1. We stated that the 14% rate increase was attributable to the cost of the Clinton construction. We were in error; despite the Commission's assertion that "unquestionably, the driving force for the requested

electric rate increase is the Company's need to generate revenue to support the construction of Clinton Unit #1," we should have said that only part of the increase was requested to pay for Clinton and the balance for general revenue purposes.

2. We also stated that the "usually neutral staff of the Commerce Commission joined in asking that the rate increase be denied." That is in error; we should have said that the staff recommended that the cost of Clinton construction not be included in the electric rate base. In short, it recommended that the part of the increase attributable to the construction be denied. (Letter from Chandler to Kelley, January 21, 1980)

Chandler's letter addressed the issues raised in Kelley's letter to stockholders and in the videotape. His point-by-point analysis concluded:

In sum, it should be clear that far from being "used" by your opponents in the rate case, we went to considerable lengths to get at the facts, which were and perhaps remain in dispute. In this letter I have cited at length from the Commission order because the Commission itself had access to all arguments and data, and was highly critical of the Clinton project, in terms of overruns, schedules, and the credibility of your own claims. We did time our broadcast just prior to the decision and said so, because that decision was to address questions in which the entire country has a stake.

There remains one final area of concern. I note that you take pains to point out to users of your videotape that the "60 Minutes" material contained in the tape is copyrighted by CBS, and you proscribe limits on its use. While I appreciate your own concern and efforts to avoid the abuse of our rights by others, I am nonetheless obliged to point out that your own use and distribution of the material constitute in themselves an infringement on our copyright.

Illinois Power, in response to the CBS letter, performed an extended analysis of the letter asserting that CBS's admission of inaccuracy on "two rather insignificant points was entirely unsatisfactory." The 15-page document went on to identify what IP believed were nearly 20 specific examples of unfairness, inaccuracies, invalid and nonrepresentative comparisons, and misleading though technically correct comments. The analysis document contained a number of accusatory remarks concerning responsible journalism, calculated use and omission of selected information, and questionable ethics. The document concludes with a discussion of how difficult it was for IP to "accept the '60 Minutes' presentation . . . as balanced and unbiased journalism." Furthermore, IP consulted its attorneys, who advised that redistribution of the CBS broadcast within the IP tape constituted "fair use" as part of "comment and criticism," and not an attempt to profit by its use.

Harold Deakins, IP public affairs manager, attempted to correspond personally with Harry Reasoner of "60 Minutes" concerning the company's treatment at the hands of the program. Reasoner responded that the correspondence from CBS executive Chandler to IP chairperson Kelley accurately described his own position. Although Reasoner "personally" regretted the way IP officials felt about the coverage, he also stated, "I think we were fair," and "treatment of Illinois Power as a strong example was proper and reasonable." Reasoner maintained the network position, citing cost overruns in the nuclear business as "horrendous and endemic." (Letter from Reasoner to Deakins, February 28, 1980)

YOUR ASSIGNMENT

1. What are the organizational communication issues contained in this case? Describe the responsibilities of both Illinois Power and "60 Minutes" to communicate with the general public.
2. Describe the various communication constituencies of Illinois Power. Specifically, consider stockholders, the general public, regulatory agencies, and the media.
3. Describe the various communication constituencies of a program such as "60 Minutes." Specifically, consider the agenda setting and persuasive roles of the "60 Minutes" story with regard to the general public and Illinois Power's stockholders and regulatory agencies.
4. How can communication theory help us understand what happened at Illinois Power? Consider persuasion theory, media effects research, the public relations literature, and general systems theory.
5. What would you have done if you were in top management at Illinois Power? At "60 Minutes"? Discuss the value and ethical implications of your choices.

WHAT HAPPENED NEXT?

Just over a year after the initial broadcasts, "60 Minutes" ran an update on the original telecast citing a new completion schedule and cost estimate for the IP Clinton facility. Illinois Power sent a letter to all persons holding copies of their rebuttal tape (estimated at that time by their public affairs office at 2,900 worldwide). The letter stated that if the CBS network wanted to clear up the controversy "once and for all" the network would air the rebuttal tape in its entirety. The public affairs office concluded "the viewing public can then decide for itself just who is telling the truth." Accompanying the letter was a transcript of the "60 Minutes" update and a copy of the news release explaining the new cost estimates and schedule.

In addition to broad distribution of the video rebuttal and accompanying materials, IP officials were pleased by media stories describing their response to "60 Minutes." Headlines such as the *Columbia Journalism Review*'s "Turning the Tables on '60 Minutes' " (May–June 1980), and the *Wall Street Journal*'s

"Illinois Power Pans '60 Minutes' " (June 27, 1980) captured broad attention in business circles. The plant construction continued with estimates for construction revised to $1.2 billion.

1985

The following excerpt is from *"60 Minutes" Minute by Minute,* by Don Hewitt, creator and executive producer of "60 Minutes" (New York: Random House, 1985):

> Have I made mistakes along the way? Sure, though never out of malice or deliberate disregard of the truth. The most glaring became a cause célèbre for Illinois Power and friends of theirs who do not like anything about "60 Minutes." It came about when we made some mistakes in a November 1979 story about cost overruns at Illinois Power's Clinton, Illinois, nuclear plant, including not reporting that one of the critics of Illinois Power—a man we interviewed for the story—had falsified his credentials—and we knew it. Really inexcusable, but we tried to make restitution by reporting the facts on a later broadcast.
>
> That didn't satisfy Illinois Power, which made and distributed throughout the country a very unflattering videotape about "60 Minutes" that is still being played for sympathetic audiences. That tape became the bible of the crowd that thinks "60 Minutes" is antibusiness and antinuclear. I've always thought that if Illinois Power had spent the same time, money, and effort holding their own feet to the fire as they spent holding ours, their nuclear plant would have come in a lot closer to on time and a lot closer to on budget. About our role in this episode: if we hadn't been brushed back from the plate by Illinois Power's spitball and had stepped into the pitch instead of flinching, we would have hit one out of the park. In the story we did—the one they took us to task for— we said, and correctly, that the plant was two-and-a-half years behind schedule and a billion dollars over budget. Well, five years after Illinois Power took us over the coals for that story, the plant is now seven years behind schedule and more than two-and-a-half billion over budget. Have we reported that? I'm afraid not. You see, their beanball worked. (At least the new figures got into this book.) (pp. 218–219)

1987

According to a 1987 publication released by Illinois Power, the first stable nuclear reaction occurred in 1987 and the Nuclear Regulatory Commission issued a license to operate the facility that same year. When the plant went on-line the cost for construction was published at $4.2 billion. This put the operative power plant eight to ten years past its originally scheduled completion date, and nearly ten times above its original reported budget estimates.

1989

"Illinois Power (IPC, NYSE, 14 1/2, 12-month range 13 7/8-22 1/8) is a fine old utility that could pay some handsome rewards in the next few years, once the company works through its current problems," notes Richard Band's Personal Finance from Alexandria, VA. "The Problems stem from a nuclear power plant built in the early 1980s. Although the plant is running well, it cost far more to build than it was supposed to. The result is that the firm will need to cut its dividend. At the June board meeting, we expect the dividend to be cut in half, to about $1.32 per share. Even so, that rate would provide a yield of over 9 percent. Now trading at the same price as its historical 1974 bottom, we are adding the stock to our growth portfolio for high-risk oriented investors. If there was ever a time to 'shut your eyes and buy,' this is it." (Steve Halpern, *Colorado Springs Gazette Telegraph,* Business Section, May 5, 1989)

1991

In updating this account of the power plant construction, we spoke to various customers, former construction employees at the plant, and representatives of the local media. Reactions were mixed, but most seemed to have resolved themselves over the past ten years to the issues raised in the original "60 Minutes" broadcast. One news director of the television affiliate most directly involved in the local reporting of the story suggested that, according to recent news reports, only now have IP customers stopped paying for the "construction work in progress" at the plant. Of course this work was used as justification for many of the original rate increases. Although aware of the actual completion and budget figures for the plant, the director also seemed resigned to the fact that any large construction project would suffer similar problems.

Chronological Summary of Case Events

Date	*Event*
11/25/79	CBS airs original "60 Minutes" critical of IP, estimating cost and construction overruns.
11/26/79	Ten thousand shares of IP stock are traded with the price dropping over $1 per share.
12/3/79	IP creates " '60 Minutes'/Our Reply" for distribution to CBS, IP stockholders and securities traders, and the local press. Along with the tape is a letter to stockholders from IP chair, Wendell Kelley, explaining that the video provides interview footage not seen in the original telecast, which points out unfairness, inaccuracies, and innuendo.
1/21/80	Robert Chandler, CBS News vice-president, responds to the chair's letter by defending the broadcast's accuracy in estimating cost overruns and construction delays. He

	maintains the story's accuracy was confirmed by Illinois Commerce Commission testimony.
1/27/80	"60 Minutes" airs correction of two "errors." IP spokespeople dub this a correction of "two rather insignificant points" and "entirely unsatisfactory."
4/21/80	The *Wall Street Journal* runs story entitled "Illinois Utility Sparks Widespread Interest in its Videotape."
5/80	IP's rebuttal tape is examined in the *Columbia Journalism Review.*
6/27/80	The *Wall Street Journal* runs story entitled "Illinois Power Pans '60 MINUTES.' "
12/5/80	IP releases new construction schedule and cost estimates.
1985	Don Hewitt, creator and executive producer of "60 Minutes," describes rebuttal tape as "the bible of the crowd that thinks '60 Minutes' is antibusiness and antinuclear." He maintains that the original story depicted the plant as "two-and-a-half years behind schedule and more than two-and-a-half billion over budget." According to Hewitt, "The plant is now seven years behind schedule and more than two-and-a-half billion over budget."
1987	The first stable nuclear reaction occurs and a license is issued for operation by the Nuclear Regulatory Commission (NRC). Costs are estimated by IP at $4.2 billion. According to critics, the plant comes on-line eight to ten years past its scheduled completion date and at ten times its original estimate.
1989	Business columnists recommend IP stock for "high risk investors," citing a cut in dividends to $1.32 per share, still leaving a yield of over 9 percent.
1991	"Construction Work in Progress" reported by local media as paid in full. (Telephone conversation with David Shaul, News Director, WCIA-TV, Champaign-Urbana)

Organizational Communication: Italian Style

This case is partially based on the author's experiences as a research colleague and organizational communication consultant to the Institute for Management Research and Development (IFAP) for the Institute for Industrial Reconstruction (IRI) Group, based in Rome, Italy. The case asks readers to assume the position of a U.S. communication professional invited to contribute to an organizational culture project within the IFAP.

BACKGROUND

Described as the fastest growing of the European Economic Community economies, Italian industry is a complex mixture of state- and privately owned enterprises. The IRI Group, the founder of the IFAP, is a state-owned conglomerate operating in manufacturing, utilities, transports, infrastructures, and banking. The group's three-tier structure includes a global holding agency with control over the individual sector holding companies, which are the majority stockholders in their respective operating companies and hence responsible for strategy and control. The IFAP, founded in the late 1950s, is responsible for planning, developing, and presenting training to update and reorient IRI managers. Today the IFAP, operating on an annual budget in excess of U.S. $10 million, presents a variety of public offering courses and seminars; custom designs activities for specific companies; coordinates meetings, conferences, and short courses to brief top executives; and conducts ongoing research on organization, management training, and development issues. Today the size of the IFAP's structure and its diverse activities make it the leading Italian institute for management education and also contribute to its reputation as one of Europe's finest research and training organizations.

You have been asked to contribute your knowledge of organizational culture and organizational communication to IFAP researchers, who are charged with developing a program to strengthen the IRI's culture across the conglomerate's various sector companies. You have been told that companies within industrial sectors have relatively strong cultures but that few shared realities exist at the global holding company level. With the advent of a unified Europe, IRI and IFAP leadership are interested in the impact of organizational culture on competitiveness. Moreover, IRI companies increasingly are involved in joint ventures with U.S. corporations such as AT&T.

IRI GROUP HISTORY

Leading Italian expert, Joseph LaPalombara (1987) describes the emergence and growth of the IRI Group:

> State or public ownership of large-scale industrial enterprise was a spontaneous, accidental occurrence that began with the stock market crash of 1929 and the Great Depression that followed. . . . With the crash, all of the leading economies were in dire straits, and in Italy the fascist state came to the rescue. It saved the banks by acquiring from them the more or less worthless securities they held in bankrupted corporations. Through their salvage operation, the state became either the sole or partial owner of the industries involved. . . . There was no Marxist or other socialist ideology at work here that argued that the state should be the owner of the instruments of production. No one welcomed the move on the basis of any ideological principle. In effect, the state

backed into public ownership, and apologized for doing so. In order to bring some semblance of orderliness to these new holdings, the state created, in the early 1930s, the Institute for Industrial Reconstruction (IRI). It was designed to be a temporary public corporation. The idea was that as soon as the economy turned around, the acquired industries would be turned back to private ownership. It never happened. Not only is IRI still very much around; it is immensely larger. Indeed, it is one of the world's largest holding companies, whose various branches do tens of billions of dollars of business each year. . . . Today IRI owns 100 percent of the shipbuilding industry, all of the airlines, four-fifths of the steel and metal-working sectors, almost all of telecommunications, a good chunk of the automobile industry, and a lot more. (pp. 74–76)

In 1985, the IRI employed roughly 500,000 people, held majority shares in more than 500 companies, and held minority participation in another 500.

YOUR CHALLENGE

You have been contacted by a leading researcher within the IFAP to determine your interest in a research and consulting project investigating whether organizational culture work done in the United States has applicability to the IRI's evolving needs. You have limited awareness of Italian business, you do not speak the language, and you are uncertain about your capabilities for the assignment. Furthermore, you have not worked with state-owned enterprises or organizations of the magnitude and scope of the IRI.

You are challenged by the project and decide to accept an invitation to present a seminar in Rome to researchers and university leaders based on U.S. experiences in organizational culture work. You outline issues for consideration and begin to develop your approach for understanding the expectations of your assignment.

YOUR ASSIGNMENT

1. Describe your approach to clarifying expectations for your presentation. Consider what information you need from the IFAP and how you will select material appropriate for their needs.
2. Describe how approaches or perspectives for organizational communication will guide your thinking. Define how this case contributes to an understanding of organizational communication.
3. Speculate about how cultural differences and similarities will impact exchanges of information. Identify your perceptions and expectations of the Italian culture. Attempt to understand potential perceptions of the United States.
4. Describe your expectations of a state-owned conglomerate. Research the IRI and other similar organizations to determine the applicability of your expectations.

5. Given the history and size of the IRI Group, what is your reaction to the viability of forming an IRI culture across the conglomerate? Explain your position.

REFERENCE

LaPalombara, J. 1987. *Democracy Italian style.* New Haven, Conn.: Yale University Press.

Jean Douglas—The Former Quality Assurance Manager

Jean Douglas had worked for Reynolds Toy Company for 25 years. It was hard to believe the company was in trouble. Jean had started with Reynolds right out of college and worked her way into management, first in sales, then manufacturing, and currently as quality assurance manager for the Atlanta plant. She loved her work. The products changed yearly and, of late, the Atlanta plant had been assigned the new children's computer line. The new computer line was said to be the problem. Competitors had already introduced children's computers and the initial market share for the Atlanta products was disappointing.

Most people in the toy industry had high regard for Reynolds both as a maker of quality products and as a good place to work. Jean agreed. She took pride in being associated with Reynolds and believed most of her peers felt similarly. She respected Leon Reynolds, the company's founder, who had developed the company from a garage operation to one of the leaders in a highly competitive industry.

Jean was stunned to learn that the Atlanta plant was closing. No Reynolds factory had ever been shut down. She understood no jobs were being lost, but the computer line, the camaraderie among her team, and moving away from Atlanta were all painful realities of a changing industry. Jean wondered what she should do and how she should advise the 27 people who reported to her.

THREE WEEKS LATER

Leon Reynolds came to Atlanta to assist the management team in developing a plan to close the plant and to transfer all personnel willing to relocate. He expected approximately 30 percent of the employees to transfer, with the remainder choosing to remain in Atlanta. Jean reported that only five of her group were in a position to take transfers and she, personally, wanted to consider her options before making a final decision; others felt similarly. And so the planning began.

Within a few days of Reynolds's visit, Jean received a call from Concord Toys, a principal competitor of Reynolds. Concord officials wanted to talk with Jean about a quality assurance job in Boston. They were complimentary of her work at Reynolds and suggested they could offer her more opportunity for growth. Concord, after all, had an established line of computer toys and could use someone with her experience. The manager of Reynolds's Memphis plant also contacted Jean. He wanted Jean to join his staff as assistant quality assurance manager. She would report to Fred Reams, a capable colleague with whom Jean had frequently interacted.

JEAN'S DECISION

Jean attempted to weigh her decision. In either case she would have to move. Remaining in Atlanta was desirable, but immediate opportunities were limited. Concord's offer was intriguing. She could continue to work with the technology of her choice and it was a lateral career move. The salary offer was commensurate with that of her current position. Jean wondered if the cost of living in Boston would erode her expendable income. Concord's reputation was solid but there was more employee turnover there. She believed she would have a good future with Concord, but she was uncertain about how she would fit into a new company, especially coming in at a midmanagement level. Jean believed most midmanagers in the toy industry should have specific product line experience prior to assuming broad responsibility.

Going to Memphis was another option. She liked Fred Reams and believed he was providing good leadership for the Memphis plant. Taking a demotion, however, was a problem. What could she expect for the future? If Reynolds's growth days were over, as the Concord executives suggested, she would have limited opportunity for several years. Nevertheless, she had put all of her work life into the company. She respected top management and believed she had been supported throughout her career. However, if she ever were going to make a change, this might be the time.

Jean decided to gather detailed information to help her make the decision.

YOUR ASSIGNMENT

1. Describe the variety of considerations important for Jean's decision. Identify a problem-solving and decision-making process for this circumstance. Establish decision criteria.
2. Develop a list of information sources Jean can utilize to assist in her planning.
3. What questions should Jean ask of Reynolds? Of Concord?
4. Develop a communication plan for Reynolds as it attempts to keep good people during downsizing.
5. Models of career development have historically emphasized upward mobility for career success. Discuss what a demotion can mean both emotionally and in terms of career planning. What new models of career development should be adopted for the future?

WHAT HAPPENED NEXT?

Jean made appointments with Leon Reynolds, the Memphis plant manager, and Fred Reams. She shared her concerns for the future and asked their advice. In addition, she met with Concord executives responsible for her job offer. She visited the Boston facility and met several individuals who would be part of her team there. She left Boston believing Concord was offering her a good opportunity.

In the end, Jean decided to move to Memphis. The Memphis plant manager agreed with her that she would experience more rapid initial growth at Concord, but he also encouraged her to understand the opportunities that follow downsizing. He stressed that good people were more important than ever and he wanted her in his organization. Fred Reams also encouraged her to stay with Reynolds. Only Leon Reynolds expressed real doubt, because he did not like asking employees to take demotions. It was his genuine concern that was pivotal for Jean's decision. She wanted to continue her association with a company that understood her needs. Jean decided, although the company was changing, the basic values of the culture were intact.

CHAPTER 2

Culture and Communication

Drake Computer Corporation— A Lesson in Designing an Organizational Culture

They were in their late thirties when they met. Four men, each successful in his own way, each dissatisfied with his job, and each a little bitten by the rock-star bug known in Silicon Valley and throughout the computer industry as the Stephen Jobs syndrome. They wanted to make money, but more than that they wanted to be known, to be famous, to be important in an industry known for brilliance, burnout, distress, and dissatisfaction.

They met at a computer show in Washington, D.C. While most around them were outdoing each other with success stories, the four fell into serious conversation about their personal needs for something more, something beyond the big corporation with all its pressure and its inability to recognize talent.

Six months later they had begun serious plans to form their own company. They would be different; they would be successful without the baggage of their previous jobs, and they would be rock stars, or at least well known enough to be respected for their computer design and business expertise.

They knew where they wanted to start. They believed that most high-capacity, high-speed scientific applications computers were overpriced and loaded with feature sets with few current users. The market in scientific computing had been sluggish, in part due to the prohibitive cost of most available machines. Their prospectus and initial business plan described the competitive advantage they intended to bring to scientific and military markets by building a machine with the architecture and overall capacity of the giants at a fraction of the cost.

THE FOUNDERS

Bob Anderson, 37, went to school and worked in Palo Alto, California. Educated at Stanford, Bob was the youngest general manager in the history of a large division of a major computer corporation. Prior to becoming manager, he had been the lead design engineer on a major government contract requiring sophisticated computer applications. His work on the government contract was so outstanding that his company, in an unusual compensation decision, awarded him significant patent revenue rights along with a large bonus. Bob did not enjoy the position of general manager and found the company increasingly bureaucratic.

Dan Findley, 39, also from Palo Alto and Stanford, had worked with the famed Project Nemesus team, which was responsible for significant advances integrating diverse home computing systems. The project, a joint venture of three major companies, received widespread press attention and was financially successful. Dan's dissatisfaction stemmed from the amount of credit for the project that was given to Nemesus's lead engineer, a man known to take the ideas of others and to represent them as his own. Dan decided to leave his company the day his boss was promoted to head of the corporate research and development organization.

Chet Willis, 35, went to the University of Oklahoma and worked for a major Dallas, Texas, instrument manufacturer. Willis had worked on design teams of four industry-leading products by the time he was 32. For the last three years he had worked on a project that the company had recently cancelled; it decided his team was pushing an expensive technology too far ahead of the market. Chet was disillusioned because he thought his last effort was his best to date. He had invested three years of his life in a technology that might not see the market for years to come. His situation motivated him to think about joining a smaller organization. Chet believed that layers of management had killed his project—not the technical merits or the market.

David Parker, 38, an MIT graduate, was a laboratory manager for a Colorado division of a major computer manufacturer. Unlike the other three, David's experience was with multiple companies; he had worked for three high-tech organizations with increasing levels of responsibility in each job. David did not like being assigned projects from others. For some time he thought about independence but he lacked the initiative to begin anything on his own. Those who worked closely with David frequently described him as "in over his head but able to sell his way out of anything."

FORMING DRAKE

A major Texas investor was attracted to the plan prepared by Bob, Dan, Chet, and David. Bob Anderson, in particular, was amazed at how easy it had been to raise significant capital. Within five months of securing start-up funding, the four had resigned their positions, moved to Dallas, Texas, and had begun raiding their former employers.

Twelve of the first 15 employees at Drake had worked with the founders on previous projects. All had experience with computer architecture design with specific emphasis on scientific and military applications. The other three employees, all Dallas natives, were hired to head finance, administrative, and personnel functions. The head of personnel was recruited specifically because he worked for a firm known to have a strong and generally positive culture. Bob, who had assumed the presidency of Drake, was especially interested in building a strong culture that was different from the companies he and the others had left.

During the first six months, Bob communicated daily with all employees except for brief periods when he visited potential customers. He spent most of his time with design engineers and worked directly on certain technical issues, although Dan Findley assumed the overall responsibility for research and development. During this period, Chet Willis designed a yet-to-be-staffed manufacturing organization. David Parker traveled weekly making contacts and asking potential customers for needed features and ideas. He also spent more time than his counterparts in established firms with university professors interested in applications for this type of technology.

The work was exhausting; most Drake employees averaged 70 hours per week. Excitement was intense and a sense of energy was noted by visitors to Drake's makeshift headquarters. As others were hired, expectations were explicitly stated about the level of commitment necessary to be successful at Drake. Everyone was told they would either get rich or be without work within two years. No one suggested a secure future. In fact, Drake did not want people who needed security. One employee summed up the expectation to put Drake above all else when he stated, "I come in on Saturday whether I have work or not. Everyone is here, you have to be seen. Last Saturday I went in my office and played cards with my son."

Friday evenings were reserved for beer and pizza parties, which featured talk of the week's events even though families were invited. As the months passed, the parties continued late into the evening with fewer and fewer family members in attendance. The tradition of working on Saturdays extended to Sunday afternoons as pressure mounted to meet initial deadlines.

Close to the end of the first year, the personnel manager approached Bob and the others about the pressure and stress many employees were experiencing. He noted that most employees were given deadlines without their input or an opportunity to assess the reality of the expectations. The personnel manager suggested these early experiences were pivotal to building the type of culture that would characterize Drake in the long run. Bob laughed at the personnel manager and stated he thought he knew more about culture than the man he had hired to build one. The personnel manager asked Bob what type of culture he and the others really wanted. Although all four men could talk about the organizations they had left, they were less clear about what they wanted for Drake.

Bob asked his personnel manager to find consultants who had worked with other organizations and knew how to build a culture. The personnel manager objected because he believed you could not buy a culture. Bob insisted outside guidance was needed. He and the other founders wanted a strong culture that would help them become successful. Making that happen was the personnel manager's responsibility. If he could not accomplish this goal they believed he should look for work elsewhere.

YOUR ASSIGNMENT

1. How would you describe the culture of Drake? Describe Drake in terms of expectations of employees, participation patterns, and leadership.
2. What assumptions about culture are exhibited by the founders? What is meant by a strong culture? What are the strengths and pitfalls of this view?
3. What should the personnel manager do? Is he responsible for building the culture as Bob suggests? What role should external consultants serve?
4. Is the awareness and avoidance of what is considered undesirable from previous situations sufficient to build a more positive culture in a new organization? Why? Why not?
5. What should Bob Anderson consider as he leads Drake Computer Corporation?

IBM and Apple: Contrasting Cultures Working Together

The announcement of a joint venture between International Business Machines (IBM) and Apple Computer Inc. in late summer, 1991, sent shock waves through an industry known for continual turbulence. Big Blue IBM, known for its conservative, stable culture, and glitzy Apple hardly seemed likely partners in an attempt to set the next generation of standards for the personal computer industry. One headline writer summed it up, "Big Blue Apple Has a Weird Ring to It."

IBM, the world leader in office machine technology, and the upstart Apple had vastly different corporate histories. Yet by mid-1991 both found themselves losing market share and profits to a host of computer clones. Under the proposed joint venture, IBM would share with Apple a microprocessor it developed and Apple would provide IBM with its next-generation operating system. The two hoped to more tightly control today's personal computer market by setting standards they jointly control.

Their histories have been intertwined for the past ten years. In 1977, Apple introduced the Apple II, one of the first successful personal computers. In 1981, IBM unveiled its personal computer line and in 1983 introduced the PCjr home computer. Despite an aggressive advertising campaign, the PCjr sold poorly and was taken off the market within 18 months. The year 1984 was a banner one for both IBM and Apple. IBM introduced its first portable PC and the PC AT with its powerful microprocessor; Apple brought out the famous Macintosh, featuring a breakthrough graphics-based operating system. The late 1980s saw IBM continue to innovate in the personal computer market and finally, in 1990, successfully introduce the PS-1, a second attempt at the home computer market. Also in 1990, Microsoft Corporation unveiled its Windows software, which made IBM PCs almost as easy to use as a Macintosh. By 1991 IBM's ten-year alliance with Microsoft was souring, giving impetus to the Apple and IBM announcement for technology sharing to create the next-generation PC based on non-Microsoft software.

IBM, led by patriarch Thomas J. Watson, Sr., had developed what some have described as a vaulted corporate culture. IBM historically had shunned layoffs, stressed lifelong employment, and valued company loyalty. Fostering a conservative image (the pin-striped suit was once its trademark), IBM has been known to have a slow-moving and precise style in a fast-paced world.

During 1991, industry insiders suggested the increasing number of alliances IBM had formed was an attempt to regain technological dominance. IBM apparently avoided outright acquisitions in favor of alliances in order to foster the independence and entrepreneurial spirits of the smaller companies. Some believed IBM was the first U.S. *keiretsu,* the Japanese approach where huge companies surround themselves with a host of smaller companies.

When the IBM and Apple alliance was announced, Eric Rall, president of an organization of Apple computer owners, was quoted as saying, ''People feel that Apple has sold the family jewels'' (*Washington Post,* National Weekly Edition, July 22–28, 1991). Apple, a Silicon Valley upstart cofounded by the now-famous Stephen P. Jobs, became a U.S. business legend with revolutionary products and innovative marketing. The Apple II and Macintosh were pricey new technologies when introduced. A 1984 Apple television commercial compared IBM to Big Brother as conceptualized by George Orwell in *1984.* Early annual meetings resembled rock concerts. As an elite technology company for much of its initial 14 years, Apple has attempted to mass-market its products only since 1985. In 1985, Stephen P. Jobs was ousted from Apple by John Sculley, the former PepsiCo Inc. executive whom Jobs had brought to Apple, in a solidification of power. In 1986, Sculley took personal control of research and development from Jean-Louis Gassee, a brilliant engineer who wore a diamond stud in his ear. By 1991, analysts believed Sculley planned for Apple to improve its current line of Macintosh computers while making its future with IBM. Sculley has been quoted as saying, ''The key thing is not to become hostage of old technologies.'' Employees of both IBM and Apple have expressed concern over the joint venture. Both cultures are admired and both are considered alien and problematic. Following the announcement, in a gesture typifying the contrasting cultures, a group of unnamed Apple employees draped the Apple rainbow logo with the blue and white stripes of IBM.

YOUR ASSIGNMENT

1. Describe the issues involved in making a successful joint venture between corporate cultures as different as IBM and Apple.
2. Corporate cultures have frequently been described from a life-cycle perspective. IBM and Apple are in different stages of corporate growth and maturation. How might this affect the joint venture?

3. Is it necessary to share similar values when working in an alliance (or joint venture)? Would your answer differ if IBM had purchased Apple or the two had merged certain aspects of their operations?
4. How would you advise IBM employees working with Apple? How would you advise Apple employees working with JBM?
5. Strong corporate cultures have been associated with excellent organizations. Consider the relationship of corporate culture to organizational effectiveness. Why is this relationship important? What are the limitations of the "strong culture view" of effective organizations? What are the implications of organizational culture for organizational change? For IBM? For Apple?

To Manage, Value, or Do What with Diversity?

The following is a transcript of a meeting of top human resource professionals in one of the most progressive Fortune 100 companies, with over 105,000 employees in the United States, Japan, and Europe. These executives are considering whether to launch a major corporate effort in diversity training. They agree that the work force is changing but are divided in their opinions about the proper approach. In order to secure permission to release a verbatim transcript of their meeting, agreement was reached to identity each participant as A, B, C, or D, and to protect the identity of the company. As you read the transcript consider the organizational communication issues embedded in their discussion.

A: Our agenda today is to frame this issue. We need to get input from our personnel managers throughout the country and overseas as well. Does anyone want to give it a try?
B: Well, I think framing is going to be difficult, I mean the whole issue of diversity is too vague. We have cross-cultural international issues to deal with, we have different parts of the country, let alone race, gender, and age issues. I don't think this diversity thing is one issue but several all rolled up into one. I am not even sure we should attempt to frame it and then get blamed when we obviously fall short—and we will fall short.
A: I think that is begging my question. We have been asked to develop a diversity program to aid our recruitment and retention programs and to help prepare us for more international competition. We should be able to do that.
C: I know it is a silly question—but should we begin by identifying differences between "managing" and "valuing" diversity? Are they the same or are they different things? We should know what our intent is before we launch another program.
A: I agree. I think the things I have reviewed and my own gut sense of the issue is that valuing is more awareness and appreciation of work force diversity while managing is more proactive, includes specific programs, organizational changes,

rewarding performers who make diversity work in their own areas. Attitudes and awareness are somewhat secondary—nice but not as important as change.

D: Well, I think we need to begin by understanding where we are on this issue as a company. I just read some frightening things about attitudes in the U.S. Apparently a whole lot of white people have pretty negative images of blacks and other minorities. Most seem to support equality in theory but there is a lot of resistance to programs such as affirmative action or quotas. The report I read—and I can circulate a copy to the rest of you—said that a majority of whites in this nationwide survey believed blacks and Hispanics are likely to prefer welfare to hard work and tend to be lazier than whites, and generally less intelligent. The thing was done at the University of Chicago. I think it probably has something important to say about attitudes. I don't like it but I think we should consider where many of our people might be on these issues.

A: Yes, we have got to face the fact that this is pretty much a white male culture we have here.

B: I don't see what is wrong with that. This company has been successful and we don't need to apologize for our leadership. It shouldn't be a stigma to be a white male. I'm afraid that most of our good middle managers are worried that an increase in women and minorities in the company will only complicate their futures.

C: Don't be so defensive. Diversity doesn't mean white males are going to be eliminated. These changes are coming whether you like it or not. Being threatened only blocks us from good proactive planning.

B: I'm not threatened. But if you don't realize this is confusing you aren't in touch with a whole lot of our work force. For years we have been told to be colorblind and ignore ethnic differences. We were to be a culture of equal opportunity. Now you tell me that I must learn to manage differences on top of everything else. And there are companies who have adopted promotion criteria on whether or not a manager has people of all types and color working with him. That's a little much to take.

D: This isn't a social justice issue. This is a business issue. We are getting beaten up badly. A lot of our white males tell us they have trouble with negotiations abroad. The people they must work with understand English and a whole lot more about us than we do them.

A: So what are we saying about this issue? Is it international, valuing, managing, or what? Or is it all these things?

B: Well, I agree on the international thing. I think we should propose more cross-cultural training for anyone working with either Japan or Europe. We even have some European employees who don't want to work with their U.S. counterparts, they consider U.S. employees difficult and too short-fused.

C: Well, I for one, think we need to develop a management of diversity philosophy. We need to change some systems, structures, and management practices—we have to work on the subtle barriers which block people from their potential. And fear of all of this is certainly one of those barriers.

D: That's right, we have to treat people as important individuals. And white males can benefit. I heard the other day that George _____'s promotion was being questioned. One top exec had the audacity to say George has a "wife problem." His wife works and can't provide all the entertaining support others in the position have provided. We are paying George, not George and his wife for heaven's sake.

C: We do have an international piece of this issue but, gee, top management just doesn't understand how white and male the corporate culture is. The subtle thing that happens—and it sure hurts females and minorities but also some white males—top management seems to surround themselves with people just like them.

A: That's right and we can't continue to do that. I think we might be surprised if we began by analyzing our employees, our overall labor pool, and our current and emerging customer base. What do our employees need to be successful? Is it true that we are losing a lot of good people to smaller organizations with more individual flexibility? I don't know but I think we should find out.

B: Do the rest of you support this valuing or awareness training approach?

A: I don't know for sure—there is an awareness piece, a lot of the problems are subtle, but I am not sure we will ever know if it worked.

C: I favor some awareness stuff but more programmatic changes are needed. We may need to establish day care on premises, flexible and part-time work schedules to retain mature workers, and certainly foreign language and cultural training for others.

D: I think the real brunt of our work will be attacking hidden biases whether they are about the international marketplace or our own employee population. We have to get ourselves up to date on our own stereotyping.

B: This sounds like the 1960s to me. And I am glad that decade is far behind us.

D: Maybe so, but the 1960s didn't finish or maybe even start this job. The challenges are different. You can't dodge this issue so easily. We can't discount the problems.

B: Well, I think if we have good managers a lot of this will take care of itself.

A: You have a point but we can't leave all this to chance.

B: Good luck getting any support from the executive committee. We won't be able to agree on this one among ourselves.

C: Well, we have to start somewhere. I propose we consider a management of diversity approach that includes our international needs. What do the rest of you think?

The conversation continued until the four agreed on a management of diversity approach. They decided to hold focus groups among personnel department employees throughout the company to define specific issues that should be addressed by a management program.

YOUR ASSIGNMENT

1. What are the organizational communication issues embedded in this discussion?
2. Describe differences between valuing and managing diversity. What are the advantages to increasing diversity? Are there potential problems?
3. What communication theories and approaches apply to the issues of work force diversity?
4. What communication competencies and skills are needed for increasingly diverse organizational experiences?
5. How should an individual prepare for diverse working relationships and experiences? Think about your answer in terms of ethnic, racial, gender, age, and international differences.

Managing Cultural Diversity

James Dillard, president of Systems Computers, Inc., knows both the workplace and the customer base are changing. He has read *Workforce 2000*. In fact, he does not know anyone who has not read it. He also knows that many of his senior managers could care less about affirmative action, and many openly resent attempts at hiring with concerns for work force diversity.

James Dillard feels differently. He believes the future rests on having a work force that represents the diverse composition of Systems Computers' customers, a group that is increasingly minority and female. He believes that to design low cost computer products for the future requires a knowledge of customers that cannot come from an all-white male group or any single group for that matter. Among his senior managers, only Charlie Nighthorse agrees with him. Charlie, a Native American, has long advocated pluralism as a corporate objective of Systems Computers, Inc.

Dillard was pleased to see the article on U.S. West in the *Washington Post* (Lynne Duke, "Employer Puts Pluralism First," *Washington Post,* National Weekly Edition, August 12–16, 1991). According to the *Post,* U.S. West was assembling "pluralistic slates" of job candidates to ensure minorities and women are considered for new jobs and internal promotions. U.S. West, like Systems Computers, is heavily white male at the top. The article cited progress in attracting and promoting a diverse work force but also described concerns expressed about quotas by some U.S. West personnel, including minorities and females.

At his next staff meeting Dillard gave copies of the U.S. West article to all present. He asked the vice-president of personnel to think about a new approach for recruitment and promotions based on a "pluralistic slate" of candidates. He pointed out that A. Gary Ames, CEO of U.S. West Communications, had been quoted as saying that he would personally nix any high-level promotion that was not recommended from a pluralistic slate of candidates. Several staff members objected to Dillard's request suggesting it went too far and was not based on solid business judgment. Dillard countered he was concerned that Systems Computers did not have a sufficient pipeline of females and minorities employed to effectively penetrate top management ranks over the next several years. He persisted with his assignment to the vice-president although it was clear serious objections existed.

Six weeks later, the vice-president for personnel made his first report to Dillard's staff meeting. He suggested a new management performance appraisal system, which would give significant credit to managers who recruited or promoted from among pluralistic slates of candidates. The credit would be received even if the final selection for a job was a white male. Although no quotas were to be established, all managers would be required to attend in-house diversity training workshops. Charlie Nighthorse expressed concern that the approach was not strong enough. Several staff members seemed relieved. Dillard did not know; his concern rested with the attitudes of his senior staff. He wondered what he might do to help them understand that managing a culturally diverse work force was good business.

YOUR ASSIGNMENT

1. How would you advise James Dillard?
2. What does the increasingly diverse work force mean for organizational communication?
3. What type of training can help managers and others understand communication and diversity? Outline a training program for Dillard's staff.
4. Describe how organizations can foster cultural diversity as good business practice.
5. Describe ways to deal with the negative perceptions about cultural diversity in the workplace.

Culture Shock: The Russian Entrepreneurial Revolution

Moscow—These are gold rush days for German Sterligov. Six months ago, he dreamed up the idea of starting a private commodities brokerage and named it after his dog, Alisa. Now he estimates his fortune at "tens and tens of millions of rubles," and the Alisa logo appears regularly on the august pages of the newspaper Izvestia.

A 24-year-old college dropout and one of the self-proclaimed pioneers of Soviet capitalism, Sterligov is also the owner of the country's first professional hockey team and the founder of the Young Millionaires Club. "Oh, and another thing," he said as his secretary stooped to light his Marlboro. "We're going to take over the Moscow racetrack and bring in the Kentucky Derby people to set up some big-time international racing."

For all his bravado, Sterligov is not some Russian Donald Trump with his eyes fixed on a BMW sedan and a one-way exit visa to Wall Street.

Descended from victims of the purges of the 1930s, he is out to build a culture of business where none exists, to promote an alien psychology of commerce and work in a country that made the destruction of ordinary initiative a matter of brutal policy. (David Remnick, "New Soviet Masters of the Universe," *Washington Post,* National Weekly Edition, July 15–21, 1991)

The following conversation took place during the summer of 1991 prior to the Russian revolution, which began in early fall. A group of young Russian entrepreneurs describe their efforts, their dreams, and their differences with their parents and others who believed in another type of world. Individual and organizational names have been changed but the substance of the remarks is factual.

YURI: My family doesn't understand what I want to do to change things. I simply want to supply what is needed for other businesspeople in Russia to make important decisions. Mine is an information business. My father only understands this in a political way. He is pleased that we are seeing change in our government but he wants a society based on social principles. He doesn't like any of us becoming rich or making a lot of money. He believes that we are living off of others. For me, I am making money providing a service which many in my country have come to need. My father sees this as my getting ahead at the expense of others. [*Yuri provides computer information services to a growing number of Russian entrepreneurs.*]

OLGA: We want the old ways to go away. The system has destroyed almost all of us. Our parents and grandparents have become so used to the sameness, the poverty, that they think something is wrong with us when we actually want to make money. My grandmother is afraid, she thinks I may be doing something wrong. I do take chances but these artists have a right to be seen and have others appreciate what they do. I have broken the laws, but the laws are corrupt. In the long run the laws will change and I will already have a legitimate export business in place. [*Olga runs a small art dealership, exporting works from unknown Russian artists through a complicated black market arrangement.*]

MIKEL: We may be doing something wrong—but the past has been wrong and we must have new ways of doing things. Besides we work hard, no one has a right to question. People want to do business in Russia. I can make that happen. Governments just get in the way. I know you do that in the United States. It is no different here. [*Mikel connects foreign businesspeople with trade opportunities in Russia. Most of his contacts work without the knowledge of their own or the Russian government.*]

The three laughed when told that David Remnick's article in the *Washington Post* had compared young Russian millionaires to the first Carnegies, Rockefellers, and Goulds, and had described young Russians as entrepreneurs blazing trails without a code of behavior or common language. Although they did not know Remnick's references, they agreed there was no need for a code of behavior.

Some of them [*referring to the new Russian millionaires*] are a crude bunch, but to develop wealth, you need these people. We can't wait for angels to do the spade work," says Igor Svinarenko, a reporter for the leading newspaper of the Soviet business world, *Commersant.*

These businessmen who make their money selling rotten meat or lousy computers or patched-together trade deals, they'll accumulate money and build things and set up factories and stores. Some of them may do ugly things or act like barbarians. But they'll also educate their kids, maybe send them overseas to Harvard. And then the kids will come back with their high-minded ideas and they'll say, "Dad you are a scoundrel." And so they'll do things in a more refined way. They'll act on their guilty conscience. And so society will develop from there. (Remnick, July 15–21, 1991, p. 7)

OLGA: Our behavior is driven by the changes of the moment. We are forging a new business world for our future. We don't know how it will be, we only know what our dreams are and we won't wait longer for those dreams. Besides, what do we have to lose?

YURI: We seek information from the West. We want to know how others have been successful and I have some contact with that. We have a business newspaper, you know, the *Commersant.* [*Remnick referred to the* Commersant *in his article.*] It tells us much about what is going on, all the changes. Yet, we have to forge our own way. We have to work around the powers that would stop us and we have to take risk.

Remnick's article describes the *Commersant* as a revival of a business paper founded in Russia in 1908 and published until the 1917 revolution. Artyom Tarasov and Vladimir Yakovlev "started the weekly in the fall of 1989 using profits from Fakt, a 300,000 ruble loan from the bank and computer equipment provided by the Chicago-based Refco commodities firm in exchange for free ads" (Remnick, July 15–21, 1991, p. 7). The paper runs stories of joint ventures, scandals, prices of commodities, and even published lists of black market prices.

MIKEL: The key is to start small and have many avenues open to change direction. You have to have contacts. You watch and see who you can meet and talk into helping. A lot of what works is really an exchange—you provide service to one person and they put you in touch with someone else. Sometimes it isn't an exchange of money at all that is important, it is an exchange of goods or contacts.

YURI: It is a new culture for us. People only ten years ago would not have believed this could be possible. We want to open Russia again and we want to be the drivers. I don't know if it will be possible. Our parents will come along, they know the past is over, but they think we don't have enough concern for others. Let others work like I do. Work is the answer.

YOUR ASSIGNMENT

1. Describe the new entrepreneurial culture emerging in Russia. What values are changing? Why is the change described as culture shock?

2. Discuss the implications of the statement, "There is no code of behavior." Describe how it represents a culture in transition.

3. What role does communication play in these changes?

4. What does this new entrepreneurial culture mean for those attempting to do business with the Russians?

5. Develop a proposed model of how an entrepreneurial culture might evolve in Russia. Describe the communication processes that support the new culture.

Conversations

Minorities in the Work Force: How Satisfied?

ADELINA M. GOMEZ, PH.D.

Adelina M. Gomez, associate professor of communication at the University of Colorado, Colorado Springs (UCCS), holds B.A. and M.A. degrees from Western New Mexico University and a Ph.D. from the University of Colorado. Her main interest is in intercultural communication research, teaching, and training. Dr. Gomez is also an active consultant for both private and public sector organizations. She is the director of the Minority Graduate Education Opportunity Program (MGEOP) summer program on the UCCS campus, a federally funded program for minority undergraduates who are first trained in research methodology and then participate as research assistants for UCCS professors in various disciplines. The goal of the program is to prepare and encourage minorities to pursue graduate-level degrees.

For the most part, U.S. organizations have become increasingly more aware of a wider world of responsibility and have actively sought to diversify their work force at all levels. But they have not yet recognized that to combat resurgent racism, they must create a more accepting environment for this new and different work force. This is the biggest challenge that faces society as the racial and ethnic profile continues to change. Some evidence exists showing that many organizations, albeit well-intentioned, have not yet prepared effectively for an increasingly culturally diverse work force. If predictions for the year 2000 hold true, this society will see multidirectional changes in its cultural makeup. The ethnic composition of those entering the work force will be radically different as the numbers increase.

The mere inclusion or representation of a small number of individuals who have heretofore been denied access to resources and employment that their nonminority counterparts have had full participation in is no longer viable. The organization must prepare to diversify the work force more effectively. For example, there are some organizations in which there are hundreds of nonminorities and less than 30 minorities. Research shows that when minorities make up a small portion of the work force, the extent to which they can realize equal opportunity and equal treatment is minimal. This type of environment often spawns biased and prejudicial behaviors on both sides leading to perplexing problems within the organization. The organizational climate may be so heavily weighted in favor of the nonminority culture, that minorities often represent changes in the environment that few are able or willing to manage.

The resulting conflicts can include resorting to interpreting behaviors through racial stereotypes and condemning affirmative action policies. When minorities make up only a small percentage of the work force, a climate—consciously or unconsciously—may exist that allows evaluation of their performance based more on existing stereotypes and less on actual job performance. Affirmative action policies continue to be hotly debated because there are those who still perceive that the guidelines fill "quotas" with less competent and less deserving workers, and that affirmative action hiring is reverse discrimination. Experience and research have shown that as the percentages of minorities increase in what have been largely nonminority domains, the stereotypes and other negative factors decrease; a broader perspective and more cross-cultural alternatives help those involved to develop a more objective and empathetic awareness for all concerned.

Despite this less-than-perfect picture, there are success stories within many organizations. Some minorities have excelled in their chosen professions in spite of ethnic biases or prejudices, whereas others have had few negative experiences. What accounts for this? Is too much being made about how minorities fare in the organization? Are organizations unjustly accused of being insensitive to and ignorant of cultural differences? Have organizations fulfilled their obligation to accommodate some of the needs of a multiculturally diverse work force? Some of the responses given to the following questions would indicate that the answer is "No." Similar patterns of concern emerge from a group of individuals who represent substantially different organizational environments. Although statistically not significant, their concerns indicate serious problems still exist and can be construed as an indictment of today's organizations. How satisfied are minorities? You be the judge.

What follow are questions and responses from four professionals representing three different cultures and four different organizations. Three are employed in public organizations; one is employed in a private organization. All represent various upper-level management positions. The respondents were three males and one female; the cultures represented were two Hispanics, one African American, and one Jamaican. They ranged in age from early forties to middle fifties. Their professions are technical writer, public relations executive, superintendent of schools, and chief equal employment opportunity (EEO) counselor. Their academic credentials include one doctorate, one master's degree in progress, and two bachelor's degrees. The four have never met and live in geographically diverse locations. They were not aware how each had responded.

As the work force diversifies, what do you see as the most important communication issues in organizations?
HISPANIC 1: Equal treatment for all.

HISPANIC 2: The glass ceiling, women's salaries, quotas.

AFRICAN AMERICAN: Listening, collaboration, mentorship, coaching, facilitation, consensus, proper representation and opportunity, elimination of the glass ceiling.

JAMAICAN: Listening. The dominant culture (i.e., white males) seems to have difficulty listening to others. For example, at staff meetings I've voiced an idea or a suggestion which went unheeded. Later a white male colleague voiced the same one I had and everyone thought it was great.

What do you believe is the greatest challenge for managing a culturally diverse work force?
HISPANIC 1: Treating everyone the same and yet recognizing their cultural differences.

HISPANIC 2: Getting individuals in the work force to pull together as a team and not letting their cultural baggage get in the way of doing what's best for the organization.

AFRICAN AMERICAN: Acceptance of diversity, acknowledgment of diversity, policy change, cultural change, proper representation, potential backlash.

JAMAICAN: Managers must learn to respect different cultures and understand that a variety of cultural backgrounds makes for rich resources from which to garner useful and important information.

For years, the culture of an organization has been determined by the predominant white male mentality. Does your current organization reflect this? Yes, no. If yes, does this affect you personally? Yes, no. Please explain.
HISPANIC 1: Yes, my organization reflects this. Yes, I have been called a "taco bender" or "Cisco Keed."

HISPANIC 2: Yes, my organization reflects this. Yes, the white male mentality defines the business and cultural climate for most large U.S. corporations; therefore, it affects *everyone* in the organization, including white males. Once this is understood, it is simply a matter of "playing the game" within this context.

AFRICAN AMERICAN: Yes, it does. Yes. The organization is changing culturally and I am playing a major role in the transition. At times it can be difficult, but it is not impossible. It is inevitable.

JAMAICAN: Yes, it does. Yes. Although there are laws to encourage the hiring and promotion of culturally diverse individuals, I find that I have to be at least twice as efficient and knowledgeable just to be considered average.

As a highly placed individual in your organization, do you believe that your organization is consciously working to diversify not only the work force but also the management level? Yes, no. If no, please explain.

HISPANIC 1: Yes.

HISPANIC 2: No, the work force is diversified, but I am the lone minority in upper management, including women. The old boy network is alive and well in my organization and it is very difficult for *anyone* outside of it to crack it.

AFRICAN AMERICAN: Yes. We pay particular attention to diversity training and are planning systemwide exposure. We pay particular attention to affirmative action and report quarterly to the board of education. We set goals.

JAMAICAN: No. I am of the opinion that management gives lip service to work force diversity, for there is still a dearth of ethnic minorities in high positions. Usually at a meeting, I'm the *only* ethnic minority civilian in attendance.

YOUR ASSIGNMENT

1. Research the issue of the glass ceiling and explain why it is perceived by minorities as a barrier for upward mobility.
2. Develop two or three themes you see emerging from the previous responses.
3. What do you see as the major communication issues in an organization as the work force diversifies?
4. What recommendations can you offer to combat the resurgence of racism?
5. You are the director for training and development in your organization. Develop an outline that can be implemented into a training program for sensitive cultural diversity in a multicultural organization.

Moving Toward the Year 2000—An Italian Perspective

RUGGERO CESARIA, PH.D.

The following interview with Dr. Ruggero Cesaria, researcher at the IFAP Istituto Di Richerche E Formazione Dir Direzione Aziendale, Gruppo IRI, Rome, Italy, describes important issues of change, culture, and communication as Italian business faces the challenges of the twenty-first century. The Institute for Management Research and Development (IFAP) is the business school for the Institute of Industrial Reconstruction (IRI) Group with a mission to plan, design, and develop courses, programs, and teaching methodologies aimed at updating and reorienting IRI managers. Working with the vast and multisectored IRI conglomerate has enabled the IFAP to develop a theoretical and practical "know-how" that today endows IFAP with operational potential and expertise unequalled in Italy. The IFAP operates on an annual budget of more than U.S. $10 million, with a faculty of 25 full-time and over 200 part-time members, professionals, and experts from universities and specialized institutes in Italy and abroad. Dr. Cesaria and Dr. Shockley-Zalabak currently are collaborating on an international research project exploring relationships among communication rules, organizational values, organizational culture, and performance.

What are the most important business issues in the IRI (or Italy) during the next few years?

DR. CESARIA: It is very difficult to give a single answer because in Italy there is a very heterogeneous industrial structure. There are some large companies and a lot of very little factories that show different behaviors. However, we have not a strong network of middle size firms as in other European and American countries.

Surely, the 1993 European Common Market is the present then for all of our firms. It is both a business opportunity and a source of possible difficulties. In fact, a weak Italian infrastructure and bad public services can cause us disadvantages in a free competitive arena. But 1993 also means a new direction with other East European countries and extra-European ones [*i.e., Japan, which is just manufacturing and selling goods without production and import quotas in some EEC nations*]. This is a hard challenge for our business system and an opportunity to improve our competitive factors.

There is another challenge for large Italian companies. It is the cultural shift from an "efficiency organizational model" to an "efficacy organizational model." Large firms are slowly moving from "values" like "economy of scale," "production," "product," "specialization," "organizational structure," and so on, to values such as "customer," "total quality," "innovation," "just in time," "creativity," "flexibility," "entrepreneurship," "time to market," "organizational learning," "continuous change," and "organizational structure."

IRI firms are moving and changing as well. The IRI four-year plan shows us its objectives for the future:

- to continue both reorganization and development processes;
- productivity improvement;
- progressive emphasis on "total quality" and "market orientation";
- product, process, system of management and financial tools innovation;
- selection of investments choices;
- emphasis on group interrelation and synergies;
- internationalization, especially by means of a new presence both in advanced areas and in Eastern Europe;
- south of Italy economic development;
- reindustrialization in the "crisis areas";
- emphasis on human resources and optimal administration of industrial relations.

For the next four years we are able to sketch out nine strategic issues:

1. Financial politics
   Reduction of the short-run financial exposure by means of self-financing and disinvestment.

2. Human resources management and development
   To continue to manage redundancy, especially by means of
   "retirement facilities," "interfirm labor mobility," and "retraining."
   To improve employment in the crisis areas.
   To maintain good industrial relations.
   To continue to innovate human resources management and develop-
   ment systems.
3. IRI in the south of Italy
   To continue to commit itself into the area. The objective is to create
   conditions for economic growth in accordance with market principles.
4. Internationalization
   To strengthen the competitive position into the advanced technolo-
   gies and industries.
   To selectively penetrate into third-world countries.
   To pay a renewed attention to Eastern Europe.
   To develop more alliances, trade agreements, joint ventures,
   mergers, and acquisitions.
   To maximize the interaction between internationalization and innovation.
5. Alliances policy
   The objectives are:
   Financial and trade risks sharing
   Integration of design and manufacturing capabilities
   Exchange of technologies and R&D know-how
   Evaluation of success conditions.
6. European Common Market
   IRI is a large industrial group but it has to reach, in every industry,
   the critical dimensions that are necessary to excel in a European free
   competitive context. In this way, IRI is encouraging "concentra-
   tions," "mergers," and "agreements."
7. Innovation—research and development
   To manage know-how capitalization, preservation, and development.
   To manage know-how transfer among different companies and industries.
   To promote coordinated research programs among IRI firms.
8. Reindustrialization in the "crisis areas"
   IRI is involved in two important reindustrialization programs: Special
   program and Industrial Promotion Program. The first one is implementing
   47 different business ideas in high-technology industries. The second
   one will realize a work relief for 5,000 persons.
9. Services and product quality
   Objectives:
   to transfer and coordinate the "total quality" experiences;
   to monitor the "total quality" intra-group projects.

As you know, IRI has been a very heterogeneous group. Now, its strategies
ask for a new *group culture.* I really think that it is the hardest of challenges
for the future. I'm sure there is a critical tool to win: *communication.*

What is necessary for management to do to prepare to work with these issues?

DR. CESARIA: To explain what, in my opinion, is necessary for our managers to do, I could use the title of IFAP seminar for IRI Senior Management: **Leadership and Innovation.** Innovation is an important issue for IRI Group. Innovation in general environments, in markets, in products and services, in technologies, in competitors' contexts. These types of innovations ask for innovation in management models and in managerial behavior. This is a critical issue for our managers who have to change quickly. We need "leaders" instead of "managers." We need "problem finding—problem setting, and problem solving" instead of traditional problem solving. We need personal responsibility, flexibility, ethics, integration capability. Our "leader" must pay much more attention to communication and negotiation. Leaders have to show "cultural sensitivity" and become both an "internal consultant" and an "entrepreneur."

In this way, the effective leader can support the organizational learning process that is the base factor for company growth. Twenty years ago, the objective was to reduce uncertainty by means of standardization. Now the objective is to accept and live with uncertainty. Stability was the statement for the seventies; radical change was the statement for the eighties; continual change and improvement will be the statement for the future. However, change has many different meanings: *internal change* (our managers/leaders have to forget the old managerial paradigm and to move promptly to another paradigm following the different problems they meet); *organizational change* (they have to innovate organizational systems, creating both formal and informal flexible, and often temporary organizational units); and *proactive change* (they have to find/create the problem, they have to anticipate the solutions and to verify, in separate contexts, potential organizational innovations).

Another important competence is the cultural one. Our management has to facilitate a common organizational vision. Probably, in the future, we will have both temporary and "weak" organizational structures. In such uncertain organizational situations, culture will have to offer clear references about our common reality. I'm not asking for a "strong culture" that could even limit both flexibility and change. I'm suggesting that shared meaning, shared sense making, and shared understanding allow people to understand every daily action and to talk about them. In terms of Shimanoff's communication-rules approach, the new leader should *consciously evaluate and choose the rules (reflective behavior).*

What communication strategies are important?

DR. CESARIA: In my previous responses I've often spoken about communication. I really think this is one of the most important issues for Italian management. However, the term *communication* stands for things like integration, negotiation, leadership, decision making, culture, commitment, and so on. In my opinion communication has to become a *value* for our managers.

Unfortunately, the issue is so considerable that, in Italy, we have no clear strategies about it!

For example, in our companies there are often different organizational units formally involved in communication issues that are not able to meet both strategic and operative coordination. Internal communication is a new subject for many firms and, in some cases, there are no simple tools like House Organs or newsletters. There is an effort to improve interpersonal communication using training programs, interfunctional committees, quality circles, face-to-face formal meetings, and so on. However, in absence of clear communication strategies and leading examples, it becomes difficult to change daily behaviors.

I think that many Italian firms were used to following only one communication framework: communication thought of as "information transmission." In this cultural perspective, the problem is to send signals in an efficient way. The manager makes decisions and transmits them to his subordinates. He often uses an efficient written code. Finally, he is not interested in "meanings." So, the firm is unable to know the degree of shared understandings among the communicators and the general impact of a lot of both different and heterogeneous messages. In my opinion, an important communication strategy should be to change this old vision and accept different communication frameworks. As you know, I can't make decisions and communicate separately because *communication is decision*. In an organizational setting, communication and decision making are ways to create a meaningful organizational context (our own reality). Companies should pay attention to creating a meaningful frame of reference. In this way, top managers should always communicate and confirm the frame of reference in order both to obtain coordination and congruence and to avoid high value discrepancy. I hope these issues will be able to become ones to help us assess and select the next generation of Italian managers.

What does the increasing internationalization of business mean for Italian firms and for those working with Italian companies?

DR. CESARIA: When I answered your first question, I told you that internationalization was a very important business issue for Italian firms. IRI Group, for example, has four related strategic goals: internationalization, alliances policy, competitive position in the European Common Market, and innovation. They all ask for new managerial behaviors. In fact, I think that the increasing internationalization of business means much more alliances and joint ventures and much more innovation. Alliances will be finalized to exchange know-how by doing common research. This perspective means that managing know-how capitalization, preservation, and development will be the challenge for the culture. In my opinion, universities should support international companies by means of an international research network. Unfortunately, Italian universities usually have a domestic perspective (for example, many professors don't speak English). This is both a critical and weak area for the future. Presently, large industrial groups are trying to do international research by means of their training and research institutes (for example, IFAP-IRI and ISVOR-FIAT). Surely little companies won't have these chances. Another issue for IRI is to transfer experiences among its firms. IRI has some companies having long international experiences in different industries. So, the group will have to manage and exchange these experiences.

I think that the increasing internationalization of business asks for a new culture sensitivity. We are moving now from a product orientation to a customer orientation. Maybe we will have to move to a worldwide people orientation. People means customers, employees, suppliers, and so on, all living in different countries around the world. Nissan represents a good example of what I mean with culture sensitivity: They use different human resources management systems in their American and European plants.

What does the international manager need to consider for the year 2000 and beyond?

DR. CESARIA: I think that if there is one best managerial profile, it is both a changing and unstable one. Nevertheless, in our seminars we suggest a tentative managerial efficacy model. The international manager should have some personal qualities (flexibility, intercultural communication, creativity, helicopter view, risk orientation, goals orientation, leadership and empathy), some professional capabilities (negotiation, problem solving, market orientation, customer orientation, delegation, planning and control, cost sensitivity), some managerial knowledge (organizational design and development, quality assurance systems, management by objective systems, creativity technicalities, project management communication technicalities, human resources development systems, foreign languages). Obviously, these are temporary issues, for example, in the future, M.B.O. (Management by Objectives) systems could restrain both strategic vision and innovation.

Probably the goal for the year 2000 consists of a continual monitoring, redesigning, and improving of different effective managerial profiles. In my opinion, if we want to meet this goal, we will have to connect, by means of a global organizational development system, strategic issues, cultural and communication processes, managerial skills, and training investments. I know that some of our companies are moving along this way. I am sure that it will become a strategic issue for the future.

YOUR ASSIGNMENT

1. Describe Cesaria's view of communication. Contrast his views with organizational communication theory.
2. Contrast Cesaria's view of organizational culture with views commonly discussed in the United States. Think about similarities and differences. Prepare a training program for the IFAP describing organizational culture work in the United States.
3. How can individuals prepare for the internationalization of business? Develop a formal and an informal plan to acquire many of the competencies Cesaria describes.
4. Based on Cesaria's views, how similar and dissimilar are U.S. and Italian business issues?
5. Is there an international business culture? Describe potential common values for international business. Identify potential value differences.

Describing Our Changing Culture

The following is a transcript of a focus-group discussion with seven western region representatives of a major home products manufacturer. Group members live in different states and work together in person only during two district meetings per year. Immediately prior to the focus group, the national sales manager for the company announced numerous management changes and layoffs in other regions of the company. She stressed the successful performance of the western region and emphasized that the remainder of the company would look to the west for new ideas and innovation. The focus group was conducted by a member of the company's human resources staff as part of a team-building activity. The subject of the focus group was a description of the culture of the western region group.

What does it take to be successful in this group? [*Laughter*]

MARY: You have to be self-motivated. No one is going to be around on a daily basis to push you, and if you don't push yourself you can't make up the difference just before quarter reports.

JOHN: I think you have to be creative around solutions for the customer. It's like Mary said, no one is going to be there to help you figure things out.

JUDITH: Yeah, you are on your own, but you had better support the organizational goals and have your own goals consistent with what the district needs and wants.

BILLY: I think the most important thing is to know how to locate resources and get others in the company to do what you need.

BILLY: Actually, all you have to be is superhuman. [*Laughter and nods of agreement.*]

How do you know when someone is successful? What are their behaviors?

JUDITH: They make fast decisions. They don't have to wait on a lot of advice from Tom [*the district manager*].

JOHN: I think the people who are most successful know they are right and have that self-confidence that comes from knowing you have the right answer. However, you can't show too much ego and still be considered successful.

BILLY: The people who are viewed as most successful are able to influence this organization both up and down the chain. Also, a successful person has to influence across functions. When you are out in the field you are at the mercy of everyone else, including the customers. You have to be able to influence people you have never seen or met. Sometimes you have to rise above a lot of frustration and just stick with it.

WILL: I think you have to be nonjudgmental and listen effectively as well as know how to persuade others. You have to have professional polish. Also, your family and personal life need to be in balance. After all, you are out there by yourself and you need balance with all the pressure.

What is a mistake in your organization? [*Laughter*]

JOHN: We don't make mistakes. They are not permitted. You just heard Meredith [*the national sales manager who had announced organizational changes*]. [*More laughter*]

JOHN: Seriously, you can't blame other people when you screw up.

WILL: And don't make assumptions. If you need the involvement of the research or manufacturing groups, you had better ask before you make customer commitments.

MARY: You can get yourself in serious trouble if you sit on information that other people need. Also, I have found that even if you have had a problem with someone you had better forget it and not carry grudges.

SAM: I think not changing is the biggest mistake. Look at what is happening throughout the company. We have had to change because our region was under the gun to produce. If you don't change and get management support for that change you can get yourself in big trouble.

BILLY: I think an individual can make a big mistake if they don't know how to handle frustration. You can't just fly off the handle. I yell at Tom, I figure that is what he is getting paid for. It's hard not to take some of this stuff personally, but when a customer gets mad at you they are usually really mad at the company for not performing. And we are the company.

JUDITH: I think we make a mistake as a group when we don't get speedy resolution on disagreements. We get stubborn—I think we have to be stubborn sometimes to do our jobs—but we stay stubborn when we should resolve problems.

How would you describe this group to a newcomer? [*Nancy is new to the group and the group immediately began to talk to her.*]

JUDITH: [*To Nancy*] It is character building. No question about it, working in the west is character building.

BILLY: You have to be flexible and be ready to experience many different things. This group allows you to be all that you can be without joining Apple or the Marines.

JOHN: You have to be a self-starter. When you work remote you must blow your own horn.

MARY: My first reaction to this job was frustration. You either learn or you don't survive. But this is a very supportive group of people—we just don't see each other very often and it is hard to pick up the phone and ask for help.

JUDITH: I think this is a good group, but Nancy should know that in this company there are still some problems with attitudes toward women. We have some difficulty in valuing differences, in letting people grow and develop. Some of the management across the organization are really difficult.

What are the strengths of this group?

BILLY: We understand the business. We know there is a need for change and to better understand our customers. We are way ahead of the rest of the company in knowing customer needs.

SAM: We are innovative in our solutions to problems, we are loyal and yet on the cutting edge. And we never give up. We are stubborn—this is where stubborn is positive, I want you to know.

What are the weaknesses of this group?

MARY: We need more communication and more teamwork. Some people who work in this district don't want to change, they resist everything. They form cliques.

JOHN: I think a big weakness is although we are successful we are not very visible to the rest of the company. [*The west has only 10 percent of the employees of the company, 90 percent of the company's employees are in 12 east coast states.*]

Why did you want to work in this district?

NANCY: My other job went away. I needed work and this was the only opening I could find. [*Laughter*] But I really do want to work here.

MARY: I needed a challenge. I wanted to stay in a technical focus but really be in a job where you have to produce.

SAM: I thought the district management had the best handle on customer needs. This group doesn't live in the past.

You seem to be positive about the numerous changes in your processes and in the entire organization. Is that correct? If so, what has contributed to your ability to accept change?

BILLY: Our management has strongly represented the need for change to us. We were stubborn at first but the message has been stubborn and consistent.

MARY: Our numbers have improved as we see the need for more customer focus.

SAM: We have strong management. They own the problem of change. Others in the company won't or can't do that.

JUDITH: The nature of our jobs forces change.

WILL: Also, we are fortunate in that our management is presenting change as positive. They are enthusiastic about change.

NANCY: I have heard that this is the one group in the sales regions that doesn't say, "We will never do this."

BILLY: I think the big thing is that as we change our ways of doing things our customer credibility has gone up. We can see the success. We get positive feedback when we take risks. Risks are rewarded.

YOUR ASSIGNMENT

1. Reading the transcript, how would you describe this group? How would you describe their culture?
2. Identify the type of communication expectations described in the transcript. For customers? Peers? Management? Problem solving?

3. What additional questions might you ask about this group?
4. Based on their comments, what concerns do you have?
5. What are their strengths?

Singapore: Impressions of Cultural Climate in a Distance Learning Program

BARBARA MCCAIN, PH.D.

In this interview, Dr. Barbara McCain describes her experiences during the summer of 1991 while teaching a graduate marketing management course in Singapore. Dr. McCain is an assistant professor of business communication and marketing at Oklahoma City University. Dr. McCain received her Ph.D. in communication from Oklahoma University and has consulted with both profit and nonprofit organizations throughout the Midwest. Her research focuses on multinational firms and organizational culture issues. Dr. McCain describes this interview as a simple ethnographic view of her experience and the students with whom she worked.

What was your first impression of Singapore?

McCAIN: If David Copperfield had levitated me to Singapore—rather than experiencing a 21-hour flight—discovering I was in Southeast Asia would have been a tremendous shock. Clearly the environment was Western if not American. Evidence of tourism, trade, and financial development flourished. Cultural artifacts of Malaysia, India, and China permeated daily life but the pervasive culture was unified and representative of a society dedicated to growth and prosperity. English is the primary language spoken and written so mobility and conversation was easy. Automobiles were European and architectural design was a blend of historical cultural design and contemporary futuristic. This could have been San Francisco!

What was your assignment in Singapore?

McCAIN: The teaching assignment in Singapore involved 30 students participating in a graduate program in business from the United States. Curiously I observed these students for similarities and differences from domestic students in the U.S. While seeking clues of their organizational as well as educational concerns, attitudes, and values, it became apparent to me early on that their perceptions were kept oddly closed to me. I was used to dialogue and discussion from students. I wondered why they were reluctant to discuss issues and concerns of education, management, and communication. Perhaps conceptual filters—cultural, sociocultural, psychocultural, and environmental—were operationalized to the level of consciously choosing not to interpersonally interact.

How did you approach the classes?

McCAIN: Night after night I lectured and conducted small-group activities yet received minimal feedback. The class sessions operated without a hitch—students were punctual, prepared, and polite. However after five nights, I felt discouraged. I was experiencing a consequence of ethnocentrism. Communication distance had been established, and I needed to figure out why and what could be done.

I remembered some of the blue print for intercultural communication from my own college days and decided to develop a strategy based on self-disclosure and acculturation.

Tell me about the potential for acculturation.

McCAIN: Acculturation potential appeared minimal considering my age, gender, education, and cultural naivete. My strategy rested on expressing to the class on a daily basis each new adventure and restaurant that I experienced. I told them about my impressions of their city-state. During our evening tea, I told them about my background, experience, and family. As the first week culminated, I observed a slight appreciation in casual conversation initiated by them and specifically directed toward me.

What did you think was happening?

McCAIN: *Aha!* Acculturation was in process. Cognitively, behaviorally, and affectively there was evidence of an effort toward assimilating our cultural differences. Each session dialogue increased. By the end of the ten-day session, there was obvious change in our communication distance. An environment of free exchange and open discussion took place the last night, which ended with a celebration dinner and perceived sadness that we would not meet again as a class.

Now that you have had time to process the experience, what do you think?

McCAIN: As I reflect on this experience, our central cultural difference was empowered by their attitudinal difference toward the cultural climate of the classroom. Because the educational system in Singapore, as well as other Asian countries, is sufficient to meet the population needs only through the secondary levels, opportunities for postsecondary education are limited. These students value education intrinsically and extrinsically. They view education as important for their career advancement in Singapore or globally. These students had a passionate desire to learn American business practices. They thrived on analyzing and solving business problems presented in the class. I realized their serious approach to learning was culturally bound by this goal of collecting as much information as possible within the time limits. Their approach to learning left out the gray area of discussion. They were interested in concrete methods and strategies of the successful business person—and I was to provide that, not ask them to discover that through discussion.

What were their main concerns?

McCAIN: Issues and concerns voiced by the group informally rang familiar to those of domestic students in the U.S. Major concerns include:

1. career opportunities—Where will I find advancement opportunities?
2. personal marketing—Should I move to Canada, U.S. . . . ?
3. minority limitations—How do women deal with the glass ceiling?
4. communication concerns—How do I talk to my boss?

What did you learn?

McCAIN: Their questions suggested to me that issues and concerns of professionals worldwide are more alike than different. These issues filter down to the graduate student level. Perhaps the value of these impressions lies in the ability to trust and learn from students of all countries who may be and probably are the harbingers of our future organizational cultures.

YOUR ASSIGNMENT

1. If you were assigned in a foreign country to exchange information with a group of students, professionals, and so forth, how would you approach your preparation?
2. In a foreign setting, if you were to get unexpected responses to information you were charged with providing, how would you attempt to understand the responses and/or how would you alter your behavior?
3. Do you agree with Dr. McCain that professional similarities in business cross many cultural boundaries? Can you give examples? If you do not agree, why?
4. Describe important communication competencies for intercultural situations.
5. In Singapore the language was English. Describe how Dr. McCain's experience might differ with more significant language barriers.

Getting Beyond Monologues: A Cross-Cultural Meeting of Organizational Consultants

GAYNELLE WINOGRAD, PH.D.

Gaynelle Rothermel Winograd (Ph.D. in Communication, University of Colorado; M.A. and B.S. in Speech Education, Northwestern University) is an organizational communication and development consultant based in Colorado Springs, Colorado. Since 1980, she has worked in both the public and private sectors on such issues as corporate culture, career development and transition, and problem assessment during rapid growth and downsizings. In addition, she has served on the faculties of Pennsylvania State University and the University of Colorado.

It was an atypical day. For one, the cool, rainy morning was an anomaly for June on the front range of Colorado. For another, four resident consultants in organizational development (OD) anticipated meeting with three foreign consultants.

There was Ruggero Cesaria from the IRI, a confederation of Italian corporations. Prompted by a study of IRI's organizational culture, Ruggero came to Colorado Springs to work with Pamela Shockley-Zalabak, a professor and consultant who had developed a model to study organization culture with a focus on communication rules. Together, over the next week, they were going to conduct an actual cultural study in a high-tech firm. Thus Ruggero would learn firsthand how to collect and analyze data using Shockley-Zalabak's model. Their collaboration laid the groundwork for anticipated cross-cultural studies comparing Italian and U.S. companies.

And there were Tanya Kramchentkova and Sergei Lebedev from Russia, who were apparently the first two practicing organizational development (OD) consultants in that country. Their visit to Colorado Springs reflected only a tiny segment of their three-month sojourn throughout the United States. They were sponsored in Colorado by Bob Rehm, an internal OD consultant with StorageTek and co-chair of Associated Consultants International (ACI).

Their trip had three major objectives. First, they wanted to meet with OD professionals in the United States as a step in building a professional network to share experiences and expertise. They also came to learn and gather as many materials as possible. They planned to create an OD information center in Leningrad (or St. Petersburg, given the historical vote for the city's name change that had taken place just that week). Finally, they envisioned sponsoring an OD conference in Leningrad. Such a conference, in their dreams, would introduce OD concepts and processes for change to Russian political and industry leaders.

Squaring off the table that morning were three other local OD consultants. Serving as internal consultants for their respective firms, Hector Arambulo from Digital Equipment Corporation and Connie Jenkins from Hewlett Packard saw major implications for such a gathering, both personally and professionally. As an independent consultant, Gaynelle Winograd provided the link between ACI and the Russian consultants to the OD professional community in Colorado Springs.

As can be imagined, many expectations bloomed in the minds of all the consultants. In the future, such meetings may be less atypical.

What follows are the retrospective thoughts of the four U.S. consultants who participated in this meeting. Each consultant was asked a protocol of questions in separate interviews. Before reading these comments, however, consider: What would you expect if you were going to participate in this meeting? What kind of expertise would you expect from IRI's Ruggero? Tanya? Sergei? What level of experiences conducting OD projects? What professional and cultural similarities would you anticipate? How about professional and cultural differences?

What were you expecting?

HECTOR: I wanted to learn about their perspectives, issues, and processes.

CONNIE: I went in trying not to have anything firm in my mind. Well, I didn't have any specific expectations other than I was very excited to meet with people who were doing similar work from different cultural backgrounds and experiences.

PAM: I was having trouble even knowing what to expect. I was expecting high energy. . . . I was expecting more formality in terms of interpersonal relationships. I was expecting the Russians to be more formal. I found them to be informal and willing with an excellent grasp of English. Although we couldn't speak Russian, I was amazed how we could still enter the conversations in a free flowing way. The most surprising thing was the lack of defensiveness by any group: the lack of this, people not saying one way is better or worse, but rather this is the way it is and here's what we're trying to do. And no sense from the Russians that there is a sense of failure, but rather a sense of opportunity.

GAYNELLE: I guess what I was expecting was either my worst case scenario or it could be the opposite, in which I would discover that they are just people like we are and doing some really innovative work. What I found was the latter.

What expectations were met?

HECTOR: Lots of opportunities to interact, but I don't think I got a handle on their individual perspectives. Wished I had more time to crack their heads open.

CONNIE: And I expected to see new and different approaches. I guess one thing that was a surprise was how similar our approaches and thinking were and how we were all trying similar things.

PAM: And I was expecting that everyone would be very participatory and wanting to give information. Those expectations were met.

GAYNELLE: As I discovered, they were very open and warm. . . . In our initial conversations, they commented on the warmth and openness they felt from everyone that they were meeting in the United States. It was going beyond their expectations: the willingness of people to go out of their way to help them. Immediately I felt a common ground with them on a personal level. And as I found out, they were people excited about the changes on the horizon within Russia. My whole experience went beyond my expectations in a positive way.

What expectations were not met?

HECTOR: The expectation that wasn't met was I wanted to listen for new ideas and I don't think that was met. That was a disappointment. I was hoping that some magical thing would crop in and I could say, "Ah, that's it." And that didn't happen.

CONNIE: I didn't have any expectations not met because I tried to go in with an open mind. I just wanted to be open—doing a lot of listening, watching, and understanding of what they do—what kind of people they were. I felt that was more important: to know what kind of people they were.

PAM: I was expecting more differences. But the processes that we described and talked about were very similar and familiar. And I just suppose that with the stereotypes that we've had with the [former] Soviet Union for many years that their OD approaches would be different. But they weren't; they were similar.

GAYNELLE: In terms of the former, what I was expecting when I met them, given my worst fear, was drawing into a Russian stereotype that on a personal level

I might be put down because of having bourgeois, material items. . . . What I actually experienced was far from my fear.

What was the greatest surprise?

HECTOR: Probably the thing of the Italian perspective, the socioeconomic blend—their confederation, their economy thing. The other thing was that my working theory said that the Italians would be more psychologically oriented and much more emotional. That wasn't true. That was a surprise for me. I don't know that if that was just Ruggero doing that or it was more pervasive in terms of their academic approach. Even though Pam had set me up, to actually experience it was still a surprise. . . . It was a 180 with the Russians. I expected the Russians to be more like the Italians and the Italians more like the Russians. [The] Russians [were] very warm and open. I expected them to be more nationalistic . . . defensive—not, open, wanting to share. I just wish I had more time.

CONNIE: I guess the number of similarities. As I said, their thinking and their excitement about their work is very similar. There were some cultural things, especially in terms of how they positioned their work. The Russians used their background in psychology extensively, which triggered in me the thought in the United States that we work more at a superficial level. Their designs went more in depth and worked more with individual dynamics. And that's an area that I think we need to take a look at to make changes.

PAM: Two things were a surprise. I think the greatest thing was that the Russians were doing self-managing teams since we had just started to talk about self-managing teams in the last 18 months to 2 years in the United States. The notion exhibited by Tanya and Sergei of upward influence and of taking control as a way of liberating the upper structure of an organization from having to make decisions. Now while that's a concept that we're familiar with in the United States, I was surprised coming out of the strong bureaucratic, dictatorial traditions as we have assumed them to be that they were doing self-managing teams. Also surprised that there was not as much dialogue between Ruggero and Sergei and Tanya. . . . It was as though it seemed that it was the Italians and the United States talking and the Russians and the United States talking. I not sure that I fully understand that dynamic.

GAYNELLE: The extent to which they have developed an expertise that is a synchronous kind of path. Many people in many different places are thinking about the same kind of issues. The fact that the concepts of organizational development, facilitating change in organizations, or developing teams and leadership were recurring points of discussion. It was demonstrated with Sergei and Tanya when they discussed the interpersonal and intrapersonal issues that they had to wrestle with at a group level in their work. . . . Tanya and Sergei appeared to be more process oriented and skilled in that. Their stories about their interventions demonstrated this. Ruggero was oriented more to the research end. I was very impressed as he described the kind of programs funded and expectations that Italian businesses had for their managers. They provided and expected continuing education and training for their managers. This surpasses what we provide here in the United States. U.S. businesses don't seem to demand this level of individual, ongoing development in their leadership.

What was the greatest confirmation?

HECTOR: The confirmation was that we were all so similar. And in terms of management models, how pervasive the bureaucratic model is. It's incredible. It works—over time. Then changes.

CONNIE: Well, I've had this feeling for a long time and sometimes I think I'm being a little Pollyannish—but people actually aren't really very different. I think one thing helped was with Ruggero—their culture and their approach to work drove his style and approach to his work. And I saw the same thing happening with Tanya and Sergei. They really did adjust. They are probably people who are emotionally driven. Probably something that I didn't expect. Because you always think of them as being cold—right? That was very different than probably I realized. . . . One more comment: I think we need to find a way to reach more into the individual in the organization. Too much of what we do is too superficial. Watching what they do was a learning experience for me.

PAM: I thought, in fact, that it was very reassuring professionally to see the common need for leadership, the common need for trying to understand motivational processes in groups, the common need for helping people to understand individual responsibility in groups. And I thought all the consultants were moving in that vein. And there was a very similar theoretical underpinning. Another confirmation comes from Italian experience. I am very impressed that the Italians are so committed to research before practice because that does not confirm my experience of how we do things in the United States. There is a real tendency to act anecdotally as opposed to having a real sound theoretical base. So I was pleased to see such strong research connection.

GAYNELLE: What was confirming was the fact that indeed we are a global society. There's going to be an increased need for knowing about and accepting differences in cultures for consulting professionals. Cross-cultural teams of OD consultants have much to offer international businesses and endeavors.

What were the professional similarities?

HECTOR: Probably psychological theories, group processes, team building, and all the way down to trust. I thought that was very similar in terms of our approach. The incorporation of theory, interpersonal, group processes, and back to the theory. The Russians were more psychological and historical in their approach, while the Italian was more academic, abstract, and opposite end of the spectrum.

CONNIE: Their approaches were not that conceptually different. They apparently had done a lot of the same reading we do. They were very familiar with some of the same theories, concepts, and expects. That seems to be more universal than just the United States.

PAM: First, the processes that people were using: helping groups to diagnose their own problems and taking an active participatory role in solving their own problems. Second, the importance of understanding our cultural traditions of organizations as they influence behaviors. Similarity from my research bias, when one of the first things Sergei said about problems in Russia was the need for better communication processes. And of course, the whole reason why Ruggero is in the United States is to look at communication rules as a way to help management and leadership understand organizational culture. Seeing the enormous emphasis on organizational communication in both countries.

GAYNELLE: All the way around there was a thirst for knowledge: wanting to know what other people were doing. . . . There's an openness and a willingness to share. I found that so true with Tanya and Sergei, since I had more personal time to interact with them as their sponsor in Colorado Springs. But again, this should be expected given the type of people they were meeting—OD people like Will Schutz, William Pasmore, Marvin Weisborg, and people at the NTL Institute, to name a few on their three-month visit. But these norms should be expected from OD professionals, professionals who teach and try to model these values and norms. . . . It was exciting to hear that the Italians and Russians were having some of the same frustrations and problems that we have, such as: Do we really make a difference? Is there sustained change? How do you monitor the balance between planned and spontaneous change? . . . It's also reconfirming that they're people just like us. I hate to admit it, but I had to process my internal expectations and stereotypes. I couldn't ignore them. Referring back to my expectations, my worst case scenario drew entirely upon negative stereotypes that I have absorbed being raised in the American culture during the, so-called, cold war.

What were the professional differences?

HECTOR: Not too many differences. I felt like I was home, as if I had worked with these people a long time. . . . I think our profession really does transcend. . . . People in our profession are six sigmas off to the right in terms of openness, skills, and competencies.

CONNIE: But their applications were very specific to the types of people they were working with—even with the Italians. Here, in most of our work, we have to work from personal power. And with this situation in Italy, it was a very structured and institutionalized process. Their people were expected to do things and certain time frames. . . . And it seemed like with Sergei and Tanya that the thing that they had going for them was that the organizations that they had to work with had a great deal of pain. They were able to leverage those situations and go in and work with people at such a level that I don't think we are able to do in the United States. In the United States, we are more short-term thinking; while both of their approaches were more long-term. In the United States, we're into short-term fixes so that we don't have large investments.

PAM: Professional differences started with very different academic backgrounds. For example, the Russians were from psychological backgrounds—psychologists. They were very interested in how we prepare people for organizational development and organizational change processes. They had no formal training. The same is true for Ruggero. If you want to do a Ph.D., you do it in something like philosophy. Then after the Ph.D., you get the business training. The business training comes after the very fundamental, highly theoretical training. There were professional training differences, but all were very highly professionally trained. . . . Another interesting difference is that Ruggero works entirely with upper management and leadership and very little with direct labor, unlike here in the United States. And, with Sergei and Tanya, I also had a sense that were working with [*upper-level*] professionals. Professionally, we here are expected to work across the entire organization and I don't think that was the case [*with the others*]. But I hesitate to say this for certain.

GAYNELLE: Professionally, I saw differences in emphasis. On the one hand, Ruggero appeared to be more skilled in the research end of the OD field, while [*on the other hand*] Tanya and Sergei were more focused on the process skills given their background in psychoanalysis and social psychology respectively.

What were the cultural similarities?

HECTOR: Three things came out. The basic economic realities that we're all dealing with. The other is gender issues. Even the Russians had different symbols for the genders, different symbols for men and women . . . . They have a way to draw the differences. . . . The last concept is the global interdependence. We all have to take care of this planet. Hands reaching out to one another. So economic realities, gender issues, and global realities. . . .

CONNIE: With Sergei and Tanya and Ruggero, they were very committed to their work. They seemed very creative. They were very open people. They were very excited to hear and learn anything they could. That was very similar to people here. . . . I thought all three were extremely open.

PAM: It's an underlying belief in the importance of people as change agents in organizations and a really positive view of people. That is, that people can be better, can work more effectively, that they can take ownership and responsibility. I think another similarity was a commitment to internationalizing individual experiences. No longer simply saying that what we do in Russia, or Italy, or the United States is enough. Maybe a need that I saw among everyone in the meeting was to have a broader understanding and experience. A recognition of value in all experiences. A striking lack of defensiveness in the group—or superiority.

GAYNELLE: The cultural similarities revolved around exhaustion in terms of the heightened awareness and alertness one needs when conversing with someone from another culture and language. Always being concerned about: "Am I being understood?" and "Am I really understanding what they intend to say?" For Tanya and Sergei, they talked about the mental exhaustion of translating, especially since they spoke both Russian and English and none of us spoke Russian. I felt for Ruggero, Tanya, and Sergei given our dependence on them for their bilingual skills. In building these types of relationships, there has to be consciously built-in time for privacy and relaxation. It's important to protect that. There was also a common concern to humanize change in organizations—and wanting to do that with feeling. . . . Another cultural similarity is the need to network, to build relationships that support oneself professionally.

What were the cultural differences?

HECTOR: Again, I think the profession overrode those. It's different because of the profession.

CONNIE: Because of the cultural differences, I think Tanya and Sergei were much more expressive. I think that [because of] the type of business and work that the Italian, Ruggero, was in or did, he was more reserved. But I still saw a lot of similarities, although they expressed it differently.

PAM: There were some obvious differences. Ruggero works in a culture that values more research and formal training than ours. They have obviously many more hours in presentations and formal training among their managers than in the United States. I think that Tanya and Sergei reflected the difficulties, the massive difficulties, of implementing these types of projects with such few people trained and such a strong business need. And a much stronger sense that authoritarianism is still present in United States but not to the extent as what Tanya and Sergei work with. They are working with such a lack of support systems in a way that we take for granted—equipment, computers, and office supplies. The other striking difference is that those of us in Italy and [the] United States have worked longer in this field than Tanya and Sergei.

GAYNELLE: I think the cultural differences lie for Tanya and Sergei in their isolation. As far as they know, they are the first OD consultants in Russia. . . . They have a real challenge to build this type of expertise in their country. They also commented on the lack of openness in their country beyond their immediate friends and business partners. However, I assured them that trust and openness is not found in many U.S. communities and organizations. Openness and sharing does not come automatically. However, within a building community of OD consultants, there's always a sensing out of competence and mutual respect. Once that's there, then the trust and openness comes more readily than otherwise. . . . I also came away aware of the potential need for downsizing and outplacement processes in Russia as their economic structure changes. Russian employees are not going to be guaranteed employment. . . . There's going to be a real need for educational programs in organizational communication and organizational development. . . . They see their most important mandate is to introduce these types of concepts to major Russian industry and governmental leaders. A final cultural difference was Tanya and Sergei's love of decks on the back of houses. They said that they do not have such spacious outdoor places built onto their homes and apartments. Also the large dinner party that Pam Shockley and her husband graciously sponsored in their home to introduce our international consulting guests would not have happened in Russia. Tanya and Sergei said that in Russia, people only entertain their closest friends in small gatherings. It was a surprise, yet interesting to them, that this is often the way that business is done in the United States. . . . Another cultural difference is their lack of materials. Materials that we take for granted are scarce in Russia, such as paper, pens, pencils—let alone computer equipment. When we visited HP [Hewlett Packard] and Digital, they were amazed to see training notebooks, containing reams of paper, that were given to all participants. In Russia, they said, this would not be possible because of the lack of access to paper. The other thing is the exigency . . . the exigency for the need for change in Russia. It's no wonder then that consultants like Tanya and Sergei meet an inherent need for action and process-oriented approaches. In Russia, it appears that things are pragmatically driven. Also the sizes of the organizations that they are working with. Tanya and Sergei were talking about millions of employees in one ministry with which they work. Also Ruggero was talking about confederations of corporations. Within IRI, for whom Ruggero worked, there are hundreds of thousands of employees.

What did your inner voice say before?

HECTOR: This is exciting.

CONNIE: Well, I love talking to people from other cultures. I always feel that I learn something from it. I gain a new insight. I love it. And I come away saying that people are just not that different. We're really not that different. So, I was really excited to talk to all three of them. I knew I'd come away with something new and different.

GAYNELLE: Excited. Hoping that my guests, Tanya and Sergei, got what they needed out of the visit.

What did your inner voice say during?

HECTOR: We can really help each other. Need to work on the technology to [do] that and the politics to get supplies to do this. . . .

CONNIE: I just thought it was great. I just thought this was so neat: These may be the only two OD people in Russia and I have the opportunity to meet them? What an experience. That was a thrill. And think I did gain a little new perspective—not a major breakthrough—but that they did do things with a different emphasis.

PAM: I can't believe that I'm having this experience. That after having so many years of working in the United States to have an actual opportunity to [experience] international exchange is very exciting. Part of it would say, "I wish we could fire all our political leaders." At a certain level, many of us could work well together. The notion . . . that we could be a part of a joint team for future international ventures. The fact that people are seeing the value of working collaboratively internationally is exciting.

GAYNELLE: Honored to be sitting at a table with this caliber of competency and international experience.

What did your inner voice say after?

HECTOR: This is fun. Probably more preparation would have been helpful.

CONNIE: At times, I wish I could meet with them in their language.

PAM: Wishing that other people could have this opportunity. That people have this stimulus—to raise their professional awareness.

GAYNELLE: Just wish there was more time. . . . They loved the beauty of [Colorado Springs]. And they also wanted to see the Olympic Training Center, which they heard a lot about in Russia, although the facilities are nothing compared to the complexes in Russia. And yes, they were somewhat disappointed in it. [*The Olympic Training Center actually consists of a cluster of unremarkable buildings and training areas, as well as quonset huts for dormitories.*] Even with the shortness of time, they felt it was important to make contacts with the people in the high-tech industries here. . . . Overall, they were glad that they came, but a two-hour drive seemed long compared to what they are used to in Russia. . . . They don't drive the kind of distances on a regular basis that we take for granted here.

What is the greatest lesson or learning for future international collaborations with other consultants?

HECTOR: The process cycle. If we had used the process cycle to help focus so that we would know what we wanted when we walked out of there.

CONNIE: Well, companies and economies are very intermeshed. So we're in an international arena whether we choose it or not. People have to be able to work in that kind of environment. So I think we have to do more of this—sharing. When the United States first started working with Japan, we made some major mistakes. OD consultants across cultures can really help with future international collaborations.

PAM: The greatest lesson is that it is genuinely possible. It's not just something for people from just established firms. It's really powerful . . . that it's a whole new arena, a whole new challenge and that's invigorating.

GAYNELLE: In terms of these types of meetings, I think that there has to be a lot more of upfront type of planning so that people can get the best out of it. Definitely, anyone who is sponsoring such foreign guests needs to be present at any appointment to act as facilitator, asking questions or clarifying the conversation, . . . [and] also making sure that such foreign consultants have time to decompress. . . . It's a very intense and exciting experience. . . . But the greatest learning is having old stereotypes voted wrong.

YOUR ASSIGNMENT

1. What were the major themes of expectations across these four consultants? How were they similar and different? How were yours similar or different?
2. What was the greatest surprise for you in reading the text of these four separate interviews? Greatest confirmation?
3. Given the professional similarities and differences discussed, which ones did you anticipate? Which ones were a surprise?
4. What cultural similarities and differences were expected? Unexpected?

5. What is your greatest lesson or learning after listening in on these consultants' afterthoughts on a cross-cultural meeting?
6. What factors exist today, as well as those on the horizon, that contribute to the need for cross-cultural consulting teams?

Through Their Eyes: Russian Reflections on the U.S. Organizational Development Community

TANTIANA KRAMTCHENKOVA AND SERGEI LEBEDEV, WITH GAYNELLE WINOGRAD, ENGLISH EDITOR

English Editor's Notes: As explained in the introduction of the prior case study, Tantiana Kramtchenkova and Sergei Lebedev are believed to be two of a handful of organizational consultants in Russia facilitating change and development. By training, Tanya is a psychoanalyst, and Sergei a social psychologist. Together, they form a consulting firm, entitled "Project," as in "we project change and a new future." Sergei serves as director, and Tanya as senior consultant. During the past three years since perestroika, *they have been making major innovative interventions in large Russian institutions.*

Tanya and Sergei's visit to the United States during the summer of 1991 was orchestrated by Bob Rehm, Chris Kloth, and Julie Harmon, partners in the consulting firm, "Changeworks." In the summer of 1990, these three U.S. consultants visited Russia on a tour organized for Organizational Development (OD) consultants. By chance and serendipity, they met Tanya and Sergei. After two meetings in Russia, these five consultants jointly began to envision the potential for Russian and U.S. collaboration in OD. Consequently, the U.S. group invited Tanya and Sergei to the United States. On their trip, they visited consultants from New England to Colorado from June to August 1991.

During the subsequent Russian revolution in August 1991, our community of OD consultants had a personal connection to Leningrad, or St. Petersburg. The U.S. visit of Sergei and Tanya during the summer of 1991 both affirmed and challenged our expectations as to what Russians were like—let alone how Russian OD consultants behaved. Many stereotypes crashed and burned. Confirmation regarding human commonality emerged amid acknowledged diversity. Nonetheless, we were curious: Which of their expectations of Americans and OD professionals remained the same or shifted?

The following responses given by Tanya and Sergei were composed and faxed to us just days prior to Leningrad's historical rebirth as St. Petersburg in September and October 1991. What follows are their reflections and impressions of our U.S. culture, in general, and the U.S. OD community, in specific. By examining both interviews with Russian and U.S. consultants, we can identify common grounds of shared understanding that simultaneously accompany parallel planes of diverse viewpoints. We can, therefore, capture a glimmer of the perceptual and communication challenges facing such cross-cultural ventures.

What expectations were met or not met when you came to the United States this summer to meet and talk with other organizational development (OD) consultants?

SERGEI: [Our] American colleagues who invited us to visit the country were almost unknown to me. But I believed my intuition; and it was saying, "these were 'right' people and these contacts would have [a] future." My intuition has not deceived me. I felt we had a lot in common [regarding] our professional approach. Even before our trip, it was evident that generally our ideas and principles were very much alike; but an anxiety also existed that, speaking more specifically, contradictions would appear. Really, it seemed to be incredible that people from different parts of the world, grow[ing] up in different cultures, would be very close not only "in general," but in the system of practical realization of these ideas. I was anxious that contradictions, which might appear, could spoil the contact and make further activity difficult.

TANYA: My experience with American consultants was not long enough— everyone would agree that two brief meetings are not too much of [an] experience. The first meeting [*was with Carolyn Lukensmeyer*] and the second [*with Julie Harmon, Chris Kloth, and Bob Rehm*]. Both of the meetings "felt" very good, people were open and friendly and, to my great surprise, the main approach and principles we spoke about seemed to be very close.

Literature on OD almost does not exist in this country. I think our library— all the gifts of our American friends and colleagues—is the most complete in Russia; and we have it only now. I would like to express again our gratitude for that priceless gift.

So, my expectations:

- to define the "borders" of OD [and] of the whole field.
- to determine if our activity is "in" the field and, if so, to see our specific place in the field.
- to define approaches, close to ours and, then, what we have in common and what is different.

Without any doubts, I thought that OD was . . . more developed in the USA than here. And it is really so. Sure, people had to be more specialized— that was true also. Books, magazines, lots of workshops and conferences, networking, possibilities to get education and in different ways—I expected that, but the reality came far beyond my expectations.

The reality of life differs so much in this country and I [now] have difficulty . . . trying to guess what name my country will have in the near future; and in America, I was anxious that the works which were similar at our [*first*] two meetings [*in Russia*] had different meanings: I was afraid that what seemed to be surprisingly alike would turn into having almost nothing in common.

Fortunately, it was not so. We had long talks with our colleagues about what they were doing and how, specifically. And we saw their work by our own eyes. If I was not afraid it would take too much room, I would be glad to thank all of them personally here.

It was unexpected that we had some problems in common. Not all managers understand [the] possibilities and importance of OD in this country—and in America too. [Most Russians, as well as Americans, do not] understand what it is all about . . . and the problems OD is working on. I expected that, but now I know [that] the people here are [not the only ones who are] afraid of changes, avoid responsibility, readily blame everybody and everything, from their boss up to black cats, . . . [for] their failures, treasure their stereotypes, and are inclined to act and—only then—think, [preferring] to talk, not . . . listen.

What was your greatest surprise? Confirmation?

SERGEI: From the very first day, I wanted to know as much as possible about our American colleagues and also to tell them about us. And the main result of our professional communication happened to be a big surprise: We had or could have common opinions about almost all important issues discussed. And then, watching Chris Kloth's real work with clients, I got a relaxed breath and realized that is true—we are close and have all the possibilities for further work. It was most important.

TANYA: The most surprising was the fact that our approach and main principles were really very close. It is always amazing, though [it] happens [more often than not], that at the very far ends of the world, people of different cultures, different political and economical reality, think and act in a similar way.

What were the professional similarities?

SERGEI: We had a goal to [build a] Soviet–American team of consultants, if it would be possible. The necessity for such a team was the consequence of development [in] Soviet–American business and other connections.

TANYA: During our first meeting in Leningrad (now, thank God, our city has it's real name [St. Petersburg]) with Julie, Chris, and Bob, we said that, most probably, our countries would have wide and intensive business connections. The culture of business, mentality, and traditions were extremely different. Businessmen have to understand each other at [the very] least to be successful. It is naive to think that joint Soviet–American or American business in [Russia] would be "as in America." To be successful in Russia, in the USSR, American businessmen have to "feel" the country, its mentality, traditions, and people's values. They have to be able to distinguish "right" people from "wrong" and really understand all of this complicated and quickly changing reality. It is not easy even for professionals. And the second task, to adapt and be adapted—to create something very new: Soviet–American or American–Soviet business.

Today, negotiating, people say the same words and have an illusion of mutual understanding. The thing is that these words often have different meanings and all the problems appear later and quite unexpectedly.

So, our proposal was to create a team of Soviet and American consultants. If we can [overcome] all the mentioned and [unmentioned] differences, being a laboratory to ourselves, we would be able to help others. Our colleagues, and now friends, invited us to the USA; and we spent about six weeks together. Their help, energy, and friendliness [were very] important steps towards [creating] this "team." I think we are ready to begin and hope that Julie, Chris, and Bob are of the same opinion.

What were the professional differences?

SERGEI: The difference between Soviet and American business culture is tremendous. Without abilities to cope with this difference, I suspect that Soviet–American business, especially situated in this country [Russia], would not be successful. All the norms, habits, attitudes are different. At the same time, Soviets and Americans use the same words, [but] with different meanings. To [overcome] these misunderstandings is difficult, though possible. I think that with the help of a Soviet–American team of consultants, businessmen will save a lot of time, effort, and money.

TANYA: OD is in its beginning in our country. It is quite developed in the USA. Every [little] difference is only the consequence of a big one. On the one hand, [there are] different types of education, books, workshops, networking, etc. On the other hand, the first chair of "Sociology in Organizations" was opened at Moscow University this September. An American . . . , Steven Reinsmith, is the chairman.

What were the cultural similarities?

SERGEI: If consultants themselves could overcome their own cultural differences and develop [a real] common language, mutual understanding, and an ability to work together, they would have good chances to help businessmen and managers in the international activity.

During our visit to the USA, I realized that such a team could exist. This understanding brought "Project" and "Changeworks" to the decision to take joint activities in consulting [with] Soviet–American business.

TANYA: I think I have already answered this question. The only thing I would like to add is that our approach seems to be psychological and even, sometimes, [psychotherapeutic]. The level of stress and anxiety is very high now [in Russia], and [our] people's psyche is deformed by all these decades of violence and permanent lies.

What were the cultural differences?

SERGEI: We have different backgrounds. American consultants have grown up in [a] society with [a] well-developed culture of consulting. [This] applied science [of] dealing with people individually and in organizations [has primarily been] developed in the USA. We have grown up with a "hunger for information" in these fields and without any possibility to watch how professionals work, or to have any training.

OD practitioners in this country [Russia] could be count[ed] in [the] dozens and even the name, "organizational development," is understandable for [just a small] group of professionals.

TANYA: It is, I am afraid, impossible, to describe cultural differences "in general." The USA and USSR have different strata and groups: People in huge cities live differently from people in the country and I [do not have an] idea [as to] what the life of some groups in the population looks like.

In our country there is an opinion that in your country, people are more oriented to "things" and "actions," are very specialized and efficient in their profession, but are "narrow" and rather ignorant about cultural things, such as literature, even American, music or painting. That money and "success" play the greatest role for Americans and [that] everybody pretends he is happy, but it is only the mask. That Americans are like children: naive, friendly, easy to deceive, crazy about games, bright colors, sport[ing] events, and ice cream. That they have "bad" manners like what we expect from children—eating in streets, always having something in their mouths, being very noisy, not knowing how to behave, putting their legs everywhere and going [out] in the[ir] sneakers even to [the] Philharmonic [Orchestra].

Our people, on the contrary, have "ideas," are extremely spiritual and [are] fond of "real culture." Money [is] too low a matter. Even to think of it is improper for those who have a "soul." To be successful means to "show off" and to offend others. So, noble people have to talk about "noble" things, to smoke a lot, and to be very poor and unhappy. This opinion coexists with just the opposite one: America is great; everything is great in America. Everybody who is not a fool wants to be . . . "American" [as much] as possible.

There are lots of myths about cultural differences. Americans are different; Russians are different. They differ from each other greatly . . . . But it is very dangerous, thou[gh] popular to give "general" answers.

What did your inner voice say before your visit? During? After?

TANYA: About inner voice. Once, after our coming home from the theater, my four-year-old daughter told me: "Mom, I am so small and silly." Something of that kind [of thoughts was] my inner voice . . . [talking] to me before going to America: "They will speak so quickly. You will probably understand nothing. They are so specialized, and you have to do almost everything. You will not understand each other, etc. . . . ."

Later, in America, the tune became different: "Well, these guys are so incredibly lucky. So simple, just buy a book and read it in your native language. And no need to build a flip-chart. . . . University program here, training program there, and no necessity to ride bicycles. . . . " Now, [I have a] new melody: "I wonder when you will read all these piles of books and papers? And how you will organize the OD Conference in St. Petersburg with this total shortage of everything? (Books have to be translated, [while] your current work is to be done.) Don't forget [that] with all [these] materials, you are almost as lucky as they are.

And I am really lucky: I have a lot of friends to remember, a lot of issues to [think] about, [and] lots of books to read while standing in lines. And I am even more lucky than my American friends—I have plenty of time, because [the] lines are endless.

What was your greatest lesson or learning as a result of your visit?

SERGEI: I would like to say [something] about one amazing phenomenon. In the USA . . . , I would like to emphasize [that] every OD consultant [who] we met helped us. They gave us a lot of books and other papers. I want to thank everybody and especially Tom Chase for a full box of Addison-Wesley books. [These consultants] shared information with us, helped us to contact other consultants, showed us their [places of work, including] organizations and universities, invited us to be their guests, and spent lots of time and money driving us to different places. We lived in their homes, and they were so caring and hospitable. They organized our presentations and participation in conferences, and did so much as only really good and generous people would do.

TANYA: What is my greatest learning as the result of my visit? Well, as all people are naked under their clothes, so [too] under the surface level of differences, we are not Americans or Russians—we are people. I always suspected it, but now I know it is for sure—many thanks to our American friends.

Julie Harmon, Chris Kloth, Bob Rehm, ACI [*Associated Consultants International*]—without you this trip would be impossible. Ernest Posa, the warmth of your home is still with us; Anne Murray Allen, thank you for your kind hospitality; Tom Chase, you have done so much for us; Marvin Weisbord, we remember your "future search conference"; Lola Wilcox, thank you very much for your willingness to help; Gaynelle Winograd, without you, we would have never seen the beauty of Colorado Springs, and would have never met Pam Shockley—and nobody would have ever read these lines. Many thanks to every person we met.

YOUR ASSIGNMENT

1. What was your greatest surprise in seeing U.S. culture through these Russians' eyes? Greatest confirmation?

2. What cultural and professional similarities do these Russian professionals have in common with their U.S. counterparts? Differences? (Refer back to the interview responses of the U.S. consultants.)

3. What major communication problems would you anticipate that these Russian and U.S. consultants will have to confront for effective collaboration on business joint ventures?

4. Why would it be important for this cross-cultural team of consultants to work first on their own communication strengths and challenges before tackling the problems of clients who would represent joint ventures between Russian and U.S. business?

5. If you were asked to help facilitate creating a joint Russian–U.S. consulting team, what issues would you address? How would you design a team-building effort to enhance their working relationships?

Organizational Communication Processes and Behaviors

Commentary

LEADING, MANAGING, AND PARTICIPATING: CHANGING ORGANIZATIONAL IMPERATIVES

Literally hundreds of thousands of words have been written about individual communication processes within a variety of organizational contexts. Managers and worker interactions, team performance, career satisfaction, leadership, conflict processes, and ethical behaviors are just a few of the topics of intense academic and popular interest. Organizational communication processes and behaviors can be described as the substance of organizational life illustrating the dynamic and ever-changing nature of organizing and communicating. In Part II, **Organizational Communication Processes and Behaviors,** you will explore the topics of individual behaviors in organizations, examine a variety of group problem-solving processes, and relate problem solving to leadership and management. You will confront organizational conflicts as well as value and ethical dilemmas.

The following commentary seeks to examine individual participation processes in organizations by identifying and speculating about significant changes for leading, managing, and participating. Specifically, it will explore the substance gap in leadership and describe the transition of management's role from control to anticipatory consultant. Self-leadership and team management will be examined as the participation processes of the future. Finally, notions of the ethic of personal advantage will be explored as they relate to leadership, management, and participation in the downsized and delayered organizations of the 1990s.

New Leadership Imperatives

He talks like a leader, she walks into the boardroom with confidence, he leads a massive strategic planning effort, and she publishes her vision for the organization. Nothing really changes and they move on to other organizations and new leadership challenges. They are the leaders of a failed generation of leaders. They attend executive development programs and intellectually understand that vision, strategic direction, and change are passports to the future. But they don't get it; they are process managers who can't design the process. They have style, they don't have substance. They are the answers to the questions of how to professionalize management, they are the wrong answers.

As Zaleznik (1990a) describes,

> These business executives, who used to think of themselves as leaders, potential if not actual, became professional managers and absorbed the managerial mystique. While walking blindly along the path of the corporate career, they fell into the trap that Sigmund Freud first identified as "suggestibility," one of the mental states in which thinking and feeling separate and hence widen the rift between the mind and the heart and between logic and common sense. The managerial mystique is only tenuously tied to reality. As it evolved in practice, the mystique required managers to dedicate themselves to process, structures, roles and indirect forms of communication and to ignore ideas, people, emotions, and direct talk. It deflected attention from the realities of business, while it reassured and rewarded those who believed in the mystique. (p. 2)

Zaleznik (1990b) argues that business in the United States is less competitive because of a sea of managerial mediocrity. Leadership is needed to face worldwide competition and economic challenges and should be based on a compact that binds those who lead and those who follow "into the same moral, intellectual, and emotional commitment. . . . But, by and large, the tie that binds men and women in organizations today, particularly at the professional and managerial levels, is narrow self-interest, rather than a sense of mutual obligations and responsibilities" (p. 15). Zaleznik contends managers focus on process whereas leaders seek and generate imaginative ideas.

As industry after industry downsize and European and Japanese competition heat up, few challenge at least some of Zaleznik's conclusions. Yet the new leadership imperative is less well understood than the criticisms from which it emerges.

Warren Bennis and Burt Nanus (1985) make important distinctions between leaders and managers when they suggest that "the problem with many organizations, and especially the ones that are failing, is that they tend to be overmanaged and underled. They may excel in the ability to handle the daily routine, yet never question whether the routine should be done at all. There is a profound difference between management and leadership, and both are important. . . . Managers are people who do things right and leaders are people who do the right thing. The difference may be summarized as activities of vision and judgment—effectiveness versus activities of mastering routines—efficiency" (p. 21). Bennis and Nanus further contend that the vision leaders provide is the clearest of all distinctions between leaders and managers. To provide vision requires marshaling the "spiritual and emotional" resources of the organization as reflected in its values, commitment, and aspirations. Management, on the other hand, is charged with directing the physical resources of the organization, its people, machines, and products. Competent managers can get work done efficiently, but excellence comes from leaders who inspire followers to emotional involvement with work and their organization. Bennis and Nanus state, "Great leaders often inspire their followers to high levels of achievement by showing them how their work contributes to worthwhile ends. It is an emotional appeal to some of the most fundamental of human needs—the need to be important, to make a difference, to feel useful, to be a part of a successful and worthwhile enterprise" (p. 93).

Larson and LaFasto (1989) refer to examples of leaders of successful teams as "principled leaders." They consider principled leaders as "the final ingredient in effective team performance—and one of the most critical. . . . Our research strongly indicates that the right person in a leadership role can add tremendous value to any collective effort, even to the point of sparking the outcome with an intangible kind of magic'' (p. 118). Larson and LaFasto characterize principled leaders as providing consistent messages, possessing a perspective for unleashing talent, practicing ego suppression, and creating other leaders. They conclude, ''Leadership is clearly more than just putting 'spin' on team effort. Effective leadership does, in fact, fundamentally change what the team effort is all about. Leaders make people feel connected with the mainstream of what is happening by helping them understand the organization's vision. By overcoming inertia, they demonstrate that change is possible. Perhaps most important, they create self-confidence in people, thereby encouraging them to take risks, make decisions, and act—in short, to be leaders themselves'' (p. 129).

Manz and Sims (1989) refer to leading others to self-leadership as SuperLeadership. Manz and Sims contend managers should be ''SuperLeaders.'' SuperLeadership is conceived as a set of behaviors that inculcate habits of self-leadership in followers. Managers, in the Manz and Sims view, are transformed from supervisors or controllers to teachers and coaches. The emphasis shifts from command and instruction to getting others to command and instruct themselves.

These new leadership imperatives are not without internal contradictions. On the one hand, the imperative is to move to group and team self-leadership; on the other hand, leaders are exhorted to singularly, if necessary, risk for the future to motivate follower commitment. Leadership is described as both a lonely and highly participative endeavor. The increasing complexity of an information society places new demands on leaders and managers. The sheer volume of information available for organizational decision making complicates the development of organizational vision and the direction of organizational activities. This volume of information, when coupled with fast-paced technological changes, puts a new emphasis on the need for leadership from diverse organizational positions. These fundamental changes become imperatives not just for leaders but for managers and all organizational participants as well.

Managers in Transition

The ''middleless'' organization is the new organizational design for the 1990s. Fewer managers with larger spans of control characterize organizational hierarchies in almost all industries. Work teams are given higher degrees of autonomy and control over immediate work situations. The goal is to increase competitiveness and improve employee morale. Traditional responsibilities of managers are replaced by passing power and control to lower levels in the organization. Managers become facilitators, coaches, teachers, and experts as opposed to controllers, directors, planners, and rewarders. The new responsibilities are roles, not new organizational positions. These roles are shared by those who formerly held traditional management jobs in order to support a sizeable number of self-managed teams. Morgan (1988) suggests this new approach can be described as "helicopter management" where managers hover and come in only when something goes wrong that requires their assistance. It is operating at a distance and letting others have the hands-on responsibilities.

Hansell (1991) describes the new management imperative as anticipatory management. Managers should identify and interpret broad trends and plan for their likely impact on the organization. Managers must resist what Hansell considers "the natural intuitive response to new situations is to draw on our past experience. However, the critical information for today's decisions lies in the future, not in the past. It is what will happen tomorrow—not what happened yesterday—that is most relevant in a fast-changing world" (p. 1). Hansell's position supports Morgan's (1988) overview of competencies needed for new organizational environments. Morgan believes managers need: "(1) reading the environment, (2) managing proactively, (3) leadership and vision, (4) human resource management, (5) promoting creativity, learning, and innovation, (6) skills of remote management, (7) using information technology as a transformative force, (8) managing complexity, and (9) broadening contextual competencies" (p. 2).

Changing Imperatives for Participants

Participants, leaders, and managers in organizations are all affected by change. Career expectations are altered and responsibilities shift from individual contributors to team and group settings. The downsized and delayered organizations of the 1990s have given rise to concerns about career advancement and personal growth and security. Performance expectations are raised and performance evaluation is more exacting than in past decades.

Quality circles, high-performance teams, and self-managing teams are organizational structures and processes requiring new skills and commitments from organizational participants. Problem solving, new idea generation, conflict resolution, persuasion, planning, time management, budgeting, and evaluation are only a few of the responsibilities given to autonomously operating groups. Participants are expected to become self-leaders; to establish self-set goals; and to self-administrator awards and punishments (Manz and Sims, 1989). In addition, participants are expected to engage in continual learning, providing organizations with flexibility and renewal. Larson and LaFasto (1989) suggest participating in effective teams is based on establishing a clear, elevating goal; developing results-driven structures; forming around competent team members; generating unified commitment; encouraging a collaborative climate; setting standards of excellence; and having external support and recognition.

The Ethic of Personal Advantage

These imperatives for change are challenged by what Mitchell and Scott (1990) describe as the ethic of personal advantage. They argue that much of the pressing problems in the United States can be traced to widely held U.S. values based on short-term versus long-term perspective; (2) focus on the ends versus means: and (3) individual versus community emphasis. They call this combination of values the ethic of personal advantage.

A baby food manufacturer sells sugar water as apple juice, a major bank makes loans on nonexistent oil leases, insider trading brings down a major brokerage firm, the savings and loan crisis costs taxpayers billions, an airline falsifies maintenance records, and teachers lie about degree credentials—all examples of an ethic of personal advantage. But the issues are more complex than the outright fraud and illegality that has plagued the 1980s and early 1990s. Mitchell and Scott suggest our national obsession with short-term success has contributed to survey findings indicating that over 40 percent of all employees expect to leave their current employer within three years or less; the figure increases to over 50 percent when those surveyed are managers. Mitchell and Scott conclude that the ethic of personal advantage leads to: (1) lack of job involvement and commitment, (2) increased turnover, (3) poor interpersonal relations, (4) self-absorption, and (5) unethical behavior.

The personal advantage perspective inhibits risk taking and contributes to politically correct organizational behaviors. The emphasis on the individual is in contrast with the need for high performance groups. The short-term success requirement inhibits investment in long-term solutions and the known becomes more viable than seeking new solutions. The ethic of personal advantage, therefore, to the extent it influences individuals and their behaviors, powerfully inhibits the changes we need from organizational leaders, managers, and participants. Mitchell and Scott argue that enlightened managers can contribute to change and that individuals can make a difference. The challenge, therefore, is more complex than acquiring new skills and developing new processes. The challenge is substance—the substance of values and ethics and the communication of this substance throughout organizations. It is both an individual and a societal challenge. In a very fundamental sense, it is the new leadership imperative.

REFERENCES

Bennis, W., and B. Nanus. 1985. *Leaders: The strategies for taking charge.* New York: Harper & Row.

Hansell, W. 1991. ICMA. *Public Management.* (July): 1–2.

Larson, C., and F. LaFasto. 1989. *Teamwork.* Newbury Park, Calif.: Sage.

Manz, C., and H. Sims. 1989. *SuperLeadership: Leading others to lead themselves.* New York: Prentice-Hall.

Mitchell, T. R., and W. G. Scott. 1990. America's problems and needed reforms: Confronting the ethic of personal advantage. *Academy of Management Executive.* 4(3): 23–35.

Morgan, G. 1988. *Riding the waves of change: Developing managerial competencies for a turbulent world.* San Francisco: Jossey-Bass.

Zaleznik, A. 1990a. *The managerial mystique: Restoring leadership in business.* New York: Edward Burlingame/Harper & Row.

Zaleznik, A. 1990b. The leadership gap. *The Executive* 4(1): 7–22.

CHAPTER 3

Individuals in Organizations

My Style Is My Style: Like It or Leave Me Alone

The management team at Foster Retailers in Los Angeles is composed of three strong individuals: Charles Grant, store manager; Lora Atkinson, marketing and administrative manager; and Doug James, sales manager. All are experienced in retailing and have worked for the Foster chain for many years.

Charles, Lora, and Doug report to Pam Miller, Foster's regional manager for California, Oregon, and Washington. The region is successful and Foster's Los Angeles store is one of its leaders. When Pam made a routine visit to the Los Angeles store, Charles revealed there was a severe conflict between Lora and Doug. Pam was surprised because she had assumed the two worked well together and had observed no previous evidence of trouble. Charles asked that Pam meet with each of them individually and then make a recommendation about how he should proceed.

CHARLES'S STORY

Lora and Doug are both very talented individuals but both are insecure and difficult to work around. Lora needs constant reassurance that she is making the right decision and requires a lot of my time. She wants to know what I am thinking and how I am feeling about her. I like her but her emphasis on watching every move I make to see what it means frankly gets on my nerves. Also, she has a chip on her shoulder. She thinks if anyone forgets to tell her something they are deliberately leaving her out of the group. But I believe she contributes less to the problems than Doug. Doug never wanted Lora here in the first place. He thought that he and I could run things just fine with the help of a secretary. He thought the advertising agency could handle the marketing and that we really didn't need an administrative professional to run bookkeeping, and so on. Doug wants to be successful without playing by the rules. He resents Lora asking him for time sheets on his salespeople and he doesn't like her reviewing the sales budget with him.

But the way they interact just doesn't make sense. They are like two-year-old professionals. Lora leaves Doug 10 or 12 notes per day. Doug refuses to reply. Lora asks Doug for answers in front of the people who work for him. He refuses to answer and then walks away. Doug tells his people not to tell Lora anything and to tell him immediately if she asks for anything. They drive me crazy. Lora wants me to do something. Doug tells me to get Lora off his back. They don't speak to each other in staff meetings. Frankly, I wish I could get rid of both of them without losing their basic talents.

Despite all of this, everyone in the region knows they generally turn in good numbers. I don't think I should have to deal with this. I have told them to put their complaints in writing and that I don't want to have to hear from either of them again unless they are ready to file a formal grievance.

LORA'S STORY

I am so sorry this mess can't be worked out among the three of us. I have tried and tried and tried. I know we should not have to bother a regional manager with these petty problems. Doug just won't accept the fact that I am here and here to stay. He won't give me the information I need to do my job and to help him do his. He has resented me from the day I walked in this place. He tells the others here to avoid me and some of them treat me like I have the plague.

Charles is little help. I think he is a good manager and he really has tried but he can't or won't make Doug do anything. He told us recently not to talk about this anymore unless we were ready to file a formal grievance. Well, now we are talking about this at the regional level. It just makes me sick. I am not even sure that Charles supports me. He says that he does but I'm not sure.

Doug should not be able to get away with running things his way regardless of company policy. I know his sales force performs, but it does so at the expense of everyone else. It is certainly reasonable for me to have the financial information on time. Actually, I want you to know that I am somewhat afraid of Doug. I don't know what he might do to get rid of me.

I don't think I should have to be afraid of what might happen. My work has always been good and I have never experienced anything like this. I have asked Charles for help but nothing happens.

DOUG'S STORY

We should not be here talking with a regional manager about this. We should have been able to solve this ourselves. I will take my share of the blame but the others won't. Sure, Lora drives me crazy. She has to know every little thing. And

I don't like paperwork. I know it is necessary but she bugs me about it all the time. She also wants to give orders to the people who work for me. Well that won't work and I have told them not to respond to her. That just drives her up and over the wall. She has even told other people she is afraid of me. Afraid of what? Yes, I wish she had not come on this team; everything has gone down hill since her arrival. But what am I going to do? Right now I want her to stop making remarks behind my back about how she is afraid.

I will do my part but she has to do hers as well. Charles is no help. He just shuts the door of his office and tells us to put it in writing. He puts everything in writing. We get two- or three-page memos from him all of the time. If you ask a simple question you get a written response. You know it is amazing this store has the numbers that it has.

PAM'S FACT FINDING

Following her conversations with Charles, Lora, and Doug, Pam asked several store employees about morale and told them she wanted recommendations about ways to improve the overall operation of the store. All interviewed employees, using a variety of specific examples, told Pam that management needed to be more cooperative. Individually, Charles, Lora, and Doug were good people, but as a team they made the Foster staff nervous and concerned about how to respond to questions and requests. Most felt Charles should take a stronger role and many expressed a concern that Lora and Doug should leave their personal dislikes at home. Two employees characterized Lora and Doug as talented but insecure— the same description Charles had given. Lora had the more pleasant personality but was considered manipulative because she questioned everyone. Doug was more abrasive but was generally viewed as direct and truthful. Charles was seen as trustworthy but bureaucratic.

PAM'S RECOMMENDATIONS

Pam called Charles, Lora, and Doug together to discuss her recommendations. She told them she was convinced the basic problems were individual differences in styles and approaches. She believed all three were committed to doing a good job for Foster and that all three were capable. She advised the three to work more cooperatively in order to build a team example for store personnel. She requested they meet daily for the next several weeks to exchange needed information. And she emphasized that all confrontations in front of other employees should cease immediately. She also asked Charles to make an increased effort to spend time with all store personnel. She recommended that Lora consolidate her requests to Doug into fewer messages and that she try to make most requests at the staff meeting. She advised Doug to respond to Lora's requests in a timely manner and to cease talking to his employees about her performance. Finally, she asked for their questions and comments. Charles responded he would do his best. Lora and Doug remained silent and refused to look at each other.

SIX MONTHS LATER

Pam Miller returned to the Los Angeles store for an unscheduled visit following news that Lora had filed a formal complaint against Doug with the company's personnel office. Pam asked Charles for specific information and a report on what had happened since her last visit. Charles was clearly disturbed and told Pam he could no longer handle the situation. He said that he had attempted the meetings as Pam had requested. Things had improved initially, but as the months passed Lora and Doug renewed their disagreements. The event that preceded the formal complaint resulted from Lora calling two of Doug's subordinates into her office to ask why they did not like her and what Doug had said to turn them against her. Doug found out about the meeting and apparently stormed into Lora's office and told her that drastic measures would be taken if she ever spoke to anyone who worked for him again. Lora left the store in tears and told her secretary she was afraid of Doug and what he might do. Doug demanded Charles tell Lora to quit harassing his people.

Pam spoke with both Lora and Doug. Three employees also requested to speak with Pam concerning the problems. Pam's conclusion was difficult and painful for all involved.

Pam placed Lora and Doug on probation. They would have six months to demonstrate they could behave as professionals or be asked to find work elsewhere. Charles was removed from his position as manager of the Los Angeles store and offered a transfer to a smaller operation with less responsibility. Pam told him he must learn to be more involved in building a team and managing people; he could not just attend to the more technical aspects of his job. None of the three were pleased, but Lora expressed relief that changes were actually taking place. Doug said he could behave professionally but was not sure if Lora could handle the task.

Pam left Los Angeles believing that all three talented people had been lost to the organization. She wondered what she should have done differently. She wondered how she should supervise Charles in his new position. She was concerned for the new manager of the Los Angeles store and knew her support would be needed. She asked her secretary to arrange a monthly Los Angeles visit for the next six months. Pam concluded that everyone, including herself, had failed.

YOUR ASSIGNMENT

1. Describe the communication style differences and problems in this case. How does conflict theory help us understand what happened?
2. How does Charles contribute to the problems? Lora? Doug? Pam?

3. What could Charles have done prior to Pam's intervention? What could Pam have done differently?
4. Based on conflict and negotiation theory, develop an intervention for Charles and Pam.
5. What do you think will happen to Charles, Lora, and Doug? Can individuals change communication and conflict preferences? Design a training program for Charles, Lora, and Doug.

The Coronado YERS Case

Ruth Walsh and her husband, Ralph, moved to Evergreen, Arizona, in the fall of 1991. Ralph had taken medical retirement from his position as director of the Park and Recreation Department in Summerfield, Iowa. Ruth had resigned as executive director of the Summerfield Youth Employment and Recreation Service (YERS) with hopes that a move to Arizona would be beneficial to Ralph's health.

By October 1991, Ruth began a job search in Middleton, a community of 200,000 within driving distance of Evergreen. Most permanent residents of Evergreen, a resort community, are employed in Middleton. Ruth felt pressured by large medical bills and her husband's reduced retirement income to find work as quickly as possible. During the first months of her job search, Ruth remained optimistic. However, by Christmas 1991, no promising positions had been located. With mounting apprehension, Ruth contacted the national office of the YERS in Akron, Idaho.

The National Executive Council of YERS determines governing policy for local YERS chapters. In addition, the council provides training in procedures, practices, and program development for local YERS organizations. The council establishes and publishes an approved list of consultants to work in training and a variety of problem-solving situations. Any local YERS can request a list of consultants who have experience in areas of particular need. The most frequent users of the consultant list are YERS programs experiencing financial and general administrative problems.

Ruth had been in local YERS management for 20 years in Marion, Iowa, Frazier, Iowa, and most recently, Summerfield, Iowa. She was familiar with the council's consulting program but reluctant to be put on the list because she wanted to work in Middleton. Ruth knew that becoming a YERS consultant would mean extensive travel. She worried about her decision but did not see any viable alternatives.

Within six weeks of her listing on the consultant roster, the Tulane, Oregon, YERS telephoned Ruth to inquire if she would be interested in working there for approximately three months. The executive director of the Tulane YERS had been fired and the board of directors wanted to conduct an extensive search for a new director. Ruth reluctantly agreed to act as consulting director for a period not to exceed 90 days. Her apprehension was based on leaving Ralph and Evergreen to work some 1,300 miles from home. At the last minute, Ralph decided to accompany Ruth, which somewhat eased her anxiety.

While in Tulane, Ruth learned of developing problems with the YERS in Coronado, Arizona. Margaret Rims, a professional associate and friend of 15 years, wrote to ask Ruth for a letter of personal recommendation. Margaret had been promoted to the position of executive director of the Coronado YERS in 1990 after 23 years of service with the organization. Margaret indicated to Ruth that she was experiencing difficulty with certain members of her board of directors with regard to program direction. She told Ruth the letter would be utilized to update Margaret's own personnel file. Ruth wrote a letter and made a mental note to visit Margaret when she and Ralph returned to Evergreen.

Ruth gave the Coronado situation little more thought as she worked hard updating records at Tulane for the new director's arrival. During her last weeks, Ralph began to experience increasing stomach pain that was unrelated to his other medical problems. Ruth was relieved when the time came to return to Evergreen.

Ralph was hospitalized almost immediately on their return. Surgery successfully corrected Ralph's problem but the medical bills wiped out her Tulane earnings. Although two additional consulting offers came while Ralph was recuperating, Ruth felt compelled to turn both down.

Ruth was taken by surprise when Dr. Angela Atkins, president of the board of directors of the Coronado YERS, contacted her in August 1992. Dr. Atkins indicated the Coronado program was in serious difficulty. Dr. Atkins asked Ruth to meet with the board of directors and to make recommendations for consulting services. Dr. Atkins offered to pay her travel expenses and a consulting fee to attend a meeting. Ruth agreed even though she was surprised to learn the services of Margaret Rims had been terminated.

THE CORONADO YERS

Coronado is the largest city in Arizona with a population of 1 million. Coronado is located in the middle of the state, approximately 80 miles from Evergreen. The YERS program has had a long and distinguished history in Coronado. However, in recent years minority groups of African Americans and Hispanics have continuously asked for increased services and facilities in parts of town with substantial minority populations. These requests have created dissention and growing controversy among staff and factions on the board of directors.

Margaret Rims had been with the Coronado YERS for 25 years at the time of her termination. Margaret began her career in recreational services while attending Coronado University. She continued in recreational services after graduation and saw the YERS recreational program grow from a 1-person staff with limited programs in a single location to a 15-person staff with programs in seven Coronado locations.

Margaret has been given credit over the years for the development of the recreational program. She has been asked by the national council of YERS to lead several regional and national workshops on recreation program development. It was at one of these workshops that Margaret had met Ruth Walsh.

Margaret Rims's application for the executive director position surprised several staff and board members. Most people associated with YERS assumed Margaret was happy in her position. Several board members voiced concern over

Margaret's overall administrative qualifications, but the prevailing sentiment supported her promotion.

Margaret became executive director of the Coronado YERS in a climate of mounting pressure to increase services and facilities in the heavily populated minority areas in northeast Coronado. Several local groups also questioned minority representation on the YERS staff and board. Margaret felt these pressures were best ignored. She disagreed with several board and staff members, who urged her to develop plans to increase minority member involvement.

Margaret's strongest staff support came from her friend and personnel director, Zalda Smith. Zalda has been the YERS personnel director for 18 years. She has not been pleased with increasing requirements by the National Executive Council of YERS in the area of personnel. Specifically, she disagrees with open advertisement for job vacancies, detailed job descriptions, and grievance procedures for employees. She believes employers should have much more latitude than these policies and procedures afford. Some minority job applicants have charged that Zalda was responsible for keeping them from employment at YERS.

In early 1991, several influential members of the African-American and Hispanic communities met with Margaret to discuss YERS program expansion. Margaret told the group she could not recommend program expansion in northeast Coronado. At the meeting, Bill Hillis, an African-American lawyer in Coronado, confronted Margaret with questions about Zalda Smith's hiring practices. Margaret stoutly defended Zalda.

The citizens group, however, was not content with Margaret's responses. Bill Hillis contacted Dr. Atkins and requested a formal meeting with the board of directors. The group, with Hillis as spokesperson, expressed concern to United Way officials; United Way funds, along with membership dues, are the primary source of funding for YERS programs.

The director of the United Way contacted Dr. Atkins to express his concern. He further stated apprehension that publicity of this issue might adversely affect the 1991 United Way fund drive that was just beginning.

The board of directors met with Bill Hillis and many of those who had met previously with Margaret Rims. Dr. Atkins and the board pledged support of program development in northeast Coronado and promised to look into Zalda Smith's hiring policies.

At the next formal meeting, the board informed Margaret of the need to include this promised expansion in the 1992 planning. No specific actions were taken regarding either Zalda Smith or current hiring practices. At the same meeting, the firm of Jones and Belew, certified public accountants for YERS, reported revenues from membership were down 10 percent from the previous year and facilities maintenance costs were increasing an unexpected 8 percent. Those board members who had questioned Margaret's original capabilities became vocal in their criticism.

In the next few months, the conflict between the board and Margaret Rims became open and hostile. Dr. Atkins received reports that Margaret commented in a staff meeting that she had been there before any of the board and would be there when all of them were gone.

The conflict flared into the open when Margaret submitted the YERS 1992 programming for approval of the board of directors. The promised programming in northeast Coronado was not included in the budget. Margaret walked out of the meeting in anger. She refused to return Dr. Atkins's telephone calls.

Dr. Atkins called an emergency meeting of the board of directors; sentiment ran high. The board voted to terminate Margaret over the objections of two members, who claimed the action was in direct violation of national executive council policy requiring warning and probation prior to termination of any employee. One member further expressed concern for the community impact of terminating a 25-year employee.

RUTH WALSH AND THE CORONADO PROBLEM

When Ruth met with Dr. Atkins and the board of directors the situation had generated high tension and public visibility. Community leaders active in the United Way had openly criticized both Margaret and the board. Margaret had retained a lawyer and had named Dr. Atkins and several members of the board in a defamation of character suit. She claimed specific damages in her loss of retirement benefits due to termination of employment. Membership revenues dropped 12 percent for the first six months of 1992. Staff morale and productivity were extremely low. Dr. Atkins believed Zalda Smith to be the focal point of internal disruption and also Margaret Rims's source of information.

Ruth was desperate for an assignment within driving distance of her home. She felt deep concern for Margaret Rims and was convinced by Dr. Atkins's own account that the board had violated YERS policy in Margaret's termination. Members of the national executive council urged Ruth to accept the Coronado assignment.

Ruth asked for the weekend to prepare her requirements if she were to accept the assignment. She was concerned about the difficulties in bringing the staff together while helping the board formulate clear policy to deal with pressing financial and programming problems. The telephone rang as she was drafting a list of her requirements to present to the board. Ralph told her it was Margaret Rims. Ruth wondered what to do.

YOUR ASSIGNMENT

1. Describe as many communication problems in the case as you can identify. Describe differences between the internal issues and public concerns.
2. Identify the various ethical issues illustrated by the case.
3. How would you advise Ruth Walsh? What would you tell Margaret Rims?
4. Describe the work force diversity issues in the case and describe how increasing community diversity influenced the case. Determine whether the board acted appropriately in the termination of Margaret.
5. Develop a consulting work plan for Ruth Walsh to present to the board.

Ron Arnold's Job Crisis

Ron Arnold knew he was failing. His performance appraisals were still outstanding, but he knew he was not performing up to his standards. He did not like managing the quality assurance department of Dobson Hospital and it showed in his work, or at least his stress in coming to work.

Ron had experienced success in his ten-year career at Dobson. He had begun as a trainer in customer service, where his abilities were quickly recognized. His peers considered him the obvious choice for department manager when the position opened. People throughout the hospital liked to work with Ron and, under his guidance, the training department grew by 30 percent in less than three years. When the hospital began an aggressive marketing and community outreach project Ron was a natural choice. Ron's work in marketing was praised by Dobson's chief executive officer, who personally asked him to take the quality assurance (QA) job. The hospital's QA process and the QA department were in trouble when Ron assumed leadership. Numerous errors in the pharmacy and on medical records had created concern among the medical quality boards; a lawsuit was pending against the hospital. Ron's mission was to change the processes and reduce the overall error rate.

Ron was not welcomed as manager of the QA department. The former head had been reassigned to another department prior to Ron's appointment. This person was popular with the staff, who believed problems in the hospital were beyond the QA department's control. QA could establish processes, train, and monitor, but it did not do the actual work or make the mistakes for which it was being held accountable. Ron found the group resistant to change and, for the first time in his career, resistant to him personally.

Ron researched other hospital QA departments with attention to their programs and processes. He learned that much of the industry had more aggressive standards and training programs than those practiced at Dobson. He suggested to his senior staff members that they review other approaches and make recommendations for changes to Dobson programs. He was disappointed in their minimal efforts because he felt there was little chance of significant impact. Ron discussed personnel changes with the human resources department and was discouraged when he found little support for bringing in new people.

Ron began to dread coming to work. At the end of his first year he wrote negative performance appraisals on three out of four of his senior staff. The tension in the department began to mount. Ron mandated changes in several programs and announced a new training schedule. He was dismayed to learn that members of the department openly disagreed with his decisions at meetings where he was not present.

Ron began to rethink his role as a manager. Why had he enjoyed so much early success? Was he capable of managing only if surrounded by positive enthusiastic people? What did it take to bring about change? Ron began to think about other alternatives. Should he look for another management job, or leave management altogether? How should he decide?

YOUR ASSIGNMENT

1. How would you describe Ron Arnold's management of the QA department? Consider distinctions between leadership and management. Describe the needs of the QA department.
2. Describe the factors influencing the QA staff's resistance to change. How can they be encouraged to be more participative and understanding of new expectations.
3. Describe the factors influencing situational differences in management.
4. What are the communication issues in this case?
5. Can the same individual be a good manager in one situation and not effective in another? Describe your answer in terms of contingency theory.

Karen Rhodes—On Becoming a Manager

Karen Rhodes is an artist. She teaches at a local midwestern university and maintains a studio at the Business Enterprises Center for Artists (BECA). Karen specializes in animation and currently is completing work on an original short feature requiring over 3,600 individually painted drawings. She became a manager for the Summer Youth Program at BECA in order to hire assistants to paint animation cells to provide financial support for herself and talented young people interested in her film project.

The Business Enterprises Center for Artists is supported by grants and provides summer employment to teenagers interested in art. In addition to artistic capabilities, qualifying teenagers must meet a set of federal guidelines limiting total family income and/or be identified as "at risk" students based on past academic difficulties or behavior problems. The ten students assigned to Karen were recommended for the program by their high school art teachers. All ten have problematic academic records and five have been in trouble with the police. Six of the ten come from low income families. All are males—four whites, three Hispanics, two African Americans, and one Native American. They are expected to work 40 hours per week and are paid somewhat above the federal minimum wage. Karen is responsible for all administrative details, training, work assignments, supervision, and performance evaluation. No one is guaranteed to stay in the program for the duration of the summer. She is free to terminate any employee and ask for a replacement from the agency in charge of the Summer Youth Program.

Karen had never managed before. The following transcript is taken from an interview federal auditors conducted with Karen one week prior to the program's completion.

AUDITOR: Karen, what did you expect going into this summer?

KAREN: I had a fantasy idea. I thought I could charm this group into complacency and obedience. I thought I could create an excited but relaxed artistic atmosphere. I had never worked with these types of kids. . . .

AUDITOR: What happened on the first day?

KAREN: Well, I had to do everything. The paperwork—you know you have to have that—hand out the equipment, try to teach people their basic tasks. Everybody fought, everybody walked around; it was chaos. Well, nobody physically fought; I think I should be grateful for that. The man in the studio next to mine came over at the end of the day and said, "Karen, you had better get your act together." He said, "You go home tonight and rent a copy of *The Dirty Dozen*. You watch it and figure out what to do." I did what he said and the next morning I told him—the hero is so violent. And he said to me, "Forget that—think about how he got respect." He told me I wasn't acting like I owned the project. He said I have to own this project to get their respect. Then he taught me how to reprimand.

AUDITOR: How do you reprimand?

KAREN: You have to get right in their face. (Karen is of slight build standing 5'1''.) You look them right in the eye—you act like you are going to tap them on the shoulder but you don't ever touch—and you tell them exactly how things are going to be. The guy who pushed the hardest in the beginning, he had been in a lock-up for the past two years. I told him he couldn't intimidate the others or me. I finally had to fire him. I was a little afraid; I thought, what will I do if he won't leave? He left—I did just what I have described and he left quietly.

AUDITOR: What did the others think?

KAREN: They learned I meant business. One of them said, "Karen you are a nice girl but you have got to be firm." Well, they saw I could be firm and fair. They kind of go from aggressive to self-pity on me.

AUDITOR: After the first few days, how did things go?

KAREN: Much better, we settled into a work routine. The interesting thing is, they break the routine with their group talk. Sometimes it is to get out of work and sometimes they work away while this very interesting dialogue goes on.

AUDITOR: What do you mean?

KAREN: Well, now they are talking about racism—in a way they are working out dominance, I think. The group has debates. They are relentless about who is best at what. They don't like heavy metal music—I think they are concerned about its racist tones, but their concern is also territorial, a way of discovering who they are—they are thrashing it out. When one guy called another a racist the group tried to help. They are highly verbal. When I work with them one at a time they tell me everything. I have learned a lot about their backgrounds—they are very talented. I worry what will happen [because] they have so many problems.

AUDITOR: These kids are often silent in school settings. How do you assess their verbal skills?

KAREN: They are highly verbal. They are just the group I wanted. The gloves are really off. They only really care about each others' opinions. They are now at the point that one will say to another, "You didn't do that right, do it again." I don't get shocked.

AUDITOR: You talked about how direct and specific you have had to be, it sounds as if they are the same with each other.

KAREN: You bet. It is what I call, "in-your-face management." They are terrified at being ostracized from the group. Now the group norm is missing a little work each week. Each person is attempting to prove they don't have to play as strictly by the rules as we have all summer. They are testing me, I think.

AUDITOR: Would you fire anyone during the last week?

KAREN: Sure, I would feel bad for about ten minutes. [Laughs] Seriously, I would have to, that's what they want from me, the final testing.

Karen's program was highly evaluated. Work output and quality were good, program auditors were pleased, and her employees rated their experience more favorably than any other summer program in a five-state district. She did not have to fire anyone during the last week.

YOUR ASSIGNMENT

1. What are the leadership issues in this case?
2. How would you describe Karen's communication approach?
3. What would you do in a similar situation?
4. Describe various applications of "in-your-face management."
5. How does this interview apply to more traditional organizational settings? What can we learn?

Managing Your Manager

Nick Bradley believes power comes in many forms. In most respects he seemed a strange choice to join Merv Johnson's senior staff. Johnson, national sales manager for Merton Foods, usually selected aggressive and hard-driving senior sales representatives with extensive major account experience. Bradley's background in finance and his low-key personal style were strikingly different from any of Johnson's other six managers. Insiders, however, suggest that Bradley is the one to watch because Johnson listens to him more than anyone.

Nick Bradley is a quiet, thoughtful man prone to working alone. He has made few personal friends during his seven years with Merton Foods and several of his peers describe him as a man who refuses to play corporate games. He successfully revamped major reporting practices in the finance department, which saved the company several million dollars over a five-year period. Some believe Johnson selected him for his analytical capabilities and because Bradley seems to have little personal ambition.

Few know that Johnson has known Nick Bradley for 20 years. Nick went to school with Johnson's oldest son and was in the Johnson home on several occasions as a young man. Johnson liked him then and was pleasantly surprised to learn he had joined Merton Foods. Johnson followed Bradley's career in finance, initially out of personal interest, and became increasingly impressed with Nick's solid judgment and support of his manager. Bradley seemed to look out for the best interests of his finance boss and the department with little thought to his own career. For example, he had recommended that the department he managed be reduced in personnel when the new reporting systems went on-line. Few Merton managers had ever been known to voluntarily reduce their own span of control.

Johnson's senior staff members soon learned that Bradley's reactions were important to watch. If disagreement occurred, Bradley did not attack anyone; he stated his position calmly and carefully. Most of the time Johnson ended up supporting Bradley's view. His peers began to seek his advice because they found him cooperative and helpful. He gave others credit but seemed most concerned about Johnson's success. Johnson was overheard describing Bradley to Merton's president as a man who "shares my values and judgment, I can trust his advice on just about anything." Most everyone at Merton would agree—Nick Bradley had become a powerful man.

YOUR ASSIGNMENT

1. Describe Nick Bradley's power. What power bases does he utilize? Discuss in terms of power and credibility theory.
2. Speculate as to why Johnson trusts Nick Bradley. Describe the relationship between trust and power.
3. Describe upward organizational influence as evidenced in this case. Describe what is meant by "managing your manager." Is Bradley managing his manager?
4. Is Nick Bradley's approach to his career effective? Why? Why not?
5. What organizational communication issues are raised by this case?

My Japanese Counterparts

Rick McAllister is learning to speak Japanese. As a marketing trainee for Presto Foods, Rick believes he will have many career opportunities if he can position himself to be of value to Presto in the emerging Pacific Rim markets. Rick chose to learn Japanese because of the perceived difficulty of the language and because none of the other new college hires at Presto can speak Japanese. Rick has always been competitive and believes this is the competitive advantage he needs.

Rick was not prepared for the following discussion with his Japanese instructor, Nikki Reynolds. Nikki has lived in the United States for five years and teaches at the local foreign language center. Prior to coming to the United States, Nikki had worked for one of the major companies in Japan as a translator for the chief executive officer and president. She and her husband intend to return to Japan at the end of the year.

NIKKI: Rick you are coming along well but I should tell you I believe you should also consider a course in Japanese cultural studies to assist with your understanding of Japan in a way that just language instruction will not facilitate.

RICK: Nikki, I can barely work and keep up with learning the language. Besides, how hard can it be? Once I know the language the rest will come easy.

NIKKI: Well, yes, learning the language can be important, but understanding the Japanese cultural background is just as important for business success.

RICK: What do you mean understanding?

NIKKI: Understanding how the culture influences what happens. Not judging before having more information.

RICK: Well, I just ask for what I need and want. If people will be straight with me then I can be straight with them. And I can do that if I speak the language.

NIKKI: Rick, it doesn't work that way. Japan is a shy culture. We don't talk as directly as you. In fact my parents taught me that to use the first person is bad manners. Now times are changing in Japan as well, but someone with your style and approach will be considered rude by many people I know.

RICK: Well, what about learning about Americans, learning about me. Why do I have to change to make things work?

NIKKI: Rick, no one says you have to change, but you have to understand the reactions you are getting. Historically we have been taught obligation and loyalty to our work. You have been taught more about individualism. We have been taught obedience and not to show our own feelings—that is not the case here. It is not a matter of right or wrong; it's just what is.

RICK: What other differences have you observed?

NIKKI: Well, we in Japan work more as a group than in the United States. There is not as much individual competition. You have told me, for example, that you are studying Japanese because it will make you more competitive. Do you see what I mean? Another example: In Japan if employees make a mistake they are not fired. You told me only last week about one of your peers at Presto who, what did you say, "got the axe." In Japan we transfer someone to another job.

RICK: I am beginning to see what you mean. What do you think I should do?

NIKKI: First, understand the culture. Learn to follow the rules. You have to study to understand what they are. And then, Rick, you need physical exposure to the culture. You will experience culture shock just as I did when I moved here. But, for me it has been worth it.

RICK: You are telling me language is not enough. And that my style may create problems for me—even the style we value at Presto.

NIKKI: I am not saying you are going to have problems, I am saying your style is your style. But the Japanese have a very different style and if you want to work together. . . . Rick, communication is changing all of our cultures . . . but communication is both a basis for misunderstanding and understanding.

YOUR ASSIGNMENT

1. Based on intercultural communication theory, develop a course of study for Rick in addition to his language studies.
2. Consider the statement, "Why do I have to change to make things work?" How would you respond to Rick? To his Japanese counterparts?
3. How much alteration in style should an individual attempt when working with those from another culture? Develop guidelines for effective intercultural interactions.
4. Identify important similarities and differences between the cultures in the United States and Japan. From this list, determine how an individual can prepare for effective communication and business interactions.
5. Design a training program for individuals preparing to represent their organizations in foreign countries such as Japan, Mexico, and Poland. What are the similarities for each country? The differences?

CHAPTER 4

Groups and Problem-solving Communication

Carson Products' Management Team Disaster

Tom Sellers had been with Carson Products for 16 years when he was promoted to head the small-appliance division in Akron, Ohio. Most Carson managers had worked in several divisions prior to being assigned to top management. Tom, however, had spent 15 of the last 16 years in the Akron division, first in marketing and later in research. He had spent one year traveling Europe and the Far East for Carson to evaluate small-appliance manufacture. He was promoted immediately following his return.

Akron employees had mixed responses to Tom's appointment as general manager. Some were pleased that a local person could come through the ranks and lead the division. Others who had worked more closely with Tom felt his abrasive style and interactions with his former protege, Jan Ellis, could contribute to problems at the division staff level.

Jan Ellis had succeeded Tom as head of research for Carson at Akron. She had worked for Tom in the research department since joining Akron and was known for her technical capabilities and argumentative style of communicating. The arguments between Jan and Tom about product research were legendary in the department.

Their abrasive and open disagreements often made others uncomfortable even though neither seemed to hold grudges or remain angry. Tom valued Jan's opinions and recommended her for promotion when he left for Europe.

Close observers were concerned about the problems Tom had seemingly created while head of research and then left for Jan to deal with in his absence. Many blamed Jan for cancellation of two major projects and the termination of two section heads who had a long history of low productivity. It was not widely understood that corporate research managers had requested that Tom take action prior to his departure. He delayed and suggested Jan should have a fresh look at the situation. A dip in profits put pressure on Jan to make immediate changes. She took full responsibility without reference to Tom. One of those terminated sued Jan and the company. Three senior employees quit, alleging Tom would have solved these problems more effectively. Jan's close associates knew that this time she was not readily forgiving Tom for the situation she inherited.

The division staff of Carson Products consisted of Tom, Jan, the head of marketing, the quality assurance manager, the comptroller, the personnel director, and the manufacturing manager. All were experienced managers but, with the exception of Tom and Jan, were not known for innovative and creative thinking. At the time Tom became division manager, profits had declined for three consecutive quarters. Corporate management began pressuring the group to develop a new strategic business plan rethinking their products' positions in markets increasingly fragmented by foreign competition.

Tom began the strategic planning process by asking Jan to assess the marketing and manufacturing managers' current strategies and to provide potential directions for future planning. Tom began his own review incorporating some of the information gained in his year of travel. Tom also spent considerable time talking with his boss, the group division manager who had immediately preceded him at Akron.

Tom became convinced that dramatic changes in product lines were needed. He believed that over the next five years three of the division's current product lines should be discontinued and new home appliances with greater dependence on computer technology should be introduced. Jan's group came to a very different conclusion. They recommended that these product lines remain in production with computer-assisted models added as high-ticket items for each of the lines. They also concluded that foreign competition would not continue to erode markets if aggressive marketing and pricing programs were put in place.

In a staff meeting, Tom charged Jan and her group with unwillingness to change. Jan countered that Tom's proposals lacked factual support and were too high risk for the division. The two argued so abrasively that other members of the staff became uncomfortable. Tom ended the meeting by blaming others for not joining the discussion. Jan privately told the marketing and manufacturing managers that she was "going to the mat" on this one because it meant the future of the division.

At the next meeting, Tom told his staff a vote would be taken to determine the basic direction of the strategy. The quality assurance and personnel managers objected because they felt the strategy should not be the result of a vote but of a carefully established group consensus. Tom became openly hostile and insinuated that consensus could be built if Jan would listen to reason. Jan quietly excused herself and left the meeting. Tom covered other business items and adjourned the meeting with no decision on strategy.

Tom went to Jan's office and the two argued for more than two hours. Jan told him she would not support his position and would call in corporate management before changing product lines. Tom asked her if she wanted to continue to work in the division. She said he would have to fire her to make her leave. Tom was forced to tell his boss, the group manager, that the Akron staff could not make a strategy decision.

YOUR ASSIGNMENT

1. Describe the group dynamics that have contributed to the strategy stalemate? Is this conflict productive or counterproductive for Carson Products? Develop your answer utilizing theories of group and conflict processes.
2. Which theories of leadership apply in this case? How would you advise Tom?
3. What should Jan do next?
4. What are the responsibilities of the other team members?
5. What problem-solving and decision-making processes would you recommend for this group?

WHAT HAPPENED NEXT?

John Forbes, the group manager for Akron division, joined the group for a meeting. He asked that Tom present his position with Jan responding on behalf of the marketing and manufacturing managers. After listening to both presentations, John asked other group members to propose a method for resolving the differences. The personnel manager suggested giving both proposals to teams of senior employees and asking them to critique the documents and to provide additional suggestions as necessary.

Tom objected because he believed that involving more division members in the dispute would only weaken the staff's credibility. Others disagreed. Forbes recommended that a strategy council be developed to review the five-year plan and to make appropriate recommendations. Neither Jan nor Tom were to be members of the council. Jan's senior assistant, the assistant research director, was asked to act as chair.

Over a period of five weeks, the strategy council met daily and reviewed both Tom's and Jan's proposals in addition to other information. They developed a consensus recommendation combining elements from both proposals and making additional changes in product lines. The council presented their proposal to the division staff. Jan was enthusiastic. Tom remained silent throughout the meeting. Tom accepted the proposal, and with the support of his staff, forwarded it to John Forbes. Forbes praised the plan and Tom for his leadership. Jan found this somewhat humorous but decided not to respond. She later told the marketing and manufacturing managers that Tom might become a good general manager after all.

The R & D Lab: Teams Making "Go" or "No Go" Decisions

The research and development lab at Mission Products has a long history of success in the development of industry-leading medical products. Lab scientists and managers frequently were recruited by competitors with lucrative financial offers. Most chose to stay at Mission Products in part due to the outstanding reputation they enjoyed as a group and the generally congenial work environment.

Fred Rames was promoted to lab manager at Mission following 17 years as a senior scientist in charge of the development of instruments for cardiac surgery. Fred was well liked by both scientists and managers at Mission and was expected to carry on most of the traditions of his predecessors. However, no one, including Fred, had expected Mission's successful acquisition of three major contracts on which the sales department had recently bid. Normally Mission acquired only one or two major contracts per year, requiring minimal alteration of staffing and project responsibilities. The three contracts necessitated an increased staff as well as new project assignments. Over a period of three months, the lab hired 25 new people and created two additional project teams.

Fred, along with his senior managers, Ralph Barnes and Helen Singer, felt project decisions would have to be more closely monitored with so many new people and tight contract deadlines. In the past, project schedules had been developed by Ralph and Helen in cooperation with the project manager of a particular team. Overall lab schedules were reviewed by Fred and Mission's sales department. Specific technical decisions were usually handled at the project level with project managers informing Fred, Ralph, and Helen. Fred and his staff rarely made "go" or "no go" technical decisions on individual projects.

Fred, Ralph, and Helen discussed the need to review the decision-making procedures in the lab. They were concerned that tighter reporting controls would alienate some longtime personnel, but felt controls that applied only to new people were unfair. Helen suggested that the project managers in the lab review the overall situation and make recommendations back to Fred. Fred and Ralph agreed with Helen to ask project managers for their preferences.

A meeting of all 12 project managers identified two major concerns: (1) How would decisions be made when differences arose between two teams working on the same overall design? (2) How could project staffing decisions shift personnel quickly from one design area to another? Mission project managers had rarely had to coordinate between projects or share staff in initial design phases.

The project managers agreed to recommend to Fred and his staff that a contract management team be assigned for each major contract. This contract management team would have representatives from each project team and a member of Fred's staff. It was to make all technical decisions requiring coordination between or among teams, scheduling reviews, and personnel needs. Most managers felt these new groups were necessary but dreaded the extra time-consuming responsibility.

Fred, Ralph, and Helen accepted the recommendation from the project managers and six contract management teams were created. Fred, Ralph, and Helen served on two teams each. Each team elected a chair from among its members.

Four of the management teams worked throughout the contract year without significant problems. Design groups remained on schedule and contract requirements were met. The other two teams had serious conflict over technical decisions and personnel assignments. Fred had to personally intervene and assume responsibility for conflict resolution. At the end of the year, Fred decided to evaluate these decision-making groups prior to the new year's contract awards.

YOUR ASSIGNMENT

1. What are the questions Fred should ask about these decision-making teams?
2. Describe possible reasons for different experiences in different teams.
3. All teams were formed similarly. Should all teams have had a similar process for decision making? Why? Why not?
4. If Fred uses this process again, what should he change? What should stay the same?
5. What other methods for "go" or "no go" decision making can you describe? Would you recommend any of them to Fred? Why? Why not?

Decisions, No Decisions, More Decisions

They had come together, appointed by the chancellor of the university to prepare the largest grant proposal the university had ever submitted to the Metchell Foundation. The group represented five university departments and was chaired by the director of libraries, Janice Morton. Several faculty and administrative staff told the chancellor the group could never complete its task because it would never agree to setting priorities for funding among competing departments. Furthermore, Jordan Davis was on the team.

Janice Morton is well respected among faculty, staff, and students. She is task oriented and known for her fair treatment of those with opposing views. Jordan Davis, on the other hand, is respected for his research record in electrical engineering but generally disliked for his dogged determination to build the electrical engineering program at what some believe to be the expense of the computer science and mathematics departments. Jordan is aggressive and often disruptive in meetings. Jim Wallace, head of mathematics, is an excellent teacher interested in the overall growth of the university. Joan Williams, chair of computer science, is new to the campus; Jack Rivers, head of biology, and Mark Dennis, head of chemistry, are longtime department heads of successful science programs.

When Janice Morton first convened the group she knew her major responsibility was to encourage a process that would permit good ideas to be evaluated while avoiding in-fighting, which could result in the group missing the grant deadline. Janice was aware that many believed she could not succeed.

At the first meeting of the task force, Janice presented a proposed work schedule with tight deadlines and initial fact-finding assignments for all five chairs. She did not ask the group for their approval but she did ask for alterations and additional suggestions. Jordan Davis complained he did not have time to meet frequently; Janice responded the deadline necessitated active commitment. Anyone who could not attend meetings should either provide a substitute with decision authority or agree with the decisions of the group. Janice knew from the smiles of other group members she was dealing directly with the problem most feared by everyone—Jordan's disruptions blocking achievement of the goal.

At the second meeting, Janice was pleased to find the group well prepared. They had independently identified several problems that should be addressed in the grant proposal. Joan Williams brought excellent suggestions from her previous university. Jordan had done his share of the work and the group seemed to be off to a good start.

Over the next several weeks, the task force decided they would develop a mathematics and science learning center designed to provide students placement testing, academic support, and career guidance. There was hope that it would lead to increased enrollments and retention of math, science, engineering, and computer science students. The project was designed to address two specific issues: declining enrollments—both nationally and at the university—in math, science, and engineering; and retention support for students choosing any of these majors.

Once program design was completed, Janice realized developing the budget and setting priorities for department funding levels could become a source of conflict. The program goals seemed easy to establish compared to funding decisions. Janice was particularly concerned about Jordan and whether Joan had enough experience with him to realize he would likely undercut funding for computer science.

Jordan did not attend the initial budget meeting. He sent his assistant chair, who remained silent through the discussion. The group decided that math, biology, and chemistry would be the first departments to establish testing and retention centers. Computer science would follow in year two, with electrical engineering coming on-line during year three. Grant guidelines from Metchell provided for five-year funding with a potential for two additional years based on program evaluation. Those departments on-line in year one would receive more funding than either computer science or electrical engineering. Joan had agreed these priorities were appropriate based on current enrollments in the various departments and overall campus funding of each of the five programs.

Janice was encouraged when the group was able to make decisions that all could support, which enabled them to move on to write the final proposal and then to present it to the chancellor for his approval. She was dismayed to receive a telephone call from Jordan Davis stating he was submitting a new budget and schedule for electrical engineering. He expected electrical engineering to be included in year one and to receive as much funding as both mathematics and biology combined. Janice reminded Jordan that the group had agreed their decisions were binding and his representative did not object at the meeting. Jordan hung up without comment.

Janice subsequently called an emergency meeting of the task force. Jordan did not attend nor did he send a representative. The group agreed the proposal should proceed as planned. Janice scheduled a meeting for the following week to review the final draft and plan a presentation to the chancellor.

Janice was pleased to see Jordan in the meeting room when she arrived with copies of the final draft. She was not prepared, however, for the arrival of the dean of engineering, the man to whom both Jordan and Joan report. The dean asked to speak with the group. He stated he would not support the proposal as written and he wanted both the engineering and computer science programs to receive the same funding as mathematics, biology, and chemistry. Although Joan was visibly angry, she said nothing. Janice explained about the group's prior agreements. The Dean said that those agreements did not matter—this was not a majority rule situation. He excused himself leaving the group in stunned silence.

Jordan was gleeful. He flatly stated, "Now let's get down to business." Jim Wallace stated he saw no reason to alter the group's decisions. If engineering and computer science did not want to be part of the proposal he felt that was their problem. He looked at Joan and asked her what the group could do to support her position. The group agreed an immediate appointment with the chancellor was needed.

The chancellor listened attentively to the project goals and overall timetable recommended by his task force. Janice then told him of the dean's objections and suggested Jordan was in the best position to represent the dean's views. Jordan declined comment but suggested the grant would not be funded without engineering and computer science. The chancellor smiled and suggested he believed Jordan was correct. The group left the chancellor's office discouraged and angered.

Janice was pleased when the chancellor telephoned her and authorized completion of the proposal with no major changes. She called a meeting of the task force to celebrate. Jordan chose not to attend and electrical engineering went unrepresented. One final task remained: assignment of space should the proposal receive funding.

Space at the university is at a premium. Janice expected problems as she worked with the vice-chancellor for administration, who makes classroom and office assignments for the campus. She was surprised why he authorized five classrooms for the project if funding were received. She wondered why he did not discuss this decision with others, but with the deadline for submission pending, she asked no further questions.

When the chancellor received word that the Metchell Foundation had awarded the university $7 million he called Janice and congratulated her for her good work. He asked her to head an interim planning group to bring the grant on-line. Janice responded that her original group should be the core team in charge of the project. She also recommended selectively expanding the group to include others necessary for the project's success.

Janice was not surprised that Jordan Davis was furious. He and the dean of engineering met with the chancellor and recommended that the university not accept the funds unless timetables could be altered to more appropriately support electrical engineering and computer science. Joan again was angered and met privately with the dean of engineering to express her concern about her lack of inclusion in college decisions. She complained Jordan had never contacted her with his concerns and her program was jeopardized by his thinking and actions. The dean appeared to agree with Joan and asked her to be patient.

At the first meeting of the planning team, Janice was further dismayed to learn the vice-chancellor of administration did not consider his classroom commitments binding. He told the group he had not expected them to receive funding and had gone along with their request on the assumption that if funding were received something could be done at that time. The chairs of biology and chemistry both had worked hard on the proposal and, as the most senior of the group, expressed frustration about a long-standing problem at the university of decisions not being real decisions. One commented, "We have a no decision until pushed mentality."

Janice, Jack Rivers, and Mark Dennis went to the chancellor and urged him to tell the vice-chancellor to allocate space so equipment orders could be placed. The chancellor agreed he must urge action, which gave Janice a sense of relief. She expressed to the group her belief that decision making at the top of the university was slow and difficult.

Six months after the grant was awarded, space had been allocated and the first three centers had placed equipment orders. Center directors had been hired and most felt pleased with their work. Janice and the group decided it was time to advertise for a permanent project director.

Over 100 applications were received. A selection committee was formed with team members reluctantly agreeing that Jordan and the dean of engineering should be part of that team. After all, the new person would have to deal with these two important and difficult people.

Jordan vetoed hiring any of the three candidates who visited campus. He insisted their engineering backgrounds were weak and they would favor program expansion in the sciences. Jordan told the group he had a right to his way on this one because the others had overridden him during every other stage of this project. The others reluctantly agreed; they were convinced that although they had good candidates, none of the finalists was strong enough to stand up to Jordan. In a surprise move, Joan submitted her application to the committee.

Janice and the chancellor were secretly pleased and believed Joan was capable of handling both Jordan and the dean of engineering. The interview team met to decide whether to reopen the search or hire Joan as project director. Jordan appeared angry as the meeting began.

YOUR ASSIGNMENT

1. Based on problem-solving and decision-making theory describe the critical decisions in the case.
2. Describe how the task force approached decision making and problem solving. Should the consensus have been eliminated at the first meeting? Why? Why not?

3. What can a group do to effectively include a person with Jordan Davis's style and approach? Evaluate how effectively the group worked with other "powerful" individuals in the case.
4. What were the "no decisions" in the case?
5. Predict how the group will approach the project director selection. Compare your predictions to "What Happened Next?".

WHAT HAPPENED NEXT?

Joan Williams was hired as project director. Jordan Davis voted against her selection and the dean of engineering abstained based on what he described as a conflict of interest. Joan succeeded in having her assistant chairperson appointed the new chair of computer science to ensure the continuation of many of the programs she had begun.

Joan took a no-nonsense approach to project budgets, time schedules, and evaluation. She publicly criticized Jordan when he was late with reports and asked the dean of engineering to hold him responsible for any problems the grant might incur due to his lack of cooperation. By year three of the grant, all programs were on-line and the first comprehensive evaluation by the Metchell Foundation was successfully completed. Jordan Davis began to interview for positions at other universities. The dean of engineering was pleased with the two programs in his department. By year four student enrollments had increased in two of the departments and retention had improved by 6 percent in all departments. Joan credited the success of the program with the commitment of the original task force; she revealed to Janice that it was Janice's leadership that inspired her to pursue the job of project director. The group continued to have occasional conflict and disagreements but generally considered themselves successful.

The Wisdom of "The People"

LaDONNA HARRIS

The Wisdom of "The People" is a special contribution to this book from LaDonna Harris, president of Americans for Indian Opportunity and well-known activist for human rights and world peace. Before you read her contribution, reflect for a few minutes on her life and times. Consider how her experiences and the experiences of others have helped shape the strategic-planning processes she describes.

LaDonna Harris speaks with the authority and depth of a lifetime's experience initiating constructive change in issues of self-determination and human rights. Her concern and her impact have reached out to tribal peoples and all humans. Her Comanche grandparents, one an active member of the Native American church and one a devout Christian leader, modeled a life of mutual respect for personal choice and gave her an *abiding belief that there is room for all traditions. She spoke Comanche until she entered grade school, which allows her to view all things from "two worlds" with great empathy for the value in diverse cultures.*

LaDonna Harris took an active part in the integration of her hometown—Lawton, Oklahoma—and was a principal organizer of the first statewide organization to bring together over 60 Oklahoma tribes in an historic coalition. Her national visibility began in the 1960s when, as the wife of a leading U.S. senator, she was active in the civil rights movement. Appointed to serve on presidential commissions by presidents Johnson, Ford, and Carter, she has represented the United States to the United Nations Educational, Scientific, and Cultural Organization (UNESCO) and served as a founding member of the National Women's Political Caucus. She currently serves on the boards of the Global Tomorrow Coalition, Keystone Center, the National Urban Coalition, Women for Meaningful Summits, and is on the advisory board to the National Institute for Women of Color.

LaDonna Harris is in demand as a teacher, speaker, and resource person with organizations such as the Aspen Institute, the Woodrow Wilson Center, and the Washington School for the Institute for Policy Studies— working with over 100 organizations each year on international and Native American issues. She is the recipient of honorary degrees, a Doctor of Law from Dartmouth College, and a Doctor of Humanities from Marymount College.

Recognizing the need for a national Native American organization, LaDonna Harris formed Americans for Indian Opportunity (AIO) in 1970. AIO is a national advocacy organization dedicated to the achievement of self-determined political, economic, social, and cultural goals by the tribes. AIO serves its constituency by anticipating the issues that will be addressed in the future. Through symposiums and information management, AIO enables tribes to investigate the dynamics of effective tribal governance and works with key decision makers on the role and participation of tribal governments in the federal system. AIO's tradition in working with tribes is based on maintaining cultural integrity while taking on contemporary issues. AIO works from the premise that strong tribal communities and governments are able to make greater contributions to local and national life. The following case is an example of AIO's work in tribal issue management.

A SHARING AND NURTURING OF TRIBAL SPIRIT

Tribes have exercised incredible tenacity and perseverance in maintaining their autonomy in the face of many obstacles. It is the endurance of Tribal values that makes them unique. Now, Tribal Issue Management (TIM) forums offer Tribes a strategy for building on those values, paying particular attention to culturally-relevant ceremony, posturing, bonding, participant respect, consensus building, ownership of contributions and shared responsibility for implementation. TIM restores the kind of broad participation in governance that was valued traditionally but obscured with the onset of constitutions and representative forms of government.

Background

Tribes have persevered through a period of unrelenting transition as they have moved beyond their isolated rural settings to active participation in global development issues in little more than a generation. As a result, today's Tribal governments frequently find themselves paralyzed with indecision, caught between the conflicting cultural values of communal versus individual, consensus versus representation, and responsibility versus control.

Many of the pressing problems facing the Tribes are symptomatic of deeper frustrations, key among them being the limited participation in the overall Tribal government system. Traditional Tribal society was dependent on participation but the effect of representative government has been to reduce the number of active participants to an elected few. This can be critical in a society where group identity is strong and participating in promoting the common good is seen as a way of giving back to the numuhnuh, "the people," in a never ending cycle of reciprocal exchanges. In such cases, participation becomes a basic need common to all who share in Tribal identity. The Tribal government system provides some members deep satisfaction and status associated with giving back to the Tribe. But to draw a line between those who can fulfill that need and those who cannot, violates cherished egalitarian principles.

It becomes predictable, then, that those who can demonstrate their capacity to give back to the common good will come under attack from those who cannot. Broad participation, therefore, in shaping the future of the Tribe and carrying out related Tribal activities should be encouraged as an important means of reducing dysfunctional attacks on the Tribal government while creating new pathways for alienated members to again own their Tribal identity.

In fact, this link between culture and power is gaining attention, not only among Native Americans, but with other groups around the country and internationally as well. People everywhere are beginning to understand that our values, attitudes, and relationships work either to enhance . . . or to limit . . . our participation and the participation of others in the process of both community and nation building.

Tribal Issue Management (TIM) forums provide an opportunity to reexamine these values and the issues that arise from them; it provides an opportunity to aggregate opinion on future directions for the Tribe and to set priorities for achieving them; and it provides an opportunity to place the welfare of the numuhnuh back into the hands of each contributing Tribal member.

Overview

Tribal Issue Management forums begin with a clarification of where the Tribe is at the moment and move on to a description of where the Tribe eventually wants to be. Then comes defining the activities needed to bridge the two. This is followed by the assignment of roles and responsibilities for carrying out those activities.

The first round of forums outlines a vision for what the Tribe wants to become. It begins with a forum involving the Business Council and selected community representatives which is followed by similar forums in each of the participating communities. The results of each of these forums are then aggregated into a common vision statement at a general combined structuring session.

The second round follows a similar pattern, focusing this time on generating a set of activities that will enable the Tribe to become what they have envisioned. In the final round, participants at all levels assume various roles and responsibilities for carrying the first steps of implementing the activities that have been selected. Once this first cycle is complete, the Tribe can select that aspect of their plan with the most complexity and public interest for the next phase of their on-going series of Tribal issue management forums.

A three-member TIM facilitation team receives training (currently provided by Americans for Indian Opportunity) in how to conduct the forums. As facilitators, they have the delicate task of remaining neutral to the issues and options being discussed as they guide the participants through the issue management process. They learn to use a computer software program designed to speed up the consensus building process and to generate and display graphically information that assists the group through each step of the method.

Larger Tribes may want their own TIM facilitation team in order to institutionalize the forums and make them an on-going part of the Tribal government system. Smaller Tribes may need to band together and train one composite team to serve three or four Tribes.

Ceremonial Beginnings

Opening the forum with a locally appropriate ceremony is the first of several mechanisms that recognize the critical role Tribal identity and Tribal values can play in discovering new ways out of complex and deeply rooted problems. Gift giving and the public recognition of service in the interest of the Tribe are appropriate additions that add to strengthening Tribal identity.

Blessings, pipe ceremonies and/or prayers go much deeper then the typical greeting or statement of welcome. For Tribal participants, their attention is drawn to their common bond and all that means. If outsiders are involved, the ceremony tends to elevate the status of Tribal identity and values, and places participants in a mode of mutual respect for one another.

Legitimizing the Forums

The attempt to adjust the decision-making process of any group runs the risk of challenge by the status quo. The adjusted process may well strengthen the position of incumbent decision-makers but unless fully convinced of the value of the emerging changes, they will certainly resist.

This potential resistance is part of the rationale behind Tribal Issue Management Forums beginning with the Tribal Council Members themselves before moving on to participating communities. Having experienced the impact of the forums themselves, they readily perceive the forums' potential for reviving Tribal identity and Tribal initiative.

Once the Council members realize how the forums empower participants to take charge of creating their own future and to focus less on receiving services, they happily endorse the forums. Its potential in terms of expanding Tribal resources and as complementing their capacity to achieve Tribal objectives becomes apparent. But, more than that, Tribal members begin focusing on how they can contribute to our communities and to making the Tribe stronger again.

It is important, even following the initial forum involving the Tribal Council members, that links to the Council be nurtured and maintained. It is a good idea, then, to involve some member of the Council in each community-based forum and to offer them a role in the opening and closing of each forum. Recommendations should be presented to the Tribal committee along with regular progress reports on roles and responsibilities by various participants and groups.

The Comanche Tribal Chairman consented to putting his opening remarks on video for one of the sessions that he was unable to attend. His examples of Tribal values regarding respect for elders, honoring valor, and children as a resource for the future, showed the young how culture creates the opportunity for belonging.

The greater the involvement and commitment of the Tribal government, the greater the chances of the process eventually achieving credibility as part of the overall government process.

Bonding

Tribal values and Tribal identity becomes the focus of the group's attention by calling on each of the participants to track their kinship ties to the rest of the group. Cross-links between individuals and their inherent relational obligations immediately begin drawing the group together.

It is understandable that the strongest component of Tribal vision statements is often the continuation of the numuhnuh . . . a continuation of "the people." Group identity is synonymous with being Tribal and where group identity is strong, preservation of the group and its value system becomes all important. This reiteration of kinship terms calls forth those values and practices that set the group apart and immediately bonds the group around a common cause.

At the same time, participants are asked to express what being a member of the Tribe means to them. From this comes a positive affirmation of deep cultural values, often expressed subliminally. These values, if captured and clarified, become a useful reference point during all the subsequent steps of the process.

The traditional circle is another feature of Tribal Issue Management forums that contributes to the bonding experienced by the group. The simple circle is really quite profound in that it avoids making distinctions among the participants, placing them face to face and calling forth their common humanity in a way that minimizes the potential for overt confrontation. There is no stage to set the leadership apart and there are no rows that have come to distinguish passive recipients from those in authority who are thought to have the needed answers.

The full exposure of participants to one another in relative proximity tends to heighten their interpersonal orientation and to diffuse the kind of verbal abuse that is easier with the authoritarian arrangement of rows and stage.

It is important to note here that as much as a third of the group time spent together is spent on these preliminary activities with the chief function of binding the group together into a single collaborative group. This is a far greater amount of time than in other issue management models, but very crucial groundwork for such bi-cultural situations.

Posturing

In many Tribes, much of the discussion that takes place during the early stages of public meetings reflects a strategy by various participants to position themselves and establish a role in the group. The content, then, may not reflect a serious attempt to solve a problem so much as to make a statement of identity. Since Tribal Issue Management Forums separate the generation of issues from the generation of new options for dealing with those issues and since each participant is awarded an opportunity to address the group in turn, posturing becomes integrated with issue generation and becomes an acceptable part of the process without interfering with the more difficult generation of alternatives that takes place later in the forum. It has become clear that, if you do not allow people the opportunity to vent their emotions early on, they will not support the conclusions of the group in the end.

In TIM forums, the opinion of each participant is solicited, moving around the circle in turn. Interruptions are avoided and unnecessary. The net effect is that each participant is deeply affirmed by the fact that his or her opinion is so valued.

Respect for individual opinion is very important among Native American Tribes and underlies a pattern of consensus that does not strive for agreement, but values each opinion as another perspective on the whole, one that further clarifies an issue that no one participant can fully appreciate on his or her own. By definition, then, each perspective is needed in order to get a clearer view of the real situation.

Building Consensus

Consensus continues to build, then, if all clarification or any aggregation of opinion first goes back to the originating participant or the group, as the case may be, to be sure that they concur with the new path that contribution is taking. If the originator(s) objects, there is further clarification after which opinion may coalesce or perhaps divide and continue down more than one track. Here again, the respect accorded the original contributor is a deeply affirming element that contributes to his or her commitment to the final outcome.

In Tribal Issue Management Forums, meaning is never frozen in time and place. It is never a question of holding participants to what they have said, but of uncovering what was meant and allowing for that meaning to evolve as the group interacts and creates its own meaning. The consensus that emerges, then, reflects the wisdom of the group, the wisdom of "the people" . . . inevitably more than the sum of the contributors. Such forums are ideal for Tribes where group identity and the importance of contributing back to the group are highly valued.

The Historical Perspective

A key piece of the TIM forum is the historical overview which puts the immediate situation in the context of the evolution of Tribal governments generally. It inevitably provides an element of psychological relief that comes from realizing just how ingenious Tribes have been in persevering through continual upheaval and in managing the virtually unmanageable situations that have been imposed upon them.

The historical perspective tends to create a spirit of optimism about the potential for overcoming the immediate set of problems, given all they have overcome in the past. Ideally, this piece of the process immediately precedes the period of generating options for dealing with the issues the group has identified.

Vision Statements

The TIM forums rely on a Tribal elder or visionary leader to interject from time to time statements like the historical overview to keep the sights of the group high as they deal with a myriad of complex local problems that are very close to their everyday life. The vision statements provide periodic reminders of how much the Tribe has overcome through the years and how great their potential remains for dealing with the current reality. Both the historical statement and the affirmation of cultural values may well become a series of shorter statements strategically placed to help the group maintain their momentum. They are particularly useful immediately prior to the voting on prioritizing issues or proposed activities.

Ownership

The advantage of the TIM forums is that the participants themselves assume responsibility for implementing the results. Their sense of ownership of the outcome is strong, in part, because their opinion has been respected and cultivated in accordance with cultural values.

The facilitator plays a key role here. Ownership is fragile and can be lost if the ideas are manipulated by the facilitator or if the discussion is managed directly by the elected leaders. There is always a greater response in implementing the recommended actions if the participants genuinely feel the conclusions reached were theirs.

Shared Responsibility

Shared responsibility is a common value among Native American Tribes, reflecting the obligation of Tribal members to contribute back to the Tribe. While the frustration of this value can lead to considerable strife for the Tribal system of government, restoring participation through consensus and sharing responsibility has just the opposite effect. Frustration turns to fulfillment as Tribal members respond to the new pathways created for participating once again in nurturing the development of "the people." Because of the reaffirmation of Tribal values, the respect shown for individual opinion, and the building of consensus within the group, participants find they are eager to have a part when it comes to the final round of the forums where roles and responsibilities are assigned.

Other Contexts

TIM forums are easily adapted for use in nonIndian contexts. They are especially useful where Indians and nonIndians are participants working together to solve issues of joint concern between them. In these cases, the historical and cultural statements play an even more important role as the dominant group is exposed to and impacted by another valid perspective on an issue they may have thought they understood.

YOUR ASSIGNMENT

1. Describe key communication processes in TIM forums. Identify key concepts from organizational culture, group, nonverbal, and intercultural communication theory.
2. Contrast LaDonna Harris's description of consensus to common understandings of the term in other types of organizations.
3. Discuss the similarities and differences between TIM and other strategic planning processes with which you are familiar.
4. Describe how you believe the use of historical perspective influences group decision-making processes.
5. How might TIM be adapted to other types of organizations? What are its strengths? What else is needed?

The Power of Empowerment: A Case History of Organizational Communications

LARRY KOPERSKI, LINDA HERTZ, JIM JOST, AND ARNIE BERGER

This case describes a new model of product development utilized by the Logic Systems Division of Hewlett-Packard Company located in Colorado Springs, Colorado. The model is a design for organizational communication *based on the concept of empowerment, the authorizing and enabling of people and groups to take responsibility and authority. This process of project management resulted in the introduction of a new product that was 30 percent under budget (saving over $100,000) and shipped to market in six months, one month ahead of an already aggressive schedule.*

INTRODUCTION

It is no secret to anyone in the electronics industry that a steady stream of new products is necessary for survival and growth against global competition. Unfortunately, the industry is a victim of its own success. The fierce competition that is the norm in this industry has forced the players to streamline their product development cycles in order to just keep pace with each other.

The authors of this case study were all part of the Logic Systems Division (LSD) of Hewlett-Packard Company during the time period when the subject of this study was evolving. LSD designs and markets Microprocessor Development Systems (software tools and microprocessor emulators). As a semiconductor manufacturer develops a new generation of microprocessor or microcontroller, the designers at LSD must move with the same or better efficiency to have the development tools in place for the users of these new processors at the time of introduction.

Each of us was part of this study, so we use our initials to refer to ourselves and to our specific involvement in the process. A rather complete treatment of the tactical aspects of this process has been discussed in Berger and Jost (1991).

At a recent conference, sponsored by the Institute of Electrical and Electronic Engineers (IEEE), one of the speakers remarked, ''Most barriers to successful product introduction are related to people, not technical problems.'' This particular conference had focused on the impact the changing global business environment was having on U.S. industry.

In 1990, a number of people involved in the new product introduction process at LSD made this same observation. They engaged in concerted efforts to see if they could change the pattern. This is a case history of their process and activities, and a record of some of their discoveries about communicating in a complex, highly technical environment.

The HP workers first asked themselves a series of challenging questions about how to make a truly effective team. They considered whether they had ever experienced such a team, and found personal examples from team sports. What if the people involved in the new product development process worked together like a highly coordinated basketball team—the players knowing how they fit into the game plan and what to anticipate from their team members; using a common language; trusting their teammates to play their position, but there to support when somebody gets by them with the ball? What if the team took the risk to try out some new plays, but committed itself to discussing what worked, what didn't, and what they'd like to do differently next game? What if team members let each other know they were important to the team whether they played all, or just a short part of the game? What if the team had a common goal so clear and compelling that the members were energized to eliminate any obstacles to success; to challenge previous job roles; to set-up well-thought out, widely communicated plans, ready to respond with creative solutions when new issues emerged?

The HP team members felt this scenario would be a program manager's dream. But would it take just the right people, with years of training in advanced team skills, and lots of cash for rewards to accomplish this? And would upper management support it?

What follows is the story of how one project manager, LK, created the framework for this model of empowered teams. It beat the odds and introduced the subsequent product ahead of schedule, with all parts complete, and under-budget! It also became the prototype for all of the subsequent product development cycles. Interestingly, this was not the first attempt to create a team approach to product development at LSD. Several years earlier, AB had attempted to implement a similar concept, but ultimately abandoned the idea due to lack of support across the organization. LK succeeded because of his efforts to create empowered teams, the principal subject of this case study. Finally, we should mention this idea is not particularly revolutionary in broader circles, outside of HP. In the popular vernacular, this form of team product development is often referred to as *concurrent engineering.*

NEEDS ANALYSIS

LK did not start out with grandiose plans, or view himself as enlightened. He was asked to lead a product introduction project that already had a late start for sales during the optimal marketing window. He wanted to get the product into the hands of customers as quickly as possible, to fortify the division's business, at a time when the division's future as an independent organization was uncertain. He wanted people working on the project to have a "new and positive teamwork experience," and to really feel "part of the team."

This feeling he wanted project members to experience was similar to those he had when he was part of a wellperforming basketball team. At a time when many of the division's 500 or so members were undergoing a sense of hopelessness, low energy, and low morale—what was referred to by some as a "group depression"—he wanted people to feel good about their work on this project, and the contribution they could make both to their team members and the division's success.

He realized the interactions among members of the four departments primarily involved in the new product introduction process—research and development (R&D), marketing, manufacturing, and quality assurance (QA)—are generally the source of bottlenecks and delays in the successful release of new products. In fact, the other functional areas often referred to the R&D lab "throwing the product over the wall" to their respective areas. This humorous, but negative, description was evidence of the very real barriers that existed among these functional areas. He also observed that often people encounter barriers unwittingly raised by other project members. He knew this type of complex, highly technical project could involve a lot of hurry-up-and-wait from team members, and could degenerate into finger pointing when things did not go well.

LK realized a strong partnership with these four departments was the key to accelerating the development process to meet his time-to-market goals. After several discussions with his manager, managers from the other functional areas, the R&D lab manager, and the division's acting general manager, LK proposed that a "wheel" program management structure be used for the project. Representatives from each of these departments would serve as team leaders to communicate issues and coordinate decision making within and across the departments. He wanted to plan for concurrent instead of consecutive processes in many stages of product development. He wanted the team to understand early on how their decisions impacted other members as well as the overall project. To accomplish this, he decided, would take a strong team process and cooperation, as well as the freedom to question how they did their jobs.

IMPLEMENTATION

Coincidentally, during this time, LH—personnel liaison assigned to R&D, marketing, and QA—had an objective to improve communication and organizational effectiveness within and across these departments. Their joint effectiveness was viewed as strategically key to the division's success (and survival!). LH had recently completed a course on organizational development and change at the university, as well as HP team-building and project management seminars. Could some of the concepts she had studied be applied to a specific business need? She wondered whether "theory" could be adapted to the division's work environment, and what she and the team members involved would learn in the process.

LH contacted the R&D lab manager, and asked for suggestions about project teams that might benefit (as well as be receptive) to her team-building assistance. She explained that a team in the early stages of organizing might be the best match to her contribution. The R&D manager suggested she contact three of the project managers in his department, and discuss her proposal with them. LK was the first manager with whom she met.

LH reviewed a basic team process model with LK (Beckard's goals, roles, processes, relationships), as well as suggestions from HP's corporate engineering department for improving productivity by focusing on "doing the right things" (the product) and "doing things rightly" (the process, resources, people). Applicable elements of the HP corporate engineering approach included: "anticipate the market, design faster, communicate faster, do things in parallel, do things right the first time, leverage best practices, maximize re-use, focus on essential contributions, form seamless, cross-functional teams, provide world-class design environments."

A key ingredient for the project team's success, LH and LK agreed, would be to enlist the creativity and commitment of each individual who had a task to get the product out the door. Also key to reaching their goals would be the support of the team members' direct managers, because no changes could be made in direct reporting relationships. The team needed to be able to overcome potential obstacles from rigidly structured procedures.

It was important to avoid situations where members felt caught between commitments made to other team members and changing priorities and assignments from their managers. The goal was a "seamless cross-functional team."

To begin team development, as well as to gather practical information and ideas for changing processes, LH contacted each of the 28 people identified as having a direct part in project completion, and most of their managers. She explained the purpose of her involvement was to enhance development of effective team processes for on-schedule new product introduction. She recorded perceptions of each individual's vision of a well-functioning team for this project and some of the obstacles to that vision becoming a reality. She asked about their past experiences with product introductions, what they understood to be expected of them, what they needed from other team members, and what they needed to contribute for successful introduction. She asked them what one thing they would change about the introduction process if they could, and how they could contribute to this change. The representatives from manufacturing and marketing were both ready to try something different. They had worked together on a previous introduction and they wanted a better process.

LH summarized the results of the interviews into the themes of goals, roles, processes, and relationships. She also shared the complete, anonymous data with LK and the three team leaders identified from marketing, manufacturing, and QA. LK initiated a weekly steering committee meeting including LH and the team leaders. This group was called the planning team. They reviewed all of the interview data and suggestions and named the larger team the extended team. The subteams from each department were called the function teams. After much debate and brainstorming, the planning team outlined definitions, purpose, roles, and communication objectives for each of the teams. They also discussed how often, and through what channel they would share information and coordinate activities for each subteam. The team leaders chose different methods to match their subteam's style and needs. The result was a matrix describing the communication plan for the extended team, the planning team, and each function subteam. Figure 4.1 shows the structure of the project organization.

During the first meeting with the extended team, LK and the planning team focussed on goals and shared all of the information they had gathered. LK also presented the program's potential revenue results, and outlined a proposed six-month project schedule. LH presented the summary of the team's interview data, and facilitated a cross-functional small-group exercise. The groups discussed and then summarized each member's perspective for

1. a successful product introduction as defined by the outside;
2. what qualities project team needs to reach success; and
3. what enables individuals to feel proud of being on the team.

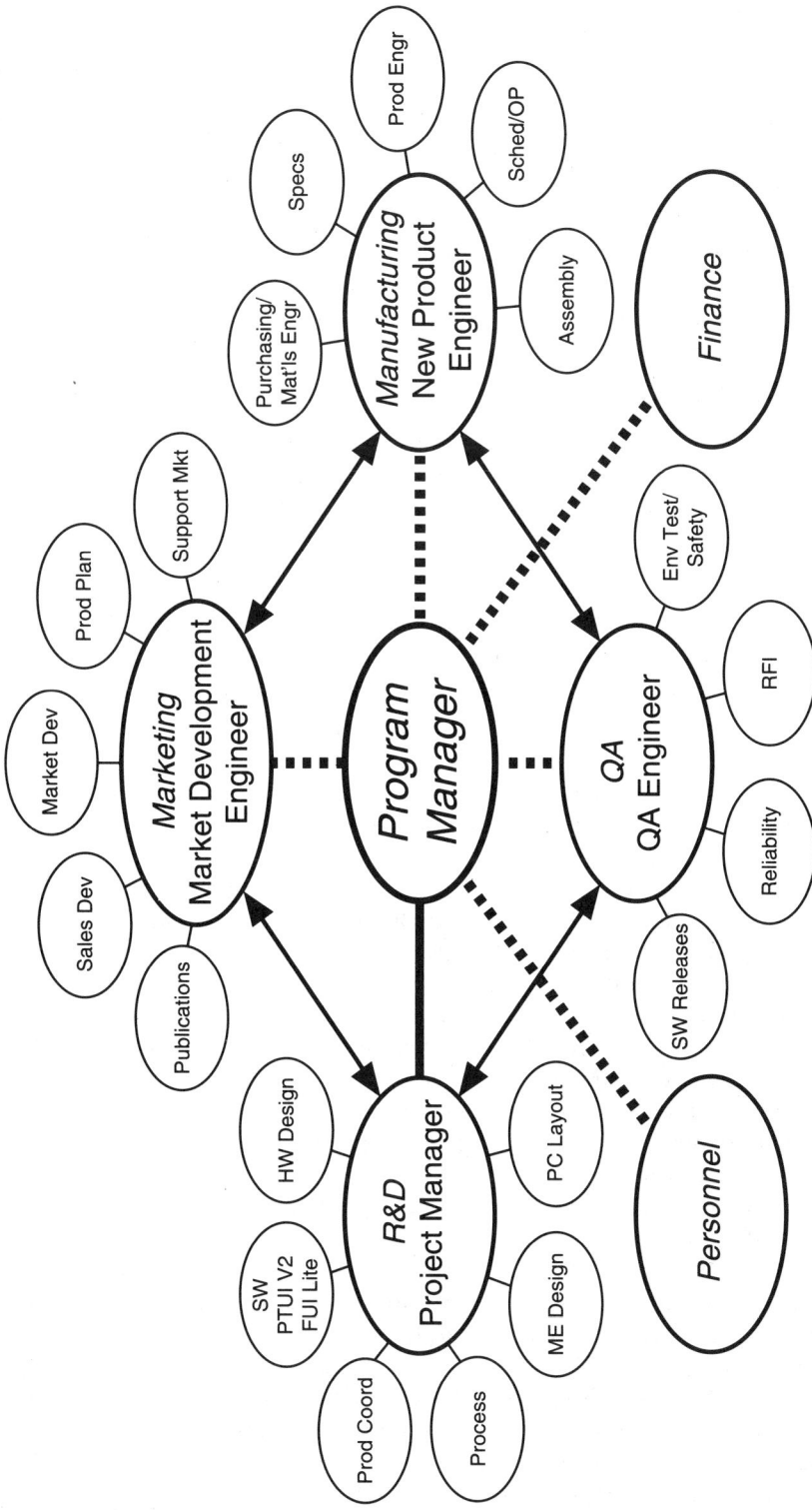

FIGURE 4.1 The product development team.

Each group elected volunteers, who met together and combined the summaries into an overall goals statement for the project. Also, a survey was composed from the groups' summaries, which was used as a baseline of team members' satisfaction during this early stage of the project. Specifically, each person was asked to rate how much they felt the project team was currently demonstrating the qualities identified as needed for success. The same survey was repeated at the project's end.

The second extended team meeting focused on roles. In preparation, each team leader met with their function team and prepared a brief summary of each person's role and responsibilities. Also, each team member was asked to consider:

1. Who are my customers? What outputs do they expect from me?
2. Who are my suppliers? What inputs do I need from them?
3. Where are the gaps? How can we close them?

During the small-group part of the meeting, each function team combined its answers to these questions. In order to identify potential gaps, team members had to think through their process flow, and ask themselves why they performed certain tasks. The importance of cutting out unnecessary steps was emphasized by using the term *Deliverables.*

After the deliverables lists were drafted by the function teams, the planning team reviewed them for duplication and gaps. They discovered by sorting these into lists of deliverables for each team member, and by tying them to specific dates in the project schedule, they had created a new project tracking tool. JJ, the process engineer responsible for R&D's project process development, joined the planning team and incorporated the deliverables lists into his data base. More than just a tracking tool, the deliverables served as an overall project process flow, and as a personal commitment list for team members.

Team members publicly named who they expected to give them specific deliverables. If there were disagreements, they were asked to personally contact the individual to discuss who was responsible for the ''inputs'' and ''outputs.'' This served as a very strong empowerment tool. Direct communication of expectations and interdependencies was practiced at this early stage in the project, and the team members were encouraged to negotiate their roles. This helped to minimize misunderstood expectations and to build personal relationships between team members necessary for team trust. (The deliverables data base and process are discussed further later.)

Using the deliverables data base to track progress for this project was the most visible example of a breakthrough. But the deliverables tool in itself did not create the empowering environment. It was developed through the participation of the extended team. This fostered the personal relationships and one-on-one communication that gave this project team ''a new and positive teamwork experience.'' The systematic updating of the commitments helped keep the team highly coordinated. The team had set itself up for success.

The third extended team meeting focused on processes. Plans for tracking project progress were reviewed, and the old project tracking tool was provided

(Gantt chart). Team members could compare the current to the proposed process, which made it easier for many team members to take the risk and try a new tool. Next, small cross-functional groups worked on metrics (performance measures) for the project. The purpose of this exercise was to specifically define and make visible how the team would measure its success on the project, both for the completed product and the team's process. The groups reviewed the initial project goals they had set, considered properties of good metrics, and listed some of the factors already measured in their departments for work quality and output. The goal was to produce a set of metrics that were:

1. clear and focused on what was important;
2. complete and with balanced emphasis on each departments' requirements;
3. timely in providing feedback on the project's progress; and
4. user friendly, providing maximum insight with a minimum need for time-consuming data taking.

The outcome of this work was a set of preproduct introduction and post-product introduction metrics, defined for each department (R&D, marketing, manufacturing, QA, finance, personnel). The overall project metrics focused on:

1. the ultimate goal to ship a complete product by the target date; and,
2. the financial results to be achieved during the product's lifetime.

Each metric specified both a goal and acceptable level. The QA planning team member took the initiative to ensure the metrics effort was completed and communicated to the team members and their managers.

However, even more important to the team's success than the achievement of these specific metrics was once again the process used to develop them. The participation of individual team members, the brainstorming and negotiating as the group's efforts were combined, and the visibility of each group's issues and constraints were key to both communication and team development. Also, the metrics provided a concise advance definition of what would constitute a finished product. LK was able to take this to his managers and get their approval, knowing that he was really representing the team's commitments.

The fourth extended team meeting focused on a demonstration of the prototype product, and a report of specific customer and field sales force interest. This feedback helped to sustain the energy and perseverance of the project team, and also provided some recognition to key team contributors. A round table session helped to surface any current problems and keep the informal communication lines open. This meeting was shorter and more informal, with the key objective of supporting the team's momentum.

The fifth extended team meeting was a celebration luncheon held on the day the first product was shipped. The top manager from each functional department signed an oversize product release document and team members received specific recognition for their contribution. Certificates had been prepared for each person, noting the unique role each had played, with humorous anecdotes cited. The lead R&D designer was especially recognized for spending long, late hours working on the project, and given a customized overnight kit to tide him over on future projects. There was a spirit of camaraderie and accomplishment; the team had exceeded its goals, and had realized a "new and positive teamwork experience." The team members owned this project and their joint success.

The final extended team meeting was a postmortem, during which the team discussed in small groups: (1) what they did right, (2) what they did wrong, and (3) what should be changed and how?

The planning team also had a detailed postmortem discussion. The results of these two sessions formed the basis for a presentation by the planning team in which it shared its processes and experiences with other project teams. The "Power of Empowerment" presentation was given to each of the division's departments, as well as by request to several other forums.

SELLING THE DIVISION

Considerable discussion began at the division—why was this team and its project so successful? What variables were key? Could success be repeated? Should the team's processes be more widely adopted? Some skepticism and even some resentment were directed at the project team from other teams. However, through divisionwide management forums and department meetings, a certain amount of consensus emerged. A "management teams' team" steering committee was formed to further the development of empowered, cross-functional teams for new product introductions. The division's upper-management staff acted as its champion. Having this high level of support from upper management made the selling job much easier across the divisional boundaries.

DELIVERABLES PROCESS AND TOOL

Prior to completion of the development project mentioned earlier, most development projects were basically handled on an exception basis; that is, things got discussed when they became a problem. There was no formal mechanism for tracking when things should be completed. Even though project managers typically created Gantt charts/task lists for the engineers on projects, and all of the participants were aware of "R&D schedules," project slippages still occurred because of issues arising in areas outside of R&D.

The effects of the typical phased project development process can be summarized as follows:

1. People's time is wasted at long meetings with low information content.
2. Project participants tend to wait until an item becomes an "exception" before taking action.

3. The project moves forward on the basis of the project manager's ability to get team members to commit to resolving exceptions by the next meeting, or whenever. Thus, communications and responsibility is "radial" in nature, with the project manager in the eye of the hurricane.
4. Things that are done x times before on other projects often fall in the cracks or have to be reinvented with each new project.
5. There is very poor correlation between the actual progress of the project and the progress defined by the Gantt Chart schedule.

The "deliverables process" attacked these problems in several ways:

1. Document and control each "quantum" of information and milestones that occur on every project as it moves from the investigation phase to manufacturing release. These information quanta were given the name deliverables.
2. Base the project on the actions necessary to complete the deliverables on or before critical time crunches hit. Force people to make decisions and communicate, as needed, without the participation of the project manager. Or, in today's popular parlance, "empower the employees" to make decisions at the lowest level needed.
3. Utilize the "paperless office" concept of electronic mail (EMAIL) to communicate and manage the deliverables. This includes sending them to appropriate people and tracking their completion (and their rate of completion). Finally, when they are slightly or critically late, elevate them to the appropriate decision maker. Managing the deliverables also entails tailoring a Data Base Management System (DBMS) to handle the information and information flow.
4. Give the project planning team much more control over the people and processes needed to make the project a success. In essence, the project team contracts out to functional areas for services, but is fully responsible for making the product a success.

What constitutes a deliverable? We don't really have a formal definition of a deliverable, but we have come to some understanding by asking the people with project responsibility the simple question, "What do you do?" They answered this question by providing us with a list of all the discreet and identifiable "things" that they need to accomplish, either by themselves or in conjunction with another team member, in order for the project to proceed. Some of these tend to be very significant, such as the hardware designer listing, "Turn on Lab Prototype." Others are relatively mundane: "Assign unique part codes to new circuits."

However, the ensemble of these deliverables is a very extensive list of what approximately 25 people need to do to make an idea a product. Within LSD, there are some 700 to 1,200 deliverables associated with any given product development cycle. Each deliverable has a projected completion date. This is essentially a way for the team members to make commitments to the team. Each deliverable has a giver and a receiver so that the person(s) responsible for that deliverable are very clearly spelled out.

A printed circuit board designer might have the deliverable, "Send Netlist to HW Designer." This quantum of data is a piece of information that the hardware designer must get back from the printed circuit board designer in order to verify that the netlist is correct before the printed circuit design data base is sent out to fabricate a printed circuit board.

Obviously, no project progress occurs until the netlist is checked. Also, the hardware designer has a deliverable to notify the PC designer that the netlist is correct, because the printed circuit board designer is not going to commit to PC board fabrication unless the PC design data base (netlist) matches what the hardware designer has created. An example of a list of deliverables is shown in Table 4.1. The deliverables shown in this table are extracted from the actual list sent to the hardware designer. We have substituted generic names for the actual people involved. The information shown is described more fully in Figure 4.2. Notice that the list of deliverables includes those produced by an individual as well as those given to an individual.

In practice, a typical project planning team might have a meeting each Tuesday afternoon. Issues are discussed as needed and the team reviews any late deliverables to see if there is a problem waiting to "jump up and bite them." On Thursday, the newly updated list of deliverables is electronically mailed to all members of the project as an update for the next team meeting on the following Tuesday. The electronically mailed list includes only those deliverables that directly affect a particular team member.

TABLE 4.1   Turning an idea into a product: Sample deliverables list for a lab engineer.

Andy								
Date due	I/O	Description	Target	Person	Subclass	Lag	Stat	Number
10Jan91s	O	LP Fdf/xrf file	to:	Elaine	LP layout	−1	d	3218
16Jan91e	I	Enclosure studies	from:	Bob	I/L		d	3266
16Jan91s	O	LP preliminary ML	to:	Barb	LP load	−30	d	3228
16Jan91e	O	PCB source supprsn	to:	Bob	I/L		t	3279
24Jan91s	O	LP net-list	to:	Judy		−1	d	3211
24Jan91s	O	LP raw board layout	to:	Judy		−1	d	3212
08Feb91s	O	LP updt ref des/ML	to:	Barb	LP load	−13	d	3249
11Feb91s	I	LP bdd file	from:	Elaine	LP PC fab	−2	d	3217
14Feb91s	O	Unreleas prt cost	to:	Don	LP PC fab	1	d	3225
21Feb91s	I	LP snd ldd bd ML frz	from:	Barb	LP load	−11	d	3260
21Feb91s	O	LP prog PAL masters	to:	Barb	LP load	−8	d	3292
21Feb91e	O	ZodSPA specs	to:	Grant	SQA deadline	−60	d	3360
21Feb91e	O	ZodSPA specs	to:	Dave	SQA deadline	−60	d	3361
27Feb91s	I	LP raw boards	from:	Judy	LP PC fab	10	d	3243
28Feb91s	O	LP del D2 supp pts	to:	Barb	LP load	−6	d	3295
28Feb91s	O	LP final excep list	to:	Barb	LP load	−6	d	3296
08Mar91s	O	Bd material list	to:	Carmen	LP load		t	3224
11Mar91s	I	LP raw bd costing	from:	Judy		15	d	3247

FIELD	DESCRIPTION
project	Name of the project that the deliverable applies to
ID number	Unique data base number used to easily retrieve a deliverable from the data base
status	Status of the deliverable (to do, started, or done)
to person	The name of the person who will receive the deliverable
from person	The name of the person who will produce the deliverable
description	Brief description of what the deliverable is
subclass	A phase in the project's schedule that the deliverable's completion date is tied to
lag	A deliverable can be tied to a subclass plus or minus x days—the lag is the offset from subclass end date
edate	The date the deliverable will be completed—it can either be entered directly or be entered using the subclass and lag to calculate a date. It is recommended that most dates be entered using subclass/lag because these dates will be automatically adjusted by the system when the project's schedule changes.
days	Working days needed to complete the deliverable
touch date	The last date that a field was changed for this deliverable

FIGURE 4.2 Deliverables data base description

Finally, the project manager also sends along a textual message giving the extended team a picture of the project's overall progress and any general issues that might be appropriate. This could include special praise for someone's extra effort, notification of any changes in key dates or milestones, progress in the R&D lab, and so forth.

The deliverables system is implemented on an HP 9000 workstation with a relational data base management system and 4GL. The system allows a user to sort the data in a variety of ways and to make summary reports of this information. It also allows the project manager to make weekly mass EMAIL mailings to everyone on the project. In addition, different views of the deliverable data are made for the project manager, planning team members, and extended team members. Anyone in the organization can access the system via LAN (Local Area Network) from either workstations or PCs. Currently, the only people that can directly change the data base are the people on the planning team. Other members of the team must give their weekly changes to planning team members for input into the data base. This has created a burden for some planning team members to find the time to collect and enter this data weekly. Therefore, one of our anticipated improvements will be to give a log-in to everyone on the team so they can directly make updates to the data base. The information that is kept on each deliverable is summarized in Figure 4.2.

Typically, extended team members give deliverable information updates to their planning team member by Monday afternoon. The planning team member inputs this information into the data base by Monday evening. Shortly before the meeting on Tuesday, a "late list" is sent out to all planning team members showing all deliverables in "to do" status with delivery dates earlier than that date. This gives the planning team members time to check on the status of these deliverables before the meeting. The whole cycle then repeats itself.

TACTICAL APPLICATION

The importance of communication within the planning team and the extended team is certainly crucial. However, of equal importance are the communication channels upward in the organization, informing upper management about the current status of the project and its anticipated completion date. This is crucial because the projected revenue stream of a manufacturing entity (such as LSD) depends on accurate sales and new product availability data.

Historically, projects often missed their forecasted completion date by wide margins. This resulted in lost revenues and wasted resources. A deliverables-based management scheme has the not-so-obvious advantage that it has the unexpected ability to predict to a much higher degree of accuracy the expected completion date for the product development cycle. This is a very significant result of this development process and deserves some discussion.

In a paper given at HP's first conference on project management, Wiemann (1990) noted that the traditional Gantt chart approach to project management and tracking progress was not sufficient for accurate forecasting of completion dates. Wiemann introduced the concept of "state variables" to measure progress. The rate at which his project team "closed" the state variables became a forecaster for the project's progress.

AB realized that deliverables could become Wiemann's state variables. Even though some deliverables are more significant than others, the ensemble tends to smooth out the differences. Thus, if a project starts with the extended team having identified 1,000 deliverables for a project, and these deliverables are being closed out at a rate of 20 per week, then a reasonable forecast would be that the project would take 50 weeks to complete. There may also be a nonlinear relationship between the closing of deliverables and the project's progress (e.g., deliverables may be closed at a slower rate at the beginning of the project and at a faster rate toward completion).

The deliverables approach is inherently more accurate than a simple task-based schedule (Gantt chart). By definition, when all the deliverables have been closed, the project is done. Everything that the extended team has to do to get the project out the door has been completed. Obviously, there are complex interdependencies. Managing these interdependencies is the job of the project planning team. The deliverables list in its comprehensiveness is the complexity, but the complexity of getting the job done is reduced to a step-by-step procedure.

YOUR ASSIGNMENT

1. Describe the model of organizational communication presented in this case. What are the specific organizational communication issues?
2. How can team members become truly empowered?
3. Discuss the combination approach of face-to-face meetings and electronic communications.

4. Contrast this approach to more traditional approaches to organizational communication.
5. What types of communication capabilities do individuals need for this type of problem solving and decision making?

REFERENCES

Berger, A. and Jost, J. 1991. Managing with compressed schedules *Electronic Engineering Times* 649 (July 8): 131.
Wiemann, A. 1990. Improve schedule accuracy by quantifying goals and progress. Proceedings of the HP Conference on Project Management, June 26–29, 1990, San Jose, Calif., 233.

Managing the Self-Managing Team

The group had been pleased that the accounting department was implementing the self-managed team concept. After all, they knew their jobs and one way for their department to help the company stay competitive was to eliminate a layer of management. John, Joyce, Paul, and Ed knew each other well and had been in accounts payable for a long time. How hard could it be to plan their work and be accountable for results?

John, Joyce, Paul, and Ed attended the initial training for self-managing teams provided by human resources. The trainer stressed the importance of meeting management, good problem solving and decision making, and timely conflict resolution. All of that seemed reasonable and not too difficult to put into practice. Paul, in particular, was somewhat concerned when he learned the team would complete performance appraisals for each other and would be expected to deal internally with any disciplinary problems. Ed told Paul there was no need for concern—they were all good performers, so why worry?

The group was surprised when Emily Jenkins was transferred to their team. Emily was reasonably new to the accounting department and had no previous experience in accounts payable. John told his peers he knew they needed more help but was not pleased to have to take on self-managing team responsibilities at the same time they were training a new member. The others generally felt the same way.

Emily's presence at group meetings immediately created tension. She asked a lot of questions and did not readily agree with the decisions recommended by the others. She asked for clarification on their problem-solving and decision-making process and refused to agree with scheduling changes even though the other four found them acceptable. Emily proposed several work-related changes and was openly hostile when the group refused to implement her suggestions. The facilitator (formerly called supervisor) for the group recommended the team adopt formal meeting management and problem-solving procedures that all of the members could accept. Emily agreed with the suggestion but the others resisted. They claimed Emily had created problems and they did not want to change what was working for them before she joined the team.

Joyce observed Emily altering several accounts payable processes without informing her team members. Mistakes began to surface based on dissimilar processing of bills and lack of communication between Emily and the other four. Paul and Ed spent an entire weekend correcting month-end statements. The group's facilitator refused to solve the team's problems.

At their weekly meeting, John angrily announced he was going to request that a consultant from human resources meet with the group and determine what they might do next. To everyone's surprise, Emily agreed with John and urged that they get help as quickly as possible.

YOUR ASSIGNMENT

1. The accounts payable team is having difficulty managing itself. The facilitator is correct to suggest the members must solve their internal issues as a team. Based on self-managing team concepts, analyze the problems this team is experiencing.

2. Identify at least three problem-solving and decision-making processes appropriate for self-managing teams.

3. Based on group communication theory, describe how a team can successfully orient a new member.

4. You are the human resource consultant assigned to the accounts payable team. Develop a plan for your first meeting with the group. What information do you need? What information will you bring to the group?

5. Design a training program for teams who will manage their own work scheduling, solve work-related problems, train their own members, conduct peer performance appraisals, and handle disciplinary issues.

CHAPTER **5**

Leadership and Management

Mark Waite's Disappointed Staff

Mark Waite was concerned about his upcoming department meeting. He wanted his first group presentation to be well received but suspected the tension surrounding his arrival made that all but impossible. Mark knew his appointment as marketing manager was a severe disappointment to the two internal candidates and management's decision to transfer him to Cleveland from Los Angeles had been interpreted as a sign that the Cleveland marketing function was in trouble.

At the time of his promotion, Mark had worked for Intel Corporation for ten years, first as a salesperson in southern California and later as regional sales manager for California, Nevada, Oregon, and Washington. He was well known throughout the company for establishing effective customer relationships that resulted in large orders of Intel's diverse home products lines. He had no direct experience in marketing management and no previous contact with the east coast divisions or the Cleveland marketing group.

Two of Mark's new staff, Carol Simpson and Jack Riley, had applied for the marketing manager position. Carol and Jack each had more than 15 years experience in the marketing department. Both had been critical of their former boss for her lack of creativity and unwillingness to take the necessary risks to better establish Intel products in highly competitive east coast markets. Carol and Jack both believed they were not considered on their own merits and were labeled as ineffective based on the history of the Cleveland marketing function.

Shortly following his arrival in Cleveland, Mark met with Carol and Jack individually. Both seemed competent yet hesitant to trust his ability to manage the function. Rumor had it that Carol was looking for a job elsewhere and that Jack was considering an early retirement. Mark was not sure what losing them would mean for the experience base of his staff.

Mark invited all department members to his first staff meeting. He began by briefly describing his background with the company and indicating his desire to get to know the department and all of its members. He outlined a schedule of individual meetings and made a request that department members come to these meetings with both innovative ideas and suggestions for processes and promotions that were working well and should be retained. Mark was unprepared for Carol's reaction.

CAROL: Mark that all sounds good. But you have to realize everyone in this room knows that giving good ideas to the boss is the kiss of death. Either the boss gets the credit, or worse yet, nothing happens and we get blamed. Sally [the former marketing manager] got a raise even if she is only now assigned to a special project. My career is over with Intel. I had waited for 10 years for this job to open and when it did I got labeled with her bad decisions.

Others began to support Carol's position and, although they did not blame Mark personally, most indicated a strong distrust of an outsider. Several voiced displeasure that Carol had not been selected for the job. Mark noted that Jack Riley sat quietly but seemed amused and watchful.

Mark let the group talk without interruption, thanked them for their honesty, and restated his desire to lead an effective organization. Although his calm response seemed to be well received, he wondered how much good information he could get from a staff so angry about past problems and current changes. He decided to meet with Carol to discuss the situation.

YOUR ASSIGNMENT

1. What are the leadership issues in this case? What are the change issues?
2. How would you advise Mark?
3. Describe your reaction to the staff meeting. Is the confrontation positive, negative, or both?
4. What type of information does Mark need to make effective decisions?
5. How would you advise Carol and Jack? What are their career options?

Dora Cartwright's Leadership Dilemma

Dr. Dora Cartwright had just been selected the first female president of Midwestern State University, the largest public institution in the country to have a female head. The regents had been glowing in their praise of her and the press conference she was about to enter was sure to be a lively one. After all, Midwestern State University had been searching for over a year for a replacement for President Johnson, a highly visible and popular man in the state. And Dora Cartwright had only become a candidate within the last week.

The presidential search at Midwestern State University had been criticized by faculty, staff, students, legislators, and citizens of the state almost from the very beginning. When Midwestern regents voted to hire a national search firm, many were opposed because of the firm's cost at a time when the state and the university were in financial crisis. The regents had ignored the criticism and interviewed the five finalists recommended by the search firm. None of the five received enthusiastic support from major campus constituencies. Three of the five withdrew their candidacies before the end of their interviews.

Prior to being asked to apply by the president of the board of regents, Dr. Cartwright had been Midwestern's vice-president of graduate programs. Her academic background included a variety of administrative positions at west coast universities and she was generally respected by the faculty at Midwestern. No one, however, had urged her to actively seek the presidency. She was surprised by the regents' invitation to interview and more so when after only four hours of deliberation she was a unanimous choice. She was concerned that faculty, staff, and students had not been included in the process and was relived when search committee members from these groups told her they would support the regents' decision.

As Dora Cartwright waited for the press conference to begin she reviewed what she thought was a complex and challenging leadership dilemma. First, she had not sought the position and as a result did not have a plan formulated for assuming responsibility. Second, she believed her selection was both a tribute to her past work and a compromise on which the regents' could agree without reopening the search. Third, she knew she would be particularly visible as a woman assuming the top position at an institution with a 100-year history of male leadership. Fourth, the state and university were in financial crisis making leadership difficult for anyone. She believed, for example, President Johnson's attraction to another offer was in part based on the bleak financial outlook facing the university. And finally, of immediate concern, were the two members of her senior staff that had been active candidates for the position. She believed the senior staff would be less than enthusiastic about her selection. She needed their support because many of them possessed information critical to her success.

Dora Cartwright decided she would tell the press she was launching a 90-day data collection process after which she would announce her strategy. Privately she began to think about how that process should evolve, who should be included, what she should ask, and how she should decide the leadership style and role that would make her an effective president for Midwestern.

YOUR ASSIGNMENT

1. How would you describe Dora Cartwright's leadership dilemma?
2. How might her selection affect her leadership? Give both positives and negatives.
3. What type of communication plan can give Dora Cartwright the information she needs?
4. How should she communicate her vision once a plan is in place?
5. Describe the leadership issues with which she must deal.

Organizational Problems at a Community Nonprofit Organization

BARBARA McCAIN, PH.D.

It is spring 1992, and the annual meeting for the Middleton Association for Retarded Citizens (MARC) is being planned. The MARC provides services for the developmentally disabled adult population in central Indiana. Typically, this is an uneventful meeting, attended by a collection of staff, administration, and a few of the membership from the community—usually parents. This year is a different story.

Twenty years ago, Martha Simco, the current executive director of the MARC, became the parent of a multihandicapped daughter. Kerry was her second child. There was no evidence of birth trauma or understanding of Kerry's severe physical and mental disabilities. Martha was confused and terrified at the outlook for her child's future as well as her own. It did not take long for Martha to find that there was no child care in Middleton. Motivated and energized from rejection, Martha started the first day-care facility for handicapped children in central Indiana in the basement of the Christian church.

As Kerry grew, so did her special needs, and Martha's life became the development of the MARC. Martha had attended college for one year before the birth of her first child and knew some secretarial skills. She was a driven woman with keen survival instincts. She became MARC's teacher, director, and fund-raiser, using only volunteers in the beginning. Martha was the most vocal lobby for services to the handicapped in the community as well as the state of Indiana. Her name became synonymous with aid to the disabled. The organization grew to a staff of 50 representing three related entities: workshop, group homes, and thrift shop. Middleton was proud of the MARC and of Martha Simco.

By fiscal year 1991, the MARC had an operating budget of $1.2 million. The financial resources were acquired primarily through state and federal grants, social security, medicaid, the United Way, and some local fund-raising. Nationally, program oversight existed through the National Quality Assurance Program, which is an accreditation council for programs working with developmental disabilities. State accreditation was loaded with regulations but loosely monitored. The MARC serviced 42 clients.

Over the years, the annual May meeting had evolved into a stamp of approval and election by Martha's cheerleaders of 11 board members. This governing board attended monthly meetings and approved recommendations from Martha for changes in staff, programs, salaries, and so forth. The members resided in Middleton and were honored to serve on the board. Usually they were recommended to Martha or her administrative assistant, who compiled a slate of officers two weeks prior to the meeting. Being a board member of the MARC required little outside commitment but yielded positive community recognition. Organizational bylaws did not limit the number of years one could serve on the board but the president was required to have been on the board for one year prior to election. According to the bylaws, the membership by majority vote had the power to override the board of directors.

MARC membership had grown to 150 (Middleton is a city of 56,000) through direct mail solicitation of $35 donations. Members received quarterly newsletters and an invitation to the annual meeting at a local restaurant. The members were mostly family and extended family and friends of clients. Members were grateful for the facilities and services for the clients. To the public the MARC appeared to be a model nonprofit organization with a cohesive staff, board, and membership.

In 1989, the mother of a client became concerned with the quality of care at the MARC group home housing her son, Jess. Sarah had known Martha Simco from the beginning of the church day-care program. Sarah had emotionally supported the MARC but had not used its services because her family was financially equipped to handle her son's special needs. In the fall of 1989, it became apparent that Jess needed to develop independent care skills and wean himself from a very doting family. Jess was accepted into the newest group home and workshop located within three miles of the family residence. Logistically, it was ideal. Jess appeared to thrive in the environment. He had constant attention and, because of his high verbal skills, he was the joy of the group home.

Sarah was not employed outside the home and had become involved in community activities. She decided to return to the local college to pursue a degree in special education. Sarah became acquainted with the policies for Intermediate Care Facilities for Mentally Retarded (ICFM) institutions in the region. Within three months after Jess began living at the home, Sarah heard of minor injuries sustained by the clients and mistakes with medicine disbursement. Sarah decided to discuss the problems first with the director of nursing. During her long, intense conversation with Beth, the director of nursing, Sarah discovered that internal affairs at the MARC were not as rosy as she had assumed.

Beth had been employed with the MARC for six months and was one of the longer tenured employees. She was frustrated with her job and found little relief confiding in Hal, the director of workshop and residential care. Hal had been employed by the MARC for two-and-one-half years and from Beth's viewpoint he represented the only continuity, other than Martha, in the organization. However, when she attempted to discuss her concerns for the MARC it was readily apparent that Hal would not confront Martha. He hinted his position might soon be terminated, perhaps due to his unfavorable attitude toward Martha's hiring and training practices. So when Sarah approached Beth with her concerns, Beth exploded with stories of internal strife and low staff morale, which resulted in constant turnover of direct-care personnel. The direct-care workers were 25 part-time and full-time employees paid at minimum wage to assist the clients in daily living and work schedules. They were the vital link to client services.

Sarah was reluctant to act on her new knowledge because Jess appeared happy, the location was convenient, and the alternative residential care in Indiana was a state institution. Sarah decided to get to know the workers on a casual basis, listen to their concerns, and carefully observe the activities at the MARC. She also decided to get a cohort involved.

At the May 1991 annual meeting Sarah nominated her outspoken friend, Andy, for a board position. Sarah's strategy revolved around Andy's objective appraisal of situations and her own continued observations of MARC. She wanted to be sure of her observations before acting on her concerns.

After several of the monthly 1991 board meetings, it became clear to Andy the board was not supposed to question the agenda items. Suggestions were made to decrease turnover but rarely were ideas implemented or carried over for discussion at the next monthly meeting. Andy routinely questioned new policy and old policy and was therefore ostracized by the group. Four weeks before the 1992 annual meeting, Andy received a letter from Martha Simco thanking her for her time and informing Andy that her term of board membership was ending. Andy immediately showed Sarah the letter.

Two days before receiving Martha's letter, Sarah had gotten a letter from a former social work consultant who asked not to be identified. The consultant was concerned about the qualifications of the MARC staff. Martha Simco did not have college requirements or supervised work experience in the field. An administrative license was required but could be obtained easily by attending a seminar once per week for six months. The social worker's conclusions suggested the MARC was operated by a team of unskilled and untrained personnel, which resulted in client injuries, dietary deficiencies, and dirty clients. An even greater concern arose when these problems were relayed to Martha, who reportedly told the director of nursing and the consultant that funds were not available to solve these problems. The crowning blow occurred when a client was diagnosed with lice and the direct care facilitator was told there was no money for medicine.

Sarah and her husband decided it was time to act on this ugly situation for the welfare of all the residents. Sarah realized the wheels of government grind slowly and to get the regulators involved would take months and stacks of paper documentation. Litigation might even be required. Although Sarah was not sure about the core of the problem, she believed it rested with the executive director's management. Sarah decided to try an individual approach.

Nine days before the annual meeting Sarah planned a strategy designed to challenge Martha's tight executive control. Sarah contacted every close friend she had in Middleton and anyone she felt would listen to her concerns without alerting Martha. She talked to parents, disgruntled staff, and extended family of some long-term clients. She asked them to become new members of the MARC, to attend the upcoming meeting, to vote for change, and to volunteer to be slated for a board position. The solicitation resulted in 35 new members, 8 of whom were interested in becoming active board members. Although Sarah discovered growing sentiment for change among many MARC associates, no one wanted to act. She persuaded, coached, and organized the group. She explained bylaws and rallied the new group for last-minute questions and preparation prior to the May 1992 annual meeting.

As was custom, the annual meeting was held at a local restaurant and started precisely at 7:30 P.M. At 7:20, Sarah, her family, and friends arrived at the meeting to the overwhelming surprise of Martha Simco. There were 60 people in attendance, the largest group in the history of the Middleton association. Martha appeared confused by the barrage of new people but instructed her administrative assistant to proceed with parliamentary procedure for a quick vote on the preselected slate of board officers. Immediately one of Sarah's friends, an attorney who had studied the MARC bylaws prior to the meeting, called for additional nominees from the floor.

The meeting coordinator became flustered and confused and asked for clarification of the bylaws. The presiding secretary reviewed the bylaws and discovered floor nominations were appropriate. Eight new members were nominated from the floor. Then the coordinator asked for the election to proceed with a silent vote. This would allow all officers to be voted on as a slate therefore limiting the number of new board members. The attorney again objected because he realized the probability of winning only a few positions and the continuation of a weak group unable to make changes. He argued for individual election of officers. This angered the coordinator, who realized a struggle had begun for board control. Martha felt threatened for the first time in 20 years; she knew the board had the potential power to overrule her and to ultimately call for a new executive director. The motion to elect the officers as a slate was defeated and a long night of individual board member election began.

One by one each board position was nominated and elected. One by one the new group of members proved to be a majority capable of electing their nominee. By 10:30 P.M. all board positions were filled: There were eight new members, a new president who had served as a board member the previous year, and two board members from the previous year who confidentially told Sarah of their interest to see accountability and change in the organization. Sarah and the new group cheered in victory while Martha carefully smiled and congratulated each new officer.

YOUR ASSIGNMENT

1. Explain at least four organizational and communication issues apparent in this case.
2. Describe the organizational climate at the MARC.
3. What would your immediate action be if you were Martha?
4. What would your immediate action be if you were a new board member?
5. What does this case suggest about organizational change?

Managing at Dillard Electronics

This case is reported from the perspective of Jane Perkins, the organizational consultant who assisted the research and development lab at the Chicago division of Dillard Electronics in a 26-month change project designed to improve overall organizational effectiveness. At the time of the Chicago division assignment, Jane had worked with various divisions of Dillard Electronics for over seven years. She was well respected within the company for her ability to identify problems and work cooperatively with diverse and often conflicting personalities. In the case of the Chicago research and development lab, Jane was asked by the corporate human resources manager to assist new management to understand the impact of their leadership during a time of extensive corporate-mandated organizational change.

THE SETTING

The research and development lab in the Chicago division of Dillard Electronics is involved in the design and development of computer technology for specialized measurement instruments. The lab is one of seven research and development groups that are part of Dillard Electronics' computer applications group. The lab employs 149 people in both professional and technical support roles. Although a lab manager has final decision-making responsibility, the lab typically operates with a 4-person management team (including the lab manager) with 20 middle managers reporting directly to the 4-person team. The 20 middle managers are responsible for teams of individuals working on particular aspects of four major design projects. Work teams are composed of professional engineers, designers, computer programmers, technicians, and clerical support personnel.

At the time Jane Perkins was assigned to the Chicago lab, corporate research and development management had replaced the lab manager and his top three assistants with managers from other labs throughout the corporation. Although replacement of senior management was not typical of the corporation, the crisis that precipitated the move was the lab's inability to release new products for manufacture during the previous four years. The four new managers were directed by corporate to achieve product releases in two product lines within two years. All internal operating decisions, including additional personnel changes, were to be the sole responsibility of the new managers.

THE MANAGEMENT TEAM

Lee Johnson, the new lab manager, came to the Chicago division with a reputation as a charismatic leader who had capably led the transformation of the Detroit division's manufacturing operation from an obsolete factory to a competitive factory of the future. Lee was chosen for the position even though he had not worked in a lab since his early days with the company. Corporate management believed his leadership capabilities were more necessary than recent design experience. Detroit's division manager fought to keep Lee in his manufacturing job and promised him new opportunities should the Chicago situation prove unsatisfactory.

Joining Lee on the management team were Harry Bridges, a senior manager from California; Joan Nighthorse, a highly evaluated design engineer from Maryland; and Richard Rees, a senior manager from the corporate special projects group. Although none of the four had previously worked together, each knew of the others' work.

TWENTY-SIX MONTHS OF CHANGES

Lee, Harry, Joan, and Richard spent their first month in Chicago reviewing the four major projects in progress in the lab. They met individually with all middle managers and participated in formal presentations from each of the project teams. The four conducted daily, two-hour meetings with no participation from other lab personnel.

At the end of the first month, Lee called a labwide meeting at which he made several announcements: cancellation of work on three of the four existing projects; two new projects with a development cycle of 24 months each; personnel assignments for the new projects; and formal changes in the lab's reporting systems. Specifically, middle managers would be required to hold weekly meetings with their subordinates to exchange project information and work on technical problems. Middle managers assigned by project groups would report on a bi-monthly basis to lab management. Quarterly project report meetings would include the entire lab with extensive preparation of project status reports. Additionally, a monthly technical forum was to be established to deal with particular technical issues. A schedule or product definition change would not be authorized unless presented and supported during bi-monthly reports, at quarterly project meetings, and at the technical forum. Presentations at review meetings were expected to be formally prepared with appropriate supporting materials.

There was stunned silence following Lee's announcements; he asked for both questions and comments but there were none. Lee adjourned the meeting realizing the negative impact of his words.

At the time of Lee's announced changes, the lab had operated for 10 years with few formal scheduling or reporting procedures. Despite a growth in personnel—from an initial group of 25 to the present 149—previous lab managers had operated primarily with informal reports from middle management and with quarterly product review sessions. The changes Lee announced appeared contradictory to typical practice at Dillard Electronics: Decision making usually included middle managers and affected personnel in project cancellations or assignment changes. In fact, no one in the lab could recall any similar circumstance in the corporation's 60-year history.

Jane first interviewed Lee and his team one week after the major announcements. She was interested in helping them review their decision-making processes and understand expected relationships between change and the technical creativity/effectiveness of the lab.

All four new managers expressed certainty that the decision to formally structure the lab's communication system was the only way they could take control of a highly ineffective situation. They believed they were acting in the best interest of the corporation and in the best interest of the lab. Lee stated, "We had no choice. . . . If we did not take what is considered to be drastic measures then the mandate from corporate would not be real to these people." When Jane probed further, Lee related his belief that change must occur for the need for change to be believable. In other words, if the communication systems were flexible and informal and the results were ineffective then a rigid system would communicate a sense of urgency for change. Moreover, Harry, Joan, and Richard stressed that the new system would give them the information they needed to make timely decisions about product directions and schedules. All four managers expressed confidence in the technical competence of lab personnel. They stated that Dillard would not have hired these people in the first place if there were serious problems with technical competence. Harry stated, "This has been a problem of communicating imperatives in a research environment—not a basic ability problem. These people are attempting to be elitist designers rather than researchers in a business environment where market needs can't wait on perfection."

Lee, with the other three supporting his statements, described why he had not included middle managers in the change decisions. He suggested middle managers should not be held responsible for these changes. He knew the changes would be resisted and perhaps cause outrage among many of the technical professionals. He believed that the supervisors would have less difficulty if workers directed blame to a higher organizational level. When Jane asked about commitment from management to products, schedules, and reporting systems about which they had no input, Lee simply stated middle management had no choice but to support change or leave. All four managers expressed a desire to have included others in the change process, but believed the seriousness of the lab problem precluded a more participative approach. When asked to account for their choices about projects to be cancelled, new product definitions, and scheduling decisions, Lee confirmed corporate research and development had made most of these decisions after reviewing lab performance and expenditures for a five-year period.

Jane concluded the interviews by asking why the four had agreed to take these seemingly difficult assignments. All four responded that the corporation would reward them for making the effort and would make those rewards especially visible if they were successful. Lee in particular expressed doubt that any two-year plan could be met, but he—in fact all four—had received assurances his career would not be damaged if the lab was ultimately disbanded. These types of assurances from corporate served as an important foundation for the team as it made decisions to implement procedures that others in the lab viewed as extreme and not in keeping with overall corporate culture.

Joan expressed an additional belief about technical creativity. She claimed the formal and public reporting system would stimulate the excellence that she felt was present in the lab. She believed, and perhaps more than the others, that the intelligence in the lab would be challenged if technical professionals and middle managers were put in frequent positions of peer review and scrutiny.

Following her initial interviews with Lee and his management team, Jane talked with all 20 of the middle managers regarding their participation in the new scheduling and reporting systems. Their responses were predictably more diverse than those of Lee's team. Seven of the middle managers expressed no difficulty in supporting and participating in the new systems. The seven generally expressed views that corporate had no choice in making changes and that in the long run the lab would benefit from change. Several in this group were glad they had not been consulted about changes because peer pressure to resist would have resulted in tension and conflict among the middle managers. Two of this group expressed a belief that the projects would not meet the intended deadlines but would be much closer to success than if "dramatic action" had not been taken. Three of the group expressed a belief that if the lab did not improve soon, their chances of any career advancement within the corporation were effectively over.

Five of the middle managers submitted their resignations by the time Jane interviewed them. These five based their decisions on what they described as the corporation's loss of basic values. One individual asked for a corporate investigation of Lee and his staff. He stated, "I know corporate is behind these moves but I want to go on record as stating my opposition and deeply held belief that this is not the way to build good products and keep excellent people motivated." Others expressed concern that the company was not going to build good products if this type of autocratic management could prevail. When asked to describe why the lab had not produced a new product in the last four years, three of the five cited lack of resources and the technical difficulty of the problems on which they had been working. The other two said that four years between product releases was not unusual in a research and development environment.

The remainder of the middle management group gave diverse explanations as to why they chose to support the new procedures. Several in this group believed they lacked personal alternatives. Several indicated they were looking for new opportunities both within and without the corporation. These individuals would support the current situation only as long as it took to find other jobs. Others suggested they would take a wait-and-see attitude. Jane found that most believed the new system would stimulate technical creativity for only a short period of time. They did believe the lab had talented people, and several suggested that standards for performance had become increasingly ambiguous in the past several years. The majority of the middle managers believed they should have participated in the product change decisions. Several expressed a concern the lab was becoming extremely confrontational and competitive. When asked how such an environment affected overall performance, most responded it would not improve creativity. Several managers did express moderate enthusiasm for the increase in technical exchanges.

The final stage in Jane's initial data-gathering process was a labwide communication satisfaction survey. At the time of the administration the lab was ranked as the least effective of all corporate labs. The survey indicated that feedback on performance and information—about reasons for lab changes, about how the corporation evaluates labs, about lab decisions, and about personal performance and pay decisions—were the best predictors of communication and job satisfaction during this period of high uncertainty and change.

Jane provided reports summarizing concerns and issues identified in the interviews and survey to Lee's staff, the middle management group, and to a labwide meeting. Lee promised lab personnel he would think about and respond to their concerns. He did not make any immediate changes in policies or procedures.

Eight months after the formal reporting system and scheduling procedures were initiated, Lee announced he was returning project scheduling responsibilities to middle management. Agreement on scheduling changes would no longer have to receive prior approval by his staff. Middle managers would continue the basic reporting process and would keep Lee's team informed about scheduling changes and potential impact on product releases. At the time of Lee's announcement, three of four major design projects were having significant technical difficulties and the fourth was proceeding according to the planned schedule.

Jane again talked with Lee and his staff. In describing the decision to return scheduling responsibilities to the middle managers, Lee indicated he and his staff believed the group was ready for more responsibility. His decision was based on the belief that middle management now knew the lab was being held accountable for projects. Lee stated that middle managers had always been capable but were just not committed to timely product releases. He also suggested middle managers could now get more effort from their direct subordinates if the subordinates saw them as more actively involved and influential in scheduling decisions. Richard disagreed with Lee and his peers. He believed returning scheduling responsibility was premature because of the difficult technical problems facing three of the projects. He felt progress would best be accomplished if scheduling pressures remained fairly severe. Richard believed a competitive spirit was helping the lab to work more quickly. Harry and Joan contended the sooner the lab could return to the general operating philosophy of the company—real management responsibility at the project level—the better for the long-term development of the middle managers. Lee expressed a personal concern influencing his decision. He said, "I have never been viewed for so long a time as such a bad guy and this is just not comfortable. I know these people can do the job if only they will see we aren't trying to make bad products—we just have to make products." All of the team agreed the formal reporting sessions were generating a technical exchange that was useful for their interactions with corporate management. They felt they could better defend what the lab had accomplished with more detailed information.

One year after the initial changes, Jane conducted a series of interviews with 64 technical and support staff members. Questions were asked about how influence operated in the lab, how communication occurred, and what communication behaviors were valued. Nine general themes emerged from these interviews: (1) working on tough projects defines your intellectual worth; (2) you are expected to argue your position; (3) management wants quality products only if the products meet schedules and market requirements; (4) releasing a product is how your team communicates its worth; (5) only go to management with hard data; (6) the corporation hires only the best; (7) positive feedback is nice, results are the measure; (8) responsibility for excellence is everybody's business; and (9) you can complain to middle management but not top management. Themes were reported and discussed at both management and labwide meetings.

Twenty-two months after Lee became lab manager, Jane reviewed the lab's evaluation by corporate and again administered the communication and job satisfaction survey. The lab's corporate evaluation had improved and a product release had been accomplished. Satisfaction with overall lab communication had marginally improved and feedback on performance, information on performance and compensation decisions, and information on lab decisions remained important for job satisfaction.

Jane wrote in her report to Lee and the corporate human relations manager that forceful, directive leadership had guided the lab through resisted changes. Specifically, Lee and his staff had decided the informal reporting systems that they replaced provided inadequate information to make timely decisions involving considerable technical complexity. The management team believed a formal reporting environment demanded a precision of presentation, and presumably thinking, that stimulated creativity and peer interaction. Finally, management operated from a premise that in order to stimulate effectiveness substantial change in communication procedures would be required to make other requested changes credible.

Jane's report indicated corporate evaluations of lab effectiveness did not significantly influence communication and job satisfaction for technical professionals and support staff. However, different types of information contributed to job satisfaction depending on corporate evaluations. Specifically, having more information about reasons for change and how the external evaluation was to be conducted were more important in times of low effectiveness than in periods of success. Results from both the low effectiveness condition and the improved evaluation condition supported the importance of feedback to individuals for both communication and job satisfaction.

During the period of Jane's work, five mangers left the organization and there were ten personnel changes in the technical professional staff. Exit interviews established that the latter resulted from normal attrition unconnected to lab changes. Resources remained fairly comparable to previous periods. With relatively few staff and resource differences, the major changes were new top managers, new requirements surrounding effectiveness, and new reporting systems. Jane's report was careful to note that it was impossible to determine whether the lab's evaluation would have improved without the changes. Corporate management, however, credited the new product release and the overall improvements to the dramatic changes introduced by Lee and his team.

YOUR ASSIGNMENT

1. Describe the approach to change used by Lee and his staff. Discuss within the context of change and innovation theory.
2. Describe leadership in the lab. Evaluate the early strategy to eliminate middle managers from decision making.
3. What are the communication implications of this case?
4. Describe relationships among creativity, effectiveness, and leadership communication.
5. Do formal presentations followed by peer evaluation stimulate technical excellence? Why? Why not? Design an ongoing communication plan for this lab.

WHAT HAPPENED NEXT?

Within 6 months from the date the case concludes, the Chicago lab released two additional products for manufacture. One of these products became an international market leader contributing to a lab rating of outstanding from corporate research and development. Lee was promoted to general manager of the Chicago division. Richard became lab manager but failed to gain the support of much of the management staff. He held the position for 1 year and then was replaced by Joan. At the time of this printing, Joan is lab manager, Lee is general manager, and Richard and Harry have new assignments in other corporate divisions. The lab has successfully released a product every 18 months for the past 4 years. The formal presentations remain and middle managers control most scheduling decisions. The months of change depicted in the case are described as "Twenty-six Months of Hell" to newcomers as they learn about the culture of the lab. Lee, Harry, Joan, and Richard are considered successful managers.

Leadership: Margaret Thatcher, the Iron Lady

> I must say the adrenalin flows when they really come out fighting at me and I fight back, and I stand there, and I know, 'now come on, Maggie, you are wholly on your own. No one can help you.' And I love it.
>
> Margaret Thatcher on leadership

Thatcherism, the decade some say marked the return of Great Britain to the world stage. For more than 11 years, Margaret Thatcher defined the course of Britain as the strongest prime minister since Winston Churchill. Martin Gilbert, a Churchill biographer, states, "Both of them also understood that the essence of leadership was to choose a course of action you knew to be the right one and stay with it, and not try to achieve compromise in order to have an easy ride whether in cabinet or Parliament or with the editorial writers."

Margaret Thatcher's vision was based on the virtues of capitalism, individual rights, and a strong military defense. Her leadership within Britain and Europe as a whole was noted for its support of free-market economies, disdain for the power of trade unions, and a driving sense that the former Soviet Union must be compelled to deal with the West based on the West's strength and power. She supported the Reagan era in the United States and urged George Bush to draw a hard line in the sands of the Middle East. She was never overwhelmingly popular at home and her advocacy of a flat-rate head tax as opposed to property taxes was the strategic error leading to her resignation.

Margaret Thatcher has been characterized as one of the great leaders of the last decades of the twentieth century. Reflect on the dynamics of leadership as you read the following observations and descriptions:

This case is adapted from Glenn Frankel, "Britain Contemplates Life After Thatcher," *Washington Post,* November 25, 1990 and the *Washington Post,* National Weekly Edition, November 26–December 2, 1990.

She was ardent, tenacious and combative, a visionary who scorned consensus politics and conventional wisdom, a restless revolutionary who, even when isolated, believed in her own innate rightness. Those were the qualities that defined her greatness—and finally, those were the qualities that destroyed her. (Glenn Frankel, *Washington Post,* National Weekly Edition, November 26–December 2, 1990)

The Greeks understood it all. Great men and women are not brought down by lesser mortals, they are brought down by themselves. Margaret Thatcher was never going to be slain by a Geoffrey Howe or a Michael Heseltine, but she could always kill herself. (David Owen, former foreign secretary and a longtime opponent and admirer, as reported in Glenn Frankel, *Washington Post,* National Weekly Edition, November 26–December 2, 1990)

Thatcher never won more than 43 percent of the vote in any of her three general-election victories. She continually opposed the welfare state and semi-socialistic system, which polls consistently indicated a majority of Britons supported.

She disliked humor and rarely displayed it.

She disdained consensus and believed that compromise often led to the line of least resistance.

She was direct, tough, combative, and spoke with a schoolmarm's style.

The British system provides for a cabinet system of government where a prime minister is, at least in theory, the first among equals. But over Thatcher's 11 years in power, critics complained that cabinet government became something of a private joke. Many of the strongest personalities left, driven out by her insistence on personally controlling policy. . . . In the end, she was left with a cabinet that was often reluctant to contradict or challenge her, a group of younger men who were in many ways articulate and attractive but far less experienced than she had become. And their failure to stand up to her on what seemed a relatively minor domestic issue ultimately led to her downfall. (Glenn Frankel, *Washington Post,* National Weekly Edition, November 26–December 2, 1990)

She was stubborn, refused to listen, and cared deeply about Britain. She was brilliant but did not look in the mirror.

For them it's all compromise, sweep it under the carpet, leave it for another day, it might sort itself out. . . . It is because we on this side have never flinched from difficult decisions that this house and this country can have confidence in this government today. (Margaret Thatcher after her resignation, as reported in Glenn Frankel, *Washington Post,* National Weekly Edition, November 26–December 2, 1990)

YOUR ASSIGNMENT

1. Describe Thatcher's leadership. Contrast Thatcher's views to more participative approaches.
2. What type of leadership vision is described in the case?
3. Discuss consensus, compromise, and leadership.
4. Think about the notion that great leaders destroy themselves. How would you respond?
5. Apply Margaret Thatcher's leadership approach to a university, a high-tech firm, or a hospital. How would it change? What would happen?

Leadership Takes on a Nonmanagement Look

Hudson Graphics had been hit hard by the desktop publishing ventures of many of its clients. In business since the late 1940s, Hudson had grown steadily for many years and was known for quality work and good customer service. Harvey Hudson, the current president and grandson of the founder, believed Hudson could survive only if management made significant changes in both products and service. Harvey had hoped his staff would generate creative ideas. But as weeks passed he became convinced the management team was hopelessly deadlocked and afraid to take significant risks. Harvey decided to take another approach.

Harvey had been reading in the trade press about a new form of leadership— putting individual contributors in positions to recommend significant change. The movement in part was in response to decreased levels of management but also offered the potential for individuals to bring a fresh view of organizations to those responsible for final decision making. Over the objections of his senior staff, Harvey formed a group of eight individual contributors and charged them with generating "streamlining" ideas for the Hudson Graphics of the future. The group's experience with Hudson ranged from six months to more than 15 years; there were no managers. The following is a transcript of their initial meeting. As you read the transcript consider the leadership issues that surface. Observe how these individuals redefine leadership for their organization.

HUDSON: I am glad you could all meet at this time. I think two hours per week should be adequate. I am not sure how long the process will take but I do know that everyone has other responsibilities. Let me reiterate what I have told each of you individually. I need this group to take a significant leadership role for the company. Three areas need attention; we need a new product development process. Technology has changed the normal products coming out of Hudson Graphics. We need to think to the future. We also need to revisit the quality of our customer service. It seems to me that our customers can help us meet their needs if we are sure they still see us as customer focused. And finally, I need cost savings. That is where the management staff is stuck. No one wants to eliminate any of their personal turf. I have some ideas but I need your thinking. Now, as I have told all of you earlier, only the group report will be made public. I will work with you and guarantee you that any decision that might be unpopular will come from me. [*The group laughs.*]

Now are there any questions? Also, let's define how you want to start.

JAN: Well, I want to make one thing clear to this group. I did not ask for this assignment. I have only been with Hudson for six months. I know you told me that was why you wanted my observations, but I want the others to know that.

HARVEY: Jan is right. I believe we all get used to doing things the way we have always done them. I asked her specifically because she is right out of college and new to this company. I think we all see things differently at different times in our lives.

GEORGE: Jan, it is OK. After all, if we come up with big changes you won't get blamed. The rest of us will. After all some of us have been with Hudson for our entire careers. Actually, Harvey, I do have a question. You answered it to me personally but I want to go on record. OK? There are no sacred cows? Right? I mean, we can recommend anything that we see whether it is popular with management or not.

HARVEY: That's right as long as you can tell me why.

PAM: Harvey, who are you going to appoint as our leader?

HARVEY: Well, I sort of thought I would fill that role.

STEVE: Harvey, I don't think you should be present for all of our discussions. I mean, we trust you, but we might be able to be more candid without you present. What do the rest of you think?

DORIS: Steve is right. Harvey, we all respect you but you are the president.

PAM: I agree also. I think we can handle this ourselves. We don't need a formal leader. We are all mature people and really want the company to be successful.

DON: Harvey, my real question is a tough one. I don't mean that I don't trust you but—this seems strange. Your staff makes good money. Why can't they do this job? Why are we being asked to take on more responsibility than we are paid to do?

JOHN: Harvey, Don is asking the million-dollar question? Why?

HARVEY: Well, what can I say? I tried to get my staff to bring me some new ideas. They are good guys. But, I have to respect their feelings. Each believes he is protecting those of you who report to him. Well, this is not working, but what can I say?

Also, I have come to believe that good individuals often see more than good managers. You know, the notion that we need a new form of leadership based on knowledge and expertise not position power. I trust you, I trust my staff. And they are experts of sorts, but the responsibilities and expectations are different.

NINA: OK, I can buy that, but I can't buy that important changes will not be challenged by your staff. I want to know that the time I invest in this project will mean something. Not that I expect you to take everything we might say, but I don't want some management staff second guessing everything.

HARVEY: Nina, I have known you for a long time. I wouldn't have asked you to assume this responsibility if I did not intend to listen. In fact, I will go so far as to suggest that I will take most of your recommendations and will tell you which ones I accept and which I reject before taking them to my staff. I can't give you any more commitment than that. I am asking a lot of each of you and I will give a lot in return.

[*The discussion continues. . . .*]

NINA: Why have we gotten away from listening to people with good experience and good ideas? If it can happen to a management team it can happen to us. How are we going to make sure we can do any better than those above us?

JAN: Well, it seems to me that each of us individually has nothing to lose with change. We don't have the turf issues the managers have and all of us want Hudson to succeed, so I don't see the problem. This seems like an intelligent group of people to me.

DORIS: I think we should realize up front that we may not agree much more than the management team, and that is OK. We need to come up with as many ideas as possible and then test these ideas. If we need more information we can ask the management team and others to provide us with what we need. We should have confidence in ourselves.

DON: You are right, Doris, but I am not sure how the management team is going to feel about our requests. They did not want this group formed let alone [to be questioned] about issues and data.

GEORGE: Don is right. But we have to do it anyway. They have failed to bring about change and it is now our responsibility to make something happen. I don't relish asking Dave [*a member of the management team known for his outbursts at those who disagree with him*] but he is not helping Hudson improve, so we ask him. He can only yell.

STEVE: George is right. If we don't want to do things differently then we should get out of this group. Actually, I think this is going to be fun. We can explore all of the things we have ever thought, and it is going to be our jobs, not some ''Why didn't the management think of this?'' game.

PAM: Harvey, I am beginning to see what you mean when you say leadership is everyone's responsibility.

YOUR ASSIGNMENT

1. Describe how Harvey Hudson defines the leadership he needs from this group of eight individual contributors. How does this differ from traditional views of leadership?

2. Distinctions have been made between leadership and management. Identify distinctions in this case. Describe why management responsibilities may actually impede leadership during times of needed change.

3. Develop a plan for this group to examine the three challenges that Harvey Hudson has presented to them.

4. Examine the emerging concept that effective organizations need leadership from all organizational positions. Explain the statement, "Leadership is a responsibility while management is a specific role." What implications does this statement have for this case?

5. Should Harvey Hudson accept the group's recommendations? Why? Why not? How can he influence his management team to accept the group's proposals?

CHAPTER **6**

Conflict and Communication

Change Is Ruining Our Company

Jones–Belew Brokerage was in trouble. Despite a 50-year success record, Jones–Belew was experiencing significant losses and a need to review its business operations in some 35 offices in 16 states. The Texas offices were of particular concern. With over 700 employees in three Texas cities, Jones–Belew profits had declined for the past 3 years.

The three management teams based in Texas knew change was coming. They had not expected, however, a mandate from corporate headquarters to reduce personnel by 43 percent. The reduction was unprecedented, especially in light of the fact the Texas offices were marginally profitable. Furthermore, the three Texas offices were told they should consolidate as many operations as possible, including merging the three management teams into two staffs.

Corporate management named Tom Coswell and Don Stein to head the two staffs and asked them to select the best people for their respective teams. Those not selected would have "bumping" rights to lower level positions within Texas. Coswell and Stein agreed to consolidate their human resources, quality assurance, finance, and marketing operations. Each would retain separate sales and product development departments.

The consolidation of the human resources department began first. Coswell and Stein believed the three current managers—Jerry Jackson, Tom Johnson, and Alice Simpson—should apply for head of the consolidated organization. All three had been longtime Jones–Belew employees, and although they did not stand out for their leadership and creativity, they were considered loyal to the company. Coswell and Stein were surprised when corporate management refused to consider any of the three; they urged them to give George Manatel receive strong consideration.

Coswell and Stein both interviewed Manatel, a California Jones–Belew employee who had overseen the consolidation of five offices in the San Francisco Bay area. Manatel's past leadership was praised by many, but he was sometimes described as a "hatchet" man who never looked back.

The announcement of George Manatel as site manager for human resources was a blow to Jerry, Tom, and Alice. They all knew they were not highly regarded by corporate but were concerned about exclusion from the site management choice. Many workers within the three departments were pleased an outsider had been appointed to bring the group together.

Within six weeks of George's arrival in Texas, he announced a list of 22 individuals—from among the 50 employees of the three departments—who would be asked to leave the function. He had identified specific names through consultation with the three former managers, a review of current assignments, past performance appraisals, and seniority with the company.

Outrage swept through the department. All employees were united in their dismay at the manner in which the list had been developed. Many suggested George did not adequately understand the jobs he was eliminating because Jerry, Tom, and Alice did not adequately understand the work of their own departments. In addition, some expressed concern that Jerry, Tom, and Alice (to a lesser degree than the other two) had failed to foresee needed changes. The former managers were perceived to be protected while people who had worked for them had to make significant career shifts. Others identified specific individuals who they believed to be excellent performers and who were on the list only because they were low in seniority.

George believed he had followed corporate policy in the development of his list. He met with all three departments to explain the procedure. During the meeting employees expressed both anger and distrust. Several employees offered the opinion that if human resources could not do a better job of reducing its own numbers, the rest of the company should not follow its advice or example. A small number believed George had acted properly and decisively.

George concluded some of these concerns employees voiced were valid, particularly the concern that former department heads had not been affected nearly as much as the people who worked for them. George decided he must hold Jerry, Tom, and Alice visibly responsible for excellent work in their new positions. He met with them and attempted to identify specific projects that each could lead during the department consolidation process. He was not pleased with Jerry Jackson's response. Jerry accused George of moving too rapidly and declared that change was ruining the company. Tom said essentially the same thing. Only Alice indicated a desire to work aggressively on a new project.

George wondered how he could motivate them. He could understand their disappointment yet knew their visible improvement to be important for others in the department. He also wondered how to help those individuals who would be leaving the department. They would have opportunities to work in other areas of the company. He needed their attitudes to be more positive.

George knew he was dealing with resistance to change. He felt isolated and at the same time challenged by an opportunity for human resources to be the first consolidated operation for the Texas offices.

YOUR ASSIGNMENT

1. How would you advise George? Develop a plan for the next six months.
2. What are the communication issues he is facing? The organizational change issues? The career issues?
3. How would you respond to the charge, "Change is ruining the company"?
4. If you were asked to lead a consolidation of three departments, identify all the information you would require to make staffing and organizational structure decisions. Where would you seek information? What type of problem-solving and decision-making processes would you utilize?
5. How can leaders help people accept change?

Severance Pay

Dr. Debra Wright, who had steered clear of controversy during her first 24 months as president of Eastern University, finds herself embroiled in her first public conflict because severance pay was given to an assistant football coach who quit after nine months. The amount of money—$26,000—is only a fraction of the athletic budget and is comparable to severance pay packages given to other athletic department employees. The payment, however, came only two weeks following an Eastern board of regents freeze on spending due in large part to budgetary problems in the state legislature.

Several regents, in their first public criticism of Wright, believe her timing could not have been worse, and two regents have openly questioned her managerial skills and political astuteness. The president of the board of regents has been quoted as saying the payment sends the wrong signal to university employees who have been warned about layoffs early next year.

Wright has told regents and her staff that her decision is in the best interest of the university; she continues to believe she is correct. Wright admits the current political climate makes the decision unpopular. She contends severance pay is often used to encourage people to leave the university even though they have done nothing to warrant firing. She wants to retain methods to deal with performance that is only marginally acceptable. Wright claims her severance pay for the assistant coach represents standard operating procedure. Moreover, she told the president of the board of regents that the severance pay is not of public concern because it came from athletic department funds as opposed to taxpayer money.

Several regents have been quoted as saying their next step will be to reexamine the severance pay policies of the university. One regent, Alan Moyer, has voiced concern that another president is being tested in the media. His comments specifically referenced the fact that Eastern University has had four presidents in eight years. Moyer was quoted as saying, "This university chews up presidents no matter what they do."

Wright is concerned about her relationship with the regents. She ponders how she should prepare for the upcoming week's emergency meeting called by the president of the regents.

YOUR ASSIGNMENT

1. What are the conflicting issues in this case?
2. Describe the various contexts of the conflict. What does the public have a right to know?
3. How would you advise the regents? What are the special issues for leadership in a public organization?
4. How would you advise President Wright?
5. Think about the utilization of severance pay to solve performance problems. Is this an effective way to deal with performance issues? Why? Why not?

The Revolution at Intex

Intex Advertising had been in business for over 20 years when Dave Intex decided he wanted to become less involved in the day-to-day operation of the company. His decision to hire Eddie Shephard to head his 30-person staff was based on a belief that none of his current employees could handle the position and his account executives—Linda Murphy, Andrea Kola, and Jack Kourman—were better left in their sales and service positions.

Eddie Shephard is a longtime Chicago advertising executive. He has been the lead account executive for several nationally recognized promotions and has many years of management experience at his current agency. The account executives at Intex were generally pleased when Dave announced his decision. None of the account executives wanted to run the office and they agreed they were better utilized in client contact positions.

Eddie called his first meeting of all employees and made an unexpected announcement. He told the staff he had hired Mark Simpson, a New York account executive, to bring new blood to Intex. Mark was to head an aggressive effort to acquire major retailers as Intex clients. No client changes would be made among the account executives, although shifts might occur in the future to accommodate the expected new business. The group was stunned by the announcement; the account executives, in particular, were concerned Eddie had not talked with them about his proposed changes.

The press release was even worse than the meeting. Eddie asked the office manager to circulate copies of publicity sheets that had been provided to the trade press. Mark Simpson's arrival at Intex was touted as an effort to energize the retail division under Eddie's leadership. Mark's background in New York was emphasized with no mention of current Intex business or the overall $15 million in billings handled by Linda, Andrea, and Jack. The three account executives were furious. Intex had been profitable long before Eddie or Mark arrived and now their clients and the industry in general were being told the firm needed new energy and direction. After a group discussion the three decided to confront Eddie.

Eddie met with Linda, Andrea, and Jack and was surprised to hear of their displeasure. He stated there was no cause for concern and they would soon see everyone would be better off with Mark's arrival. The three agreed to be open-minded and asked Eddie to discuss future changes with them before they became so public. Eddie agreed he would do so.

Mark Simpson did not want to work with Linda, Andrea, and Jack. He declined to attend their weekly meetings and told Eddie the less he worked with them the better. He requested priority scheduling in the creative departments and justified his requests based on his business acquisition plans. Linda, Andrea, and Jack again confronted Eddie and demanded a resolution of the scheduling conflicts. Eddie asked them to give Mark a chance.

The three account executives requested a meeting with Dave Intex. Dave was disturbed to hear their complaints and agreed to talk with Eddie about Mark and the new business initiative. Eddie told Dave he felt Mark Simpson was the future of the agency and, although he was sorry the account executives were upset, they were more expendable than Mark. Dave told Eddie he did not want to lose any of the three although he supported Mark.

Eddie and Mark spent many hours behind closed doors. Linda, Andrea, and Jack sometimes had to wait more than a week to get on Eddie's schedule. Mark continued to demand priority in the art and production departments. When a competitor called Linda and offered her a job she immediately contacted Andrea and Jack to ask if they would consider asking their clients to move to another agency.

Andrea and Jack were hesitant expressing loyalty to Dave. Linda agreed the three should again go to Dave and tell him they would be forced to leave if something was not done about Eddie and Mark. Dave again met with the group. He said he would talk with Eddie immediately.

Eddie was angry when he met with Dave. Mark Simpson had just resigned to return to New York. Mark felt Intex was too small an agency for his talents. Dave voiced his concerns about the three account executives and Eddie promised to work more effectively with Linda, Andrea, and Jack.

Eddie called a meeting with the three account executives to announce Mark's departure. He asked what he could do to build their confidence in his leadership. He did not tell them that Dave had given him six months to solve the problem or he would be looking for another job.

YOUR ASSIGNMENT

1. Describe how the conflict at Intex became a potential revolution.
2. What should Dave have done to prevent this problem?
3. What should Eddie have done to deal with this problem?
4. Can this conflict be productive?
5. How would you advise Eddie as he attempts to establish his leadership? What would you say to Linda, Andrea, and Jack?

The "What Do You Mean We Have to Retrain?" Case

Most of them have been with the company for over 10 years and some more than 20. They were competent, committed to their work, and had a good reputation throughout the company. It was impossible to think they were going to have to compete for their jobs. It was not fair and it just was not going to happen. They could not let this corporate reorganization continue.

THE GROUP

Fifty-six supervisors for Continental Plastics' Memphis division had received the notice from corporate manufacturing. Their jobs were being replaced by higher level process supervisor positions. They would be given 24 months to retrain for the new manufacturing processes and technologies, then they would be given an opportunity to interview for one of the new positions. No new people would be hired until all current supervisors had decided whether or not to compete for one of the positions. Those choosing not to compete could elect to go back to direct labor work. They would be assigned to the groups they currently supervised.

Jim Britton and Joan Kelley decided to call a meeting of the group. They were the most senior among the supervisors and believed it their responsibility to respond to management quickly before the training classes were scheduled to begin. They had no trouble attracting people to their meeting, with 49 of 56 supervisors in attendance. The group agreed to protest the decision and ask for a meeting to discuss alternatives with manufacturing management. They asked Jim and Joan to continue as their spokespersons.

THE SITUATION

Continental Plastics has been an international leader in plastics manufacturing for over 40 years. Only in the last 5 years has foreign competition begun to affect Continental's market share. Corporate manufacturing management created a task force to assess necessary changes to keep Continental competitive over the coming decade. Following an extensive examination of Continental's manufacturing processes and the equipment and processes of principal competitors, the task force recommended a number of technology changes requiring a new type of leadership in the factories. As a result, Continental created the new process supervisor positions to replace current factory supervisor jobs; manufacturing supervisors would be required to retrain.

Continental management hired consultants to design a training program for five factory locations. Courses would be taught on company time and all supervisors would have an opportunity to attend if they intended to apply for one of the new positions. Most current manufacturing supervisors were high school graduates who had been out of school for many years. The courses in the training program would include statistics, total quality control methods, robotics, group dynamics, presentation speaking, and problem solving. A comprehensive examination at the end of the training classes would be utilized as part of the assessment to determine who would be selected for the new process supervisor positions. Furthermore, all process supervisor applicants would be interviewed by a team of corporate manufacturing managers. Continental management hoped most current manufacturing supervisors would retrain and apply for the new positions. They expected, however, that some would elect to return to the production line.

THE MEETING

Jim and Joan were pleased manufacturing management asked Dave Duncan, a top manufacturing official, and Claire Norton, head of Memphis' human relations department, to meet with their group. Dave began the meeting by thanking the group for coming to talk with him about the changes. He stated Claire was present to answer questions about the training, applying for the new jobs, and returning to production line positions. The group listened attentively to Dave's presentation. When Dave finished, Jim and Joan asked to present the concerns of the group. They outlined the group's basic issues: The group understood competition meant changes and was willing to learn new skills. It did not accept, however, the need to formally retrain and test. Jim and Joan stressed the company was not exhibiting loyalty to the good work of the supervisors. They pointed out that no one else in the corporation was to be tested in this way. They were also concerned that an individual could go to class for two years and still end up on the production line. Jim and Joan finished their presentation by telling Dave and Claire the process for change was not acceptable to the group and group members were considering whether any of them would sign up for classes. Dave and Claire had not expected this level of resistance. Dave said he understood their pain but he believed the corporate approach was in the best long-term interests of Continental. Several group members joined the conversation by stating their displeasure with the way they were being treated by the company. Dave and Claire agreed they would communicate to corporate manufacturing managers the depth of the feelings among the Memphis group. One person asked whether the other company factories had supervisors who shared their concern. Claire indicated no other group had asked to meet with management.

MANAGEMENT'S RESPONSE

Corporate manufacturing management listened with concern to Dave's report and agreed the introduction of the program could have been handled more effectively. After lengthy discussion management decided it was too late to alter the basic expectations and process. Management issued a statement commending the good work of manufacturing supervisors and invited all current supervisors to become part of the retraining program; it asked for commitments within 30 days.

THE MEMPHIS RESPONSE

Jim and Joan again met with the Memphis manufacturing supervisors. Many responded with hostility to the latest corporate communication. Jim and Joan tried to get the group to see a decision was near and they must consider what action they were willing to take. Following four hours of heated discussion, the group voted to comply with the program primarily because most could not risk being fired or returned to the pay level of the production line. Several indicated they would look for jobs outside the company while pretending to go through the training program.

THE TRAINING

Forty-nine of 56 supervisors at Memphis began the training. Many privately agreed the classes were stimulating and they enjoyed learning new technologies and processes. The instructors were interesting and the opportunity to attend classes during work hours was helpful. They did complain about the study time required but were somewhat resigned to their lack of alternatives. The instructors reported to Claire and others that the group possessed the basic intelligence to learn the new skills and the head of the instructional team predicted that most would easily qualify for the new process supervisor positions. The training courses were completed in 24 months and the comprehensive test was successfully completed by 44 of the original 49. Three supervisors had dropped out of the program during the courses and 2 did not pass the examination.

THE INTERVIEWS

Forty of those who passed the examination interviewed for process supervisor positions. Thirty-eight were selected for the new positions and the two who were not selected were given feedback on their perceived deficiencies and asked to apply in the next round of openings.

THE GROUP'S LAST MEETING

Jim and Joan called a final meeting of manufacturing supervisors before the changes became official. They asked the group to evaluate the two-year process and provide feedback to corporate management that might make future transitions less painful. The group agreed the most important mistake had been the introduction of the program. Most agreed the classes had been beneficial and contended the results supported their initial position that the company should have promoted them and then required training. One person suggested their motivation to learn was probably increased by the uncertainty of their positions. Several members of the group told her not to mention this view in public. Jim and Joan were relieved the two years were over. They believed the skills of the group had increased but wondered if commitment to the company could ever return to previous levels.

YOUR ASSIGNMENT

1. How would you have handled the introduction of the process supervisor program?
2. What factors contributed to the conflict? Could the conflict have been avoided?
3. Was the program a success? How can you decide?
4. Describe the issues in this case in terms of innovation and change theory.
5. Design a different process for the introduction of the new supervisor positions and the required training. Base your process on communication and innovation theory.

The "Too Little, Too Late" Case

Joan Davis had been excited when she was offered the assistant manager position in the program development department of the National Achievement Organization (NAO), a major national nonprofit educational organization. Joan had headed an area office for NAO for seven years and believed she needed a change to develop her career.

Madeline Grant became the manager for program development for NAO three months prior to Joan's arrival in the New York office. Madeline was an experienced NAO marketing representative who looked forward to developing programs for sales representatives and the area offices. Madeline was pleased to have her assistant manager bring field experience to a staff who had worked almost exclusively in the national office.

Madeline gave Joan broad authority. She asked Joan to oversee the budget for four of the department's five programs and head research and writing for a new career development project. Joan eagerly accepted and asked for staff to report directly to her in the affected programs.

Madeline placed great faith in Joan's ability to manage both the ongoing projects and new program development. She expressed little concern when quarterly budget reports were late and research on the career development project was limited. Joan appeared confident about her progress and explained the late reports were due to new people in finance. Moreover, Joan hired a consultant who appeared competent to work on the career development project.

By the end of Joan's first year, Madeline was receiving complaints about unpaid bills and one of Joan's subordinates requested a transfer to another department. The head of finance denied the problem was in his office and the employee charged Joan was demeaning and confusing in providing instructions for projects.

Despite her growing concerns, Madeline gave Joan an outstanding performance appraisal and informally stressed that Joan should work on the finance problem at her earliest convenience. Madeline also requested a briefing on the career development project. It was at this briefing that Madeline began to see how little specific material Joan had produced for the program. Joan's idea seemed excellent but the program had not progressed.

Madeline asked her division manager, Joyce Walsh, for advice. Joyce suggested Madeline meet more frequently with Joan and set deadlines for project reports. Joyce reported Joan had complained about Madeline taking credit for her ideas. Madeline was shocked and concerned about how her own behavior could have been so misinterpreted.

Madeline began weekly meetings with Joan. Joan disliked the meetings and became increasingly sullen and defensive. Joan approached a new member of the department, John Paulson, and asked him to work on the career project. John, known for his organizational skills, was glad for the assignment and immediately met with the consultant to see what progress had been made.

Unknown to John, the consultant asked to meet with Madeline during the same week. The consultant told Madeline he must resign the account because he believed Joan's lack of direction and or contradictory directions would result in unsatisfactory work. He also complained he had not been paid promptly for over one year. He requested this meeting to explain his decision in the hope future business with NAO would not be adversely affected.

Madeline knew she must make changes. She did not understand why Joan was not performing when she continued to have excellent ideas and sounded as if projects were under control. Madeline decided to ask the consultant to remain on the project with John Paulson as the principal contact. John would report simultaneously to both Joan and Madeline. She would ask Joan to work directly with her on a new project that top management had assigned to the department.

Joan appeared to accept the transfer of the career program to Paulson. She pretended to be excited about the new program and agreed working directly with Madeline was a good idea. However, Joan told both the consultant and Paulson that Madeline was both out for her job and incompetent. Paulson and the consultant remained silent but worried the relationship between Joan and Madeline was badly deteriorating.

Madeline again went to Joyce Walsh for advice. Joyce agreed more specific action should be taken. She asked Madeline to write a formal letter of disciplinary action to Joan specifically identifying Madeline's concerns and requiring performance improvement. Although Madeline's general accounts of the situation were accurate, her record keeping made documentation difficult.

Madeline began making extensive notes of her meetings with Joan. She learned through a department secretary that Joan had been keeping detailed notes of all meetings for over a year. Madeline continued her documentation until she felt comfortable with drafting a letter of reprimand.

Joan received the letter with little visible comment. She said she understood Madeline's jealousy of her work and her desire to take all credit personally. Joan stated she believed Madeline was not as suited for the manager's job as she but that they could learn to work together despite these differences. Madeline could not believe the conversation and asked Joan to consider the implications of her remarks.

Joan hired an attorney, who filed a formal complaint of harassment against Madeline. Madeline met with Joyce and NAO lawyers to determine her personal position and the position of the association. The NAO attorney recommended initiation of termination procedures. Joyce agreed and Madeline met with human resource representatives to begin formal proceedings.

Joan was called to the director of human resources' office and presented with a formal letter of termination. She told the director her lawyer would pursue the matter.

For the last three years, the case has been pending in local and state courts. The association has spent thousands of dollars preparing a defense for Madeline. Joan has spent all of her savings on attorney fees and currently is unemployed.

YOUR ASSIGNMENT

1. What is "too little, too late" in this case?
2. Could this conflict have been avoided?
3. Describe Madeline's management/leadership style.
4. Develop a training program entitled "Working with Difficult People." Use this case as an example. Base your program on leadership, communication, and conflict theory.
5. How would you advise Madeline? How would you advise Joan?

The "Don't Rock the Boat Around Here" Case

George Davis was the newest member of the sales support division for Middlesex Insurance. Out of college only two years, George felt privileged to be hired by Middlesex from a group of some 50 applicants. Jobs were hard to find and George knew several of the applicants had more work experience than was reflected in his application.

George liked the members of his sales support team. Jean, Bill, and Scott were competent and willing to help him understand the computer systems and the most frequently asked questions by Middlesex customers. Their boss, John Standard, spent most of his days behind closed office doors but was pleasant enough when interactions did take place. George would have preferred slightly more direction and a more complete understanding of John's performance expectations, but the others assured him they would fill him in and there would be no problems.

George's first six months at Middlesex were busy and uneventful. Jean, Bill, and Scott were helpful and George felt comfortable with the amount of on-the-job training they provided. John's first review of George's performance was favorable with no suggestions for improvement.

George was surprised when John announced at a staff meeting that top management was critical of the number of customers being handled daily by the sales support division. Jean, Bill, and Scott, although not pleased about the criticism, assured George this happened periodically and he had no cause for real concern. George wondered about the accuracy of their perceptions. Middlesex had lost money for two consecutive quarters and there were rumors of lay-offs in parts of the company. George began to think of ways to streamline their customer service process and to improve the statistics of numbers of calls handled by the team.

Approximately two weeks following John's staff meeting, George proposed to Jean, Bill, and Scott a new method of accessing information for service claims. George believed his method would permit each team member to service approximately five additional customers per day. Jean, in particular, thought the idea was a good one but warned George that all changes must come from John, who was not inclined to listen to team recommendations. Bill and Scott seemed to support Jean's position.

George decided to mention his idea to John anyway. He was somewhat displeased to find that their advice seemed accurate. John thanked him for thinking about the problem but told him there was really no need to change systems because the group was doing an adequate job and criticisms would soon go away.

George became more concerned when the company newsletter announced lay-offs in two departments. Seniority and performance were the basis for determining who would lose their jobs. George knew he would be the first to go from his team. He again approached Jean, Bill, and Scott with his concerns about productivity. He told them about his conversation with John. They explained that John was not about to change his ways until top management sent him an order. Bill said if the idea had been John's something might happen, but John was unlikely to attempt anything recommended by his group.

Middlesex lost money for the third consecutive quarter and there were widespread rumors of additional lay-offs. Jean, Bill, and Scott agreed to support George in another attempt to convince John of the need for process changes to improve productivity. John listened quietly to George's presentation and then reminded the group he was the manager and he would bring about change when he was good and ready. He surprised them with his own plan to increase customer load by two calls per day for each team member.

George was somewhat relieved when John admitted the need to improve but felt discouraged at the conservative nature of his planning. Scott suggested John might not want management to think the team could improve in as dramatic a manner as indicated by George's plan. George believed the group had a responsibility to bring as much productivity to their area as possible. He also knew he would be the first to go if further declines brought lay-offs to his area.

George wondered what he should do. Jean, Bill, and Scott had supported him all they could. John's plan was an improvement but not nearly enough to avoid further criticism. George did not want to anger John. He knew he was not supposed to "rock the boat," but he believed his idea was superior to John's plan. Furthermore, George believed his own job might be at stake.

YOUR ASSIGNMENT

1. Utilizing communication and conflict theory, describe the conditions contributing to the conflict in this case. Identify how different interests and styles are contributing to George's concerns.

2. Develop a rationale to explain John's position and the positions of Jean, Bill, and Scott.

3. Based on principles of supportive communication and productive confrontation, plan a meeting between George and John where George can present a comprehensive argument for his ideas.

4. Describe the relationship between productive conflict and an organization's ability to change.

5. Develop an organizational communication plan for Middlesex Insurance to gather innovative ideas from its employees.

CHAPTER 7

Values, Ethics, and Organizational Communication

Lea Pearlman's Ethical Dilemma

Lea Pearlman had worked as a consultant to the majority of the departments in Morrison Manufacturing. She was respected and often the consultant of choice when Dick Wallace, Morrison's human resource vice-president, had difficult problems to solve. It was not surprising Lea had been asked to bid on Morrison Manufacturing's first employee communication and needs assessment survey.

At the time of the employee survey, Morrison Manufacturing had been in business for 75 years growing from a 25-person family-owned operation to its present work force of 3,500. In the company's early years, the Morrison family had designed and built small boats for primarily an east coast market. As their reputation for quality grew, opportunities for sales throughout the United States and Canada led to steady expansion of the work force and to diversification of product lines. By the 75th anniversary celebration, Morrison Aquatic Products had 14 product lines with sales and manufacturing offices in six states. Profits were good and Morrison management was optimistic about the future.

Dick Wallace sold the idea of an employee survey to Morrison's executive committee, the management group responsible for overall strategic decisions. Several on the committee resisted believing surveys only raised expectations about actions that management might not be ready to take. Particular concern was expressed about employee benefits and educational and training opportunities. Wallace persisted, emphasizing the need for continuing awareness of employee concerns as Morrison increased its work force in diverse geographic locations.

Lea Pearlman was Wallace's choice to lead the survey effort. She had a seven-year history of effective work with Morrison and had in-depth knowledge of various departments and product lines. She made a presentation to the executive committee and was approved for the project.

Lea was surprised by the morning paper on the day of her first scheduled meeting with Morrison's president, David Sutters. The lead story on the business page detailed Sutters's resignation to take a position with a principal competitor. Raleigh Enterprises reportedly had offered Sutters a compensation package he could not refuse. His announcement was brief, stating his hesitancy to leave Morrison and his obligation to think of his own career and the future of his family.

When Lea arrived at Morrison headquarters she found most people in a state of disbelief. Dick Wallace was concerned but suggested the meeting with Sutters should proceed as scheduled.

Lea and Dick met with Sutters, who recommended the survey should continue as scheduled. Lea disagreed, believing Sutters's departure would bias the results of the survey and make findings difficult to interpret for long-range planning. Dick agreed with Lea and the project was temporarily put on hold.

Within six weeks Morrison's board of directors had appointed Jim Elliot to the presidency. Elliot, a longtime Morrison employee, had served for the past several years as vice-president for marketing. Prior to his marketing assignment Elliot had worked in both research and human resources. Elliot was one of the members of the executive committee originally opposed to an employee survey. Wallace and others convinced Elliot the survey had broad employee interest and cancellation at this point would reflect negatively on Elliot's leadership.

Elliot told Wallace he wanted his budget and organizational development people more involved in the survey project than Wallace had planned. Wallace was concerned based on the generally negative reputation of the budget director and his assistant in charge of organizational development, Chris Nichols. Elliot remained firm and asked Wallace to introduce Pearlman to Nichols as soon as possible.

Lea Pearlman had known of Chris Nichols for some time. In fact, she had frequently advised Morrison departments with regard to projects Nichols recommended. Rarely had her past recommendations matched those from Nichols's department. She had commented to Wallace on previous occasions that she found it strange she had not worked more directly with Nichols. Wallace believed most department heads hesitated to involve Nichols and wanted to rely on human resources and the services of consultants such as Pearlman.

Pearlman, Wallace, and Nichols met to develop a schedule and procedures for the survey. Lea was pleased that most of her recommendations were approved by Nichols and that the project schedule seemed realistic. All agreed that employees should be informed of the survey process and especially how the results would be publicized and utilized by the executive committee. Pearlman, Wallace, and Nichols all expressed concern that Elliot was not committed to using the results to develop concrete action plans. Nichols, in particular, asked for several open-ended questions to be added to the survey. Employees were to be promised confidentiality with only Lea's staff having access to original surveys. Lea agreed to the questions with the assurance only general themes would be reported and no specific individuals would be named. Wallace and Nichols agreed and the survey process began.

Over 2,900 employees responded to both scaled and open-ended questions. Narrative comments exceeded 500 pages of typed responses. Employees were generally positive about Morrison but had many specific concerns and comments about management within the various departments. Lea concluded leadership capabilities varied across the company and two areas in particular had significant problems. She presented her report to Wallace and Nichols, who agreed the findings matched their general awareness of issues within the company. Lea was confident of the issues and recommendations she provided for the executive committee.

Employees individually received a copy of a shortened version of her report to management. Both management and employees responded favorably and were pleased when Elliot announced a series of task groups to deal with issues identified in the survey. Lea was pleasantly surprised to be asked to continue with the project and work as a consultant to the groups. She was unprepared, however, for Chris Nichols's intended use of the survey.

Nichols asked Pearlman to meet with him to discuss how the survey results could be utilized by his department. He was in the process of completing a series of management audits that would result in combining several functions within various Morrison departments. His goals were cost efficiencies and increased service for customers. The reorganization would reduce middle management across the company costing several senior managers their jobs. No one would be forced to leave the company, but several individuals would be asked to return to nonmanagerial positions. Nichols stated Jim Elliot was solidly behind his plans. Nichols wanted Pearlman to analyze survey data for additional information not requested in the original project. She was to present the findings to him for reorganization planning. The requested analysis would not be available to all employees nor were findings to be given to the executive committee. Nichols would pay for the additional work out of his department's budget. Specifically, Nichols wanted to know which departments had the most favorably evaluated management and he wanted narrative comments analyzed by specific departments to help him identify problems that his reorganization proposals might address. Although not directly stated, Pearlman believed Nichols was seeking information to help him support his list of management positions to be eliminated. Nichols jokingly suggested Pearlman could just let him read the original narratives and save everyone time and money. Pearlman stated she could not do that but would get him a budget estimate for the additional work he was requesting.

Lea called Dick Wallace with her concerns. She told Wallace the survey contained information useful for a reorganization effort but she considered it a breach of ethics to create reports where those affected were unaware of what was being compiled and that were not available to the executive committee. Wallace agreed and asked how he could help. Lea stated she did not intend to involve him but wanted his advice before she responded to Nichols.

Lea thought carefully about her approach to Nichols. She did not believe Jim Elliot wanted confidential information released to Nichols although he was in support of the reorganization project. She decided to present alternatives for Nichols to consider.

Lea began her meeting with Nichols by suggesting the additional analyses he had requested would cost approximately $12,000. She stated, however, that one of two conditions had to be met prior to her contracting for the services. First, she and Nichols could meet with Jim Elliot and one of Morrison's attorneys to determine liability for release of information where confidentiality had been promised, or, she could draft a memo for release to the executive committee informing them of the additional analyses and the intended use by the organizational development department. Lea justified her requests based on her statements to the executive committee and employee groups about the nature of the analysis and how data were to be analyzed and reported. She asked Nichols which approach he preferred. Nichols appeared surprised and stated he saw no reason to talk with Elliot. He informed Lea he would think about the requests and get back to her.

Lea left the meeting believing she had seriously damaged her working relationship with a powerful member of the president's staff. She was not surprised to receive a polite letter canceling her work with the groups. After all, Nichols controlled the budget that was to pay the contract.

YOUR ASSIGNMENT

1. What are the ethical issues in this case?
2. Was Lea correct to be concerned about Chris Nichols's intended use of survey information?
3. How could this conflict have been avoided and the information still useful to the planned reorganization?
4. How would you advise Lea Pearlman?
5. How should a consultant communicate standards for the handling of confidential information? Should those standards change when client needs change? If so, under what conditions? If not, why?

WHAT HAPPENED NEXT?

While having lunch with Lea Pearlman, Dick Wallace expressed concern about Nichols's treatment of her contract. Wallace indicated there was nothing he could do at the present but that he would defend Lea if Nichols made disparaging remarks to others. Wallace doubted Nichols would attack Pearlman based on her overall good reputation.

Several months passed while reorganization plans were formulated and discussed at the executive committee level. Chris Nichols was repeatedly criticized for his attempts to have certain people removed from management. Several members of the executive committee urged Jim Elliot to assign Dick Wallace to the project with specific responsibility for staffing the reduced numbers of management positions and the relocation of those whose management jobs would be eliminated. Elliot agreed and told Nichols Wallace was to become actively involved in the selection process for managers to fill slots available in the newly designed organizations. Wallace told Nichols he was hiring Lea Pearlman to evaluate the selection process they were to establish. Nichols did not object. Lea responded to Dick she would evaluate the process but should have no other involvement in the project. Lea thanked Dick for his support and felt somewhat vindicated because Morrison management was holding Chris Nichols in check.

U.S. Senator Williams and the Austin Manpower Administration

In late 1988, U.S. Senator Jim Williams (D., Tex.) and his wife, Mary, met with a group of political supporters, who were concerned about complaints surfacing in Austin over the appointment of Neva Turner as executive director of the local Manpower Administration program. Led by attorney Morris Wright, the group expressed dismay over Neva's dismissal of five longtime Manpower employees and her replacement of the terminated staff with appointments whose loyalties were known to be with Neva. Wright informed Jim and Mary Williams that Neva was telling critics the Senator and Mary would back her position.

Neva Turner is a controversial African-American woman who has been a supporter of Senator Williams since his 1970 election to the state legislature. Neva and Mary Williams went to high school together in Cleveland, a small town 80 miles south of Austin. Neva is a brilliant woman who organized and participated in much of the civil rights activity in Austin in the early part of 1962. Although she made enemies, both supporters and enemies alike considered her a moving force in opening Texas state employment rolls to African Americans and Hispanics. Mary Williams, an Hispanic, joined Neva in several marches and other protest activities in Austin. Neva headed an effort to get minorities to the polls when Jim Williams ran for the U.S. Senate in 1976. She was effective but made few friends among the more traditional and conservative of Williams's campaign supporters. She leaned heavily on her personal relationship with Mary during the campaign to protect herself from criticism. When Neva applied for the position of executive director of the Manpower Administration, most observers believed Senator Williams would strongly support her candidacy.

Following the meeting with Morris Wright and the other supporters, Mary and Jim Williams discussed what they should do. Wright is a heavy financial supporter of Williams and is astute about the mood of Austin politics. Jim carried Austin in 1988 by a small margin and finds his strongest opposition to be in the state's capitol city. He believes he cannot afford strong criticisms over Neva Turner. Jim and Mary decided Mary should talk with Neva.

Mary met with Neva one week after the meeting with Morris Wright. Neva seemed tense and defensive and told Mary she was under considerable pressure to ignore certain irregularities, which apparently were standard operating procedure for the previous executive director. Neva indicated she had terminated the five employees in question because they were abusing travel funds and had submitted overtime reimbursement requests that could not be substantiated. She told Mary she had not made formal charges in order to protect the reputation of the agency. Mary questioned Neva about her hiring practices. Neva admitted she may have made a political mistake in hiring people with whom she had previous experience. Neva specifically mentioned Bill Compton. Mary cautioned Neva to be careful, stressing the visibility of the Manpower executive director. At the conclusion of the conversation, Mary decided Morris Wright did not have all the facts. She did not tell Neva of his complaints to the senator.

Jim Williams was sympathetic to Neva's position but remained concerned her actions might prove to be a political liability. He told Mary they would need to keep in frequent contact with Neva and be better informed about the Austin Manpower office. Jim called Morris Wright and told him he believed the criticism of Neva Turner would soon decrease.

Six weeks later Senator Williams's Washington office received notification that the U.S. Department of Labor Manpower Administration was launching a formal inquiry into the Austin Manpower Administration. This type of notification is standard to U.S. senators and representatives in home states and districts where investigations will be conducted. Williams's staff member, Jerry Donald, was assigned to contact the appropriate Washington officials for further details. Jerry Donald, legislative assistant for Williams and campaign manager for the 1988 race, dislikes Neva Turner. He has long considered her a potential political problem. Donald has tried to tell Jim Williams he should sever ties with Neva. Mary Williams has resented Donald's statements. She knows Jerry is a good campaign manager but is not comfortable with his influence on Jim.

Donald's contacts at the Labor Department told him the department had evidence of misuse of funds by the executive staff of the Austin Manpower Administration. The evidence was dated prior to Neva Turner's appointment. The department was convinced the misuse was continuing. Donald further learned Neva had been asked to come to Washington to discuss the situation with U.S. Department of Labor officials.

Mary called Neva as soon as Donald reported to Jim. Neva seemed evasive but assured Mary there was probably nothing of serious concern. She stated again that abuses had occurred prior to her appointment and were the basis of her termination of the five employees. Mary offered Neva help and invited Neva to stay with the Williams' when she arrived in Washington. Jim was slightly annoyed at the invitation and Jerry Donald was openly critical.

Two days before Neva Turner was to arrive in Washington, an article in the *Austin Daily Tribune* described the pending investigation. The story stated Neva was under investigation for misuse of funds and improper employment practices. No mention was made of the previous director. Several members of the Austin Advisory Committee to the Manpower Administration were quoted as calling for Neva's resignation. The article detailed her political backing of Senator Williams. Morris Wright telephoned the senator as soon as he read the story. Williams agreed with Wright that the problem had escalated. Jim Williams did not respond directly to Wright's advice that he and Mary encourage Neva to resign. Williams felt Wright was implying Mary's relationship with Neva was standing in the way of necessary action.

With Neva expected the next day, Jim and Mary discussed the problem. Jim believed he should not interfere with the Labor Department's inquiry but was disturbed at being linked to the investigation. His office had received several calls from Austin reporters asking for the senator's comments. Jim had instructed Jerry Donald to issue a statement reflecting the senator's lack of involvement with local Manpower Administration policies and his concern that the investigation get to the source of any problems. Jim and Mary decided to meet privately with Neva as soon as she arrived.

Neva was visibly shaken when she arrived in Washington the following day. Neva had received a list of specific questions for response at the Labor Department meeting. Neva described the dilemma as she saw it. When terminating the five people who were close to the previous director she had not specified or documented their alleged misuse of funds. She realized that replacing the terminated staff with her friends had been a mistake, although Neva claimed the new staff was capable. Jim and Mary were dismayed when they learned all five new staff members had been members of Senator Williams's campaign group that Neva led.

Neva said the staffing issue was not the main problem. She said the main concern was in the Manpower Administration's employment training division, a program receiving nearly $1 million annually for training and on-the-job wage support for private sector employers of Manpower clients. Neva had placed Bill Compton in charge of the program. Compton was close to Neva and had been a strong supporter of Senator Williams since the early 1970s. Neva had not supervised Compton closely because she believed his judgment to be sound. She had placed him under considerable pressure to increase the number of private sector employers participating in the employment training program. However, she had not realized that Compton would contact people he had met during the senator's campaigns to meet these objectives. As a result, approximately 70 percent of the new employers participating in the wage-sharing program had, as individuals, contributed to Jim Williams's campaigns.

The political implication drawn by the Labor Department was clear. Individuals who had contributed to Senator Williams's campaigns, through their places of business, were receiving federal wage-sharing funds for employment of Manpower clients. This arrangement, though strictly legal, was questionable in terms of fairness and favoritism, particularly with strong supporters of Williams—Turner and Compton—running the program. Although the evidence was not conclusive, reports suggested Williams's supporters were given preference for the program over others in Austin. Neva felt the charges were mostly true, although her intent was not favoritism but improved statistics for the agency. Neva accepted final responsibility because she had signed all wage-sharing requests without questioning Compton.

Jim and Mary Williams saw a mushrooming problem. Jim called Jerry Donald to come to his home immediately. Calls were placed to Compton and Morris Wright. Neva stated she would not resign and would not let Bill Compton become a scapegoat. Senator Williams knew that in mapping a course of action he had become directly involved in the investigation. As Jerry arrived, a tense group of friends and enemies sat down to decide how to handle this political and administrative problem.

YOUR ASSIGNMENT

1. What are the ethical issues in this case?
2. Describe value differences and similarities among the principal people in the case.
3. How would you advise Senator Williams? Develop a communication plan to respond to this problem.
4. How would you advise Neva Turner?
5. Describe various communication strategies for the Department of Labor meeting, the press, the campaign supporters, and internally for the group of friends and enemies.

Can This Ethical Manager Survive, or Should She?

Nancy Bradley was appointed division manager of Park Products' recreational products lines following the termination of her longtime boss, Jack Stevens. Stevens was fired for budget overruns and his failure to oversee successful development of the company's new ski equipment. Three other Park executives were also fired. The trade press related the terminations to equipment failures and management inattention to quality control.

Nancy Bradley initially refused the appointment to division management. She accepted only when pressured by the company president, Jack Wallace. Wallace told Bradley she was the only person he could trust to thoroughly examine the financial strategy of the recreational division and he believed her to have the vision necessary to develop new product lines.

Nancy assumed leadership of a senior staff shocked by the terminations in their division and concerned that she was not strong enough to take control of an operation with sagging revenues and few new products ready for release. Nancy had worked for several years with all of the managers who would now report to her. She knew most viewed her favorably but that Jim Wilson and Denise Simpson, in particular, thought she was weak and too concerned for people.

Jim Wilson headed the golf and aquatic product lines. He was accustomed to reporting few if any details to division management and preferred to run his department as a separate business. He had been secretly pleased when the ski line failed, believing his visibility within the company would be improved. He was dismayed when Nancy was chosen to lead the division, although he thought he would have little difficulty in continuing his practices. Denise Simpson headed the human resources department for the recreational division. She was familiar with Nancy's tendency to give poor performers opportunities to improve before implementing either disciplinary or termination actions. In particular,

Denise was concerned Nancy had fought to keep David Mathews from being fired even though he had direct knowledge of the problems with the ski equipment. Nancy had defended David saying he had complained of problems in three memos to his boss. She believed David had exercised his responsibilities and should not be responsible for the failures of others. David and Jim Wilson had clashed in the past and Nancy believed Jim had unduly influenced Denise against David.

Nancy's initial meetings with her new staff were uneventful. She quickly realized, however, that she did not have the financial information necessary to thoughtfully examine the effectiveness of the division or assess the realistic level of expenditures for new product development. She asked her team to help her compile a detailed review of the division's operations from which they, as a group, would begin to make decisions and set priorities.

Mike Morris, the head of the track and field department, shared Wilson's concern that members of the team would begin to have input into departments with which they had little familiarity. Both men complained loudly in staff meetings and told Nancy she was creating problems. Other team members supported Nancy's position and suggested the ski incident would not have happened had the group been more involved as a whole.

Nancy persisted and asked all managers to make presentations about their operations, including comprehensive financial reports and assessments of new product plans. Jim Wilson was the only manager unprepared to deliver his report on the day it was scheduled. Nancy called Jim to her office and the two had a three-hour discussion about his responsibilities. Jim told Nancy she was too weak to lead the division and that she needed him and the others to survive. Nancy stated she needed Jim and the others but was perfectly capable of surviving. The confrontation left Nancy drained emotionally and concerned that her leadership had been challenged so early in her tenure as division manager.

Jim Wilson asked Denise Simpson and Mike Morris to join him in confronting Nancy about David Mathews. All three believed David was a poor manager who would eventually get the division into trouble. Nancy defended David and told the three he was her responsibility. Jim left Nancy's office determined to communicate his concerns to higher management. He had never seen Nancy so firm in the five years he had known her.

Jim Wilson was told by Nancy's boss, Bryan King, that the managers in the department were none of his business. Jim was pleased, however, because he sensed concern from King relative to continued problems. He believed he had achieved his goal in raising questions about Nancy's leadership.

Jim was angry when he received a memo from Nancy stating her budget analyst, Michelle Morrison, would audit Jim's accounts and prepare an independent report of his operations. He scheduled a meeting to confront Nancy. Nancy responded she had scheduled the audit based on Jim's refusal to provide her staff with needed information. She told Jim she needed his expertise but not his continual attempts to challenge her leadership.

Jim agreed to provide Nancy's staff with the needed information provided she cancel the audit. Following his presentation, the staff supported Jim's plans, which made Nancy wonder why he had resisted so strongly.

Nancy was surprised when David Mathews reported Jim was telling important customers that Nancy's leadership of the division was weak and that he, Jim, was doing all he could to help her. Nancy had believed Jim's concerns would remain within the staff. At her next team meeting Nancy stressed the importance of working within the group and stated she was displeased when others reported breaches of confidence from her meetings. Jim acted as if he did not know what she meant.

During the next six months, Nancy and her staff began to evaluate division financial operations and make important decisions about new product development. Most agreed they were better able to make informed decisions with the information generated at the briefings. Jim continued to resist but provided requested information for his peers. He often was critical of others yet refrained from publicly criticizing Nancy.

When Tom Henson resigned Nancy believed Jim was the logical person to assume control of the youth products lines. Budgets were tight and assignment of the product lines to an existing senior manager created needed salary savings. Jim eagerly assumed leadership of youth products believing at last he was becoming more visible and powerful within the division. Nancy was not prepared for Jim's actions. Tom Henson had involved his staff in decisions affecting the product lines in their department. Jim chose a much less participative approach. Within weeks, department employees complained to Nancy that Jim was making outrageous decisions costing the product line revenues and causing delays in new product development. Jim had transferred two of his aquatics and golf staff to head marketing and development for youth products. He demoted two senior managers who had reported to Tom Henson and suggested they should look for work in other Park Products' divisions.

Nancy confronted Jim about the changes. He told her he had been given the responsibility for the department and that he was exercising his responsibility in the same manner as he ran aquatics and golf. Jim complained no one challenged his success in those areas. Nancy asked Jim to take a more participative approach. She found jobs within her division for the two demoted employees.

The second time David approached Nancy regarding Jim the charges were too serious to ignore. David said important vendors had told him Jim was taking kickbacks from two suppliers whose contracts had been substantially increased during the past two years. Nancy asked corporate internal affairs to conduct an audit of Jim's accounts and set a meeting to confront him with the charges.

Jim was outraged and firmly denied all accusations. Two vendors signed affidavits substantiating David's allegations. Jim hired an attorney and filed a formal grievance against Nancy. Nancy was advised by Park lawyers that she should remove Jim from all management responsibilities during the investigation of the charges.

Jim's attorney offered a settlement to Park's lawyers. Jim would drop his grievance if Nancy verbally and in writing withdrew all charges and reinstated his management responsibilities. Nancy wanted Jim fired but was advised by top management and the lawyers that this public action was not warranted by their investigation. In addition, management was concerned about more adverse publicity in the recreation products division. Nancy finally agreed to give Jim a six-week suspension followed by reinstatement. The two vendors in question were banned by purchasing from future bids for Park Products' business.

Nancy was not pleased with the outcome of the situation. She felt unsupported by top management and believed her problems with Jim would only continue. She did not trust Jim and was convinced he was a disruptive force within the division. She was supported by many members of her staff but considered them powerless to help her.

Nancy considered resigning but did not want to bow to pressure when she believed she was working for the best interests of Park Products. She thought she was right but could she survive?

YOUR ASSIGNMENT

1. What are the ethical issues in this case?
2. How do the differing styles of Jim and Nancy contribute to their problems?
3. Was Jim unethical?
4. How would you advise Nancy?
5. Is Nancy an effective leader? Nancy believed ethical business is good business. Is she correct? If so, why? If not, why not?

Fast-Track Executive

Bill Kozak's career had advanced rapidly over the past eight years. He had gone to work for San Diego Wholesalers (SDW) following college. His first job there had provided him contact with Bernard Marcus, the most outstanding salesperson in the company's history. Assignment to Marcus's account team was coveted by most SDW salespeople.

Kozak and Marcus got along well from the very beginning. Within a month of their initial meeting, Marcus requested Kozak's assignment to his team. Within a year, Kozak was Marcus's principal assistant with responsibility for figuring major customer bids.

Working with bids on a regular basis, Bill began to understand that Bernard Marcus's success was based on his ability to work well with customers and his practice of providing customers with special favors, including cash kickbacks. The cost of these favors was figured into the bids. When Bill asked Bernard about this seemingly unethical practice, Bernard passed it off as standard in the industry and something Bill must learn to do. Bill agreed Bernard was a success and he saw no real harm in providing customers with what they wanted as long as the company was covered in the purchase price.

When a Denver competitor of SDW offered Marcus a job, he asked Bill to accompany him. He said the Denver company would take two or three of his team and Bill was his first choice. Bill agreed to move with Marcus in hopes of rapid advancement. He did not know that Marcus's practice of padding bids to include customer favors was not acceptable in Denver.

Bernard Marcus lasted exactly 26 months in Denver. His abuses of bid practices were uncovered and he was quietly asked to resign. Marcus refused and suggested that he would make public the financial holdings of several members of the board of directors if they did not accept his business practices. One board member in particular, Linda Kline, pressed for Bernard to leave. Bernard and the board agreed on a compromise; he would take a one-year leave with pay. Both agreed by the end of the leave Bernard would have located new employment.

Bill Kozak received a letter asking for his resignation. His association with Bernard was proof enough for the board to ask that he leave. Bill was stunned. When he asked Marcus for advice, he told Bill to look for another job. Bill was concerned that their association would make that impossible when it became known that Bernard was fired for abusing bid practices.

Bill decided he should examine as many of the company's contracts as he could access through the computer systems. He hoped he might find evidence in other bids to support his contention that he had been following standard industry practices. Bill was unprepared for what he uncovered; his peers were bidding contracts in strict accordance with company and federal standards. What startled Bill, however, was the apparent use of a special account within the sales department for private expenditures by the company president. Further investigation of this account indicated the president had compensated his immediate staff with bonuses in excess of $500,000 over the past five years. An examination of company records revealed no board actions authorizing these expenditures.

Bill became increasingly desperate as Bernard Marcus packed his desk and left Denver. He knew he had less than two weeks left himself. Bill decided to take a substantial risk. He wrote the president of the company a detailed letter describing his findings. He suggested he would inform no one of this information should the president find him a suitable position.

The president immediately called Bill to his office. The president stated that what Bill considered improper was actually standard industry practice. Bill responded he believed his own actions had been standard business practice. The president said he understood and, for that reason, he would give Bill a second chance. The president indicated his support would remain as long as Bill chose not to inform others about the bonus monies. Bill agreed and was relieved to retain his job.

The president assigned Bill to head a contract negotiation group in charge of finding new vendors for particular product lines. Those in the group were amazed by the promotion of someone rumored to be involved in the Marcus scandal. Bill tried hard to understand the duties of his new position. He was painfully aware that those around him were much more knowledgeable about vendor selection.

Bill worked hard for over two years. Few group members initially respected him they but grew to appreciate his efforts. An internal audit exposed to the board much of what Bill had discovered and he became afraid for his future. He was not surprised when the president resigned to take another top position. Nor was he surprised when the new CEO wrote him and asked that he submit his resignation. The two-sentence letter asking that he leave the company gave him no choice.

Bill Kozak resigned having learned a bitter lesson about "industry standards."

YOUR ASSIGNMENT

1. What are the ethical issues in this case?
2. Describe how a person can evaluate standard industry practices. Base your description on models for ethical communication behavior.
3. How would you advise Bill?
4. What are the communication issues in this case?
5. React to the statements: "Ethical business is good business," and "Ethical business practices are naive."

The "We Intended No Harm" Case

As John Davis stares out the window of his office he considers what he should tell his attorney and how much he should attempt to protect himself if things get worse. John Davis, an officer in Antero Savings and Loan, cannot believe he is going to be questioned by federal officials about his decisions in the Burning–Lewis property case. Of course, he helped Mike Frazier get over $10 million in loans from Antero, but no one could have expected the bottom to fall out of the real estate market. Everyone was making those types of loans when he supported the Burning–Lewis deal. No other savings and loan (S&L) would have asked someone of Mike Frazier's importance to personally guarantee loans. Frazier was a multimillionaire who expected the people with whom he did business to take the kinds of risks he did. And risks had paid off handsomely in the past. John believed Antero could win big if Frazier successfully developed the property. He never really considered Frazier would default on the second loan payment and have his company file for bankruptcy. Frazier's personal fortune was largely protected by family-member holdings untouched by bankruptcy. Furthermore, Davis never imagined the default, along with several other problem loans, would add Antero to the number of S&L's on the government's troubled list.

The Burning–Lewis deal had always been a gamble. The property, although near the airport, was not in the heavily developed northern section of town. To move industry south was a challenge that Davis felt Frazier's group was capable of influencing. Davis had sold the executive committee of Antero on supporting the loans with his argument that if Antero did not make the Frazier relationship their principal competitor, Northern Savings and Loan, surely would. It was true that Davis had not asked Frazier to personally guarantee even a portion of the loans. After all, several city council members had promised Davis that Frazier would be supported with tax incentives from the city. Influential council members wanted the project to move forward. Frazier had promised council members to build industry parks and housing developments designed to bring over a ten-year period some 100,000 new residents to the area.

John Davis knew government regulators could take exception to the "hand shake" deal he made with Frazier. John knew he had not required Frazier to support his loan application with enough hard data to justify the amount of the loans and, without additional support, the property itself was insufficient collateral. He had wanted the business and no one at Antero had attempted to stop him. They knew what was going on but now seemed ready to blame their "superstar" rather than admit anyone on the management team would have done the same thing. John also was worried about federal officials learning he had purchased a condominium in one of Frazier's resort properties. He had suspected at the time of the condo purchase that he had been given a "sweetheart" deal but had asked no questions. After all, that is how business is done. John wonders what his attorney will advise? He worries he will become the scapegoat to get the regulators off the executive committee's back.

YOUR ASSIGNMENT

1. What are the ethical issues in this case?
2. Think about the ethical implications of the following statement: Common business practice in a given industry becomes the ethical standard of practice for the industry.
3. Describe how business risk and ethical risk are similar and different.
4. Describe ethical standards for businesspeople to apply to highly competitive situations.
5. How would you advise John Davis?

The "Do My Values Fit?" Case

Following her campus interviews with UniCon, Inc.—a large health care organization—Connie Bradley was pleased to be invited to the corporate headquarters to interview for jobs in three departments. UniCon was known to select only those college graduates who were talented and who had potential to work in several areas of the company. Connie was to interview in marketing, program development, and human resources. She had been given the names of three contacts at UniCon and was told to establish her schedule by telephone prior to arriving in Baltimore.

Connie was surprised when she talked with Myra Corbet, the director of marketing. Myra encouraged Connie to come to Baltimore for an interview but suggested she apply only in marketing and program development. Myra called the human resources position a dead-end job. She said the director of human resources, Colin Justins, was a difficult individual. Myra suggested that once an employee went into human resources there were no other opportunities in the company. Because she did not know how to react to Myra's comments, Connie chose not to respond. The program development director made no such references and Colin Justins seemed nothing but professional in a telephone conversation. Connie chose to keep all three appointments.

The interview in marketing came first. Myra Corbet was enthusiastic about Connie's background and eagerly described several potential opportunities in marketing. When Connie inquired about the specific type of position she might fill, Myra was less specific; she said she would have to design one to best utilize Connie's talents. At the conclusion of the interview Myra asked if Connie was scheduled to meet with Colin Justins. Myra looked displeased when Connie said yes. She said if Connie were looking for a good human resources job she, Myra, might be able to steer her to one or two other companies in the area. Myra told Connie that Colin had an attitude and was not a good manager for professional women. Connie wanted more information but considered it unethical to ask Myra for specifics.

Connie's next interview was with Colin Justins. The interview was very different from her discussion with Myra. Colin had specific job requirements and he "grilled" Connie about the match of her background to his needs. Connie answered most of his questions with ease and felt she knew exactly what would be expected of her in the human resources position. She could not determine from the interview why Myra was so negative about the human resources job or Colin Justins. Colin said he wanted someone to take his position who was commited to human resources and would not immediately use the job as a stepping stone to other opportunities. Connie could not find fault with his position but was still worried about his statements based on Myra's warnings.

Connie's final interview in program development was uneventful. The program development manager was pleasant but described a position in which Connie had little interest or academic training. The program development department needed a statistician to design program evaluation. Connie would need additional coursework to truly qualify for the position.

Connie believed she would receive offers from both Myra and Colin. She was confused about how to gather additional information to make an informed decision. Connie wanted to work for an organization where honesty and openness were practiced. She also wanted an opportunity to work in more than one area of the company. Until her discussion with Myra, UniCon had seemed to be that type of organization. She could not, however, discount the fact that Myra might be trying to help her avoid a big mistake. Connie wondered whether her values, the stated values of UniCon, and UniCon's reality matched. Connie considered what she should do next.

YOUR ASSIGNMENT

1. Connie is experiencing a value conflict between the stated values of UniCon and the reality as described by a manager within the organization. Describe how such value conflicts can affect organizational performance.
2. If you were faced with these seeming contradictions, how could you gather information important for decision making? What specific information do you need?
3. Congruence between individual and organizational values has long been related to effective individual and organizational performance. Develop a process for examining and contrasting individual values and organizational values. How can this model assist in employment choices?
4. Describe the ethical standards you would apply to Myra's behavior.
5. Devise a plan of action for Connie. Identify each step up to and through making a decision about taking a position with UniCon.

Conversations

Living and Learning:
A Professor Goes Abroad

Michael Hackman, Ph.D.

Michael Hackman, Ph.D., is associate professor of communication at the University of Colorado at Colorado Springs. In June 1991, he and his family went to New Zealand, where he taught communication courses in the Department of Management at the University of Waikato. This interview reveals his observations after his first few months in New Zealand.

What was your first impression of New Zealand?

HACKMAN: My first impressions of New Zealand revolve around the people. When we arrived, the New Zealanders, or "Kiwis" as they call themselves, were incredibly welcoming and friendly. Within the first few days after our arrival, we received invitations to visit the homes of several neighbors. Hardly a day passed without someone inviting us over for "evening tea," the term used for the evening meal.

I also remember being in somewhat of a fog at work. Everything was so new. In addition to having a difficult time just understanding the accents, terminology used at the University of Waikato was quite different from what I had been used to at the University of Colorado. Courses in New Zealand are called "papers." On my first day at work, a student came into my office to ask about my leadership paper. I spent ten minutes trying to assure the student there would be no paper required in the course. The student left befuddled at my insistence that there was no paper, which to him meant the course would be cancelled. Now I think back to that episode and laugh. At the time, it was quite frustrating.

185

How has that changed or expanded after four months?

HACKMAN: My view of New Zealand has changed in many ways. But my view of how we learn about culture has changed to an even greater extent. More than anything, I now see that it takes a long time to really understand a culture. I am only beginning to feel as if I understand the ways of doing things in New Zealand. A lot of people will take short business trips or vacations abroad and return home believing they have gained enough experience to understand a culture. I think people have to totally immerse themselves in a culture, for an extended period of time, to become fluent in that culture.

What are the general business communication concerns of your students?

HACKMAN: As elsewhere, the concerns of students in New Zealand vary widely. Many seem to be aware of the importance of oral and written communication skills to organizational effectiveness and, as such, hope to improve in these areas. Because New Zealand is geographically isolated from the rest of the world, there is a heavy reliance on communications technologies such as fax machines, computer mail systems, and satellites. Students in New Zealand worry about being left behind as technology advances. In New Zealand, being left behind may mean being left out.

Describe the culture as you have come to know it.

HACKMAN: This is a difficult question as there are so many aspects of culture to consider. There are a great number of similarities between New Zealand and the United States. Most can probably be traced to shared colonial roots. The similarities are furthered by the export of United States' culture. Most Kiwis are as familiar with Madonna, George Bush, or Bo Jackson as the average person in the United States.

As far as differences are concerned, one thing I have noticed is that New Zealanders keep their emotions in check to a greater degree than people in the United States. The Kiwis pride themselves on being more British than the British and the famous "stiff upper lip" is fully evidenced in New Zealand. I remember a talk on visionary leadership I gave to a group of executives. I implored the group to develop a vision for their organizations and passionately share that vision with followers. After 20 minutes of enthusiastic presentation, one of the participants stopped me and said, "We just don't do that in New Zealand." Emotional restraint is most commonly exhibited by New Zealanders of European origin, called Pakehas. The indigenous culture, the Maoris, are highly emotive. So great differences exist even between cultural groups within New Zealand.

One fairly consistent aspect of New Zealand culture I have observed, is a tremendous respect for the environment. New Zealanders think of their country as being "clean and green" and work diligently to keep it that way. A variety of materials are routinely recycled by Kiwis. I was amazed to discover that most families are able to fit their weekly trash into one small bag.

What are you learning?

HACKMAN: I am learning a great deal about myself. I have realized how narrow my field of experience really is. Even though I lived for a couple of years in Great Britain and have traveled quite extensively, I am still very egocentric. I think it is healthy to take a look at the world from a different perspective. This experience has encouraged me to ask more questions of myself.

The one idea that has been most evident to me since I have been in New Zealand is that businesses must "internationalize" to survive. In New Zealand I see a willingness to learn about other cultures, to think globally, and to integrate new perspectives. As competition from the Pacific Rim and EEC [European Economic Community] increases, businesses in the United States will have to think more internationally. The issue really involves the entire foundation of the educational, economic, and political system in the United States. We need to prepare young people to be members of the global community. At the same time, organizations must look for outlets for international cooperation and coordination in the development, design, and implementation of products and ideas. For me, it took a trip halfway around the world for Marshall McLuhan's notion of the "global village" to ring true. The world is much smaller than we realize. My feeling is that few organizations will prosper in the years ahead unless they consider the complex interrelationships that hold the global village together.

There Is Life After Management

This conversation is with a man who at age 42 resigned as vice-president of human resources for a major manufacturer of home appliances to go back to school and become a teacher. Paul Davis (not his real name), at the time of his resignation, had a career many of his peers envied. He was in the air force until age 30. Then Paul worked for three different companies, with each job bringing more money and increasing responsibility. His opportunity with the home appliance manufacturer came two years after his appointment to the division staff of a computer start-up. A head hunter called to determine his interest in the job of vice-president of human resources, a position with a six-figure salary. Paul agreed to an interview and took the job, which he held for four years.

Paul, why did you leave after only four years?

PAUL: It was tough, I mean, I never thought I would leave when I took the job. The company is a good one, the money was excellent, but I really could not take it any more. It was eating at me, the long hours, the failure to really make a difference. The truth is, I left because I could not make a real difference and I believed that would soon catch up with me.

What do you mean, it would catch up with you?

PAUL: Several things. First, my family. I was working 70 and 80 hours a week. I wasn't seeing the children at all. My wife was patient but I could tell. She wanted me to do more with the kids and with her, and I wanted to but couldn't. Next, I came to believe I was offered the job because I had been with a company known for good employee relations. The president of [*company name withheld*] is excellent with the public, but he runs rough shod over his top managers and will bend any rules he wants to get his way. I was supposed to do his bidding, and when I fired a couple of people he wanted out of the way, I felt rotten.

Why not just go with another company?

PAUL: That's what everyone asks. That is the hardest thing to explain. I have been a manager of sorts for 20-plus years and—you know what?—I was never really that good at it. I like people, but I hate management details. I can motivate people but I have finally learned that when there are problems I don't really have the skills to get people to work cooperatively. Not just at this job. Things were beginning to unravel at my previous job. In the military it was easy, people had to do what I said.

Why do you want to be a teacher?

PAUL: It is something I am very very good at doing. I love to be in front of a group and interacting at all levels. I got my master's [degree] some years ago, and I always wanted to go on for a doctorate. I will either teach at a college or in some adult education program. I think my experience will benefit the students. I have seen a lot of the business world and I can bring that to the classroom.

I need to ask a difficult question. What about the money? You were making far more than you will in most teaching jobs. How do you feel about that?

PAUL: That is an interesting question. Actually, money is important to my family and me. I made good money and some investments have gone well. I don't intend for us to suffer—I never could have taught right out of college.

How do your peers react to your decision?

PAUL: They are nervous around me. Some think I got fired no matter what anyone says. Others, well, they want to do something like this. That is the sad thing. If I can change the subject for a minute. I know ten people right now in major management jobs who hate what they are doing and really want out but they are trapped. Or they think they are trapped. And you know what, that trapped feeling goes throughout their entire organizations. Management is not much fun anymore. The pressures are intense. Business is in terrible shape, all the change, all the international competition. A lot of us need to bail out. We might make room for those who enjoy the pressure cooker.

How did my peers react? Not really very favorably. It is a commentary on them, you know. If I walk out then they know they at least have other alternatives. And that forces personal decisions. Personal decisions are something most managers never think about. They are so busy with the business they forget they have personal options.

What would you tell other managers?
PAUL: To realize that management is not for everyone and that most of us really do have options. When I spend time with my children and my wife, I know I have made the right decision. When I read the newspaper or trade journals, I feel left out and alone. You know all of my friends were in the business. But I'm getting better.

YOUR ASSIGNMENT

1. Career progress typically involves increasing levels of responsibility. Describe career models where lateral job changes and other options become desirable. What will have to change in organizations for new models to be viable? Discuss the question in terms of organizational structure, rewards, culture, training, and communication.
2. Describe your personal reactions to Paul Davis's interview.
3. How does his message relate to your personal career decisions? Or does it?
4. Do you believe Paul Davis would make the same decision if he were not financially secure? Defend your answer.
5. Is Paul Davis a success? Discuss your answer.

Fired for Bending the Rules

This interview was granted with the guarantee of the interviewee's anonymity and alteration of enough factual material to conceal identification of the situation. The author, however, verified the circumstances surrounding this account.

Tell me what happened.
J.M.: I got caught, I mean I got caught up in doing what I thought was right and when it started to go wrong I couldn't get out.

What were the circumstances?
J.M.: Contracts. I worked for the top man in contracts. And I had two close friends bidding on jobs. I knew the group that usually got this type of work, I knew they were rumored to pay off some people in the company. That type of thing always made me mad, especially when good people like my friends struggle and really want to do a good job. So, I made sure my friends knew where they had to be on the bid. I knew it was wrong. I didn't tell my friends much; they would never have asked. I offered.

What happened next?

J. M.: My friends did not get the job. It seemed strange to me because I saw the contract award documentation. I knew they were lower than this other outfit. So I asked my boss, about, you know, how final decisions were made if it were not price. He asked me what I meant. I hedged a bit and told him I was just curious. He did not believe I was just curious. I think he suspected something when my friends came in with the low bid. They had bid on several jobs before and were high. He knew I did things with them socially, so I think he must have suspected something.

Go on . . .

J. M.: Well, apparently he called them in and asked if I had discussed the job with either of them. They did not lie. Actually, I would not have wanted them to. They said I had mentioned a range where they should stick but had not discussed the job in any other fashion. They did not know who else was bidding. Well, the next day, I was fired. I know it was wrong, but I thought they overreacted.

How did you feel?

J. M.: At first numb. I had to get out of the building. They told me to come in and pick up my things on the weekend. They didn't treat me like trash or anything. My boss said he was sorry to have to do this but had no choice. They didn't ask for my reaction. Later I became humiliated at what I had done. It didn't fit my own standards. I just wasn't thinking very clearly. I got caught up in my own way of trying to make things right for my friends. I have lost a lot of sleep over this thing.

What about your present employment?

J. M.: At first I did not know what to do. I had worked at that job for ten years and really needed references. Yet, they have government contracts. They are liable if they don't tell another contractor of the reasons for my termination. I went to work here [*an electronics company*] because I could apply on a form and not turn in a resume. I wanted to retrain to avoid having to deal with what happened in the past. Working on the line [manufacturing line] doesn't require any type of clearance.

Does your family know what happened?

J. M.: No, I couldn't tell my wife. I think she has been bothered. She couldn't understand why I "quit." But I couldn't tell her. She would have been devastated. She would have stood by me, but it would have killed her. No, only a couple of my friends know, the two who were involved.

What would you tell people about your experience?

J. M.: Nothing is worth what happened. I should have said something about the other contractor to my boss. I would never do something like this again. You lose a part of yourself. You wake up in the night and it's dark and you feel like everyone knows and is watching you. I can't imagine what these guys who are in the news do when they screw up. I can't imagine what it is like for them.

Is it better now?

J. M.: Some days. But some days it isn't. Talking to you like this, for the book, I mean. I'll probably not sleep much tonight. But I want to tell somebody else to think first—if that helps one person, well, that would make me feel better.

YOUR ASSIGNMENT

1. Describe your reactions to this interview.
2. Discuss how individuals get "caught up" in circumstances that they later regret.
3. J. M. has little personal support for what happened due, at least in part, to his self-imposed isolation. Discuss how you would handle a similar situation.
4. J. M.'s company has government contracts, which influence how the company must respond to his behavior. Develop an approach for management to communicate "ethical" requirements to employees. How should J. M. have handled his concerns about the vendor reported to be giving kickbacks?
5. Discuss ethical implications in this case and how they relate to organizational communication effectiveness.

Entering the Profession: An Attorney Begins Her Career

Evelyn Hernandez Sullivan

The following interview with Evelyn Hernandez Sullivan, attorney, describes her experiences during the first two years following her graduation from the University of Colorado law school. A 1986 undergraduate in organizational communication from the University of Colorado at Colorado Springs, Ms. Sullivan attended law school from 1986–1989 and became a Member of the Bar in 1990. Ms. Sullivan currently is deputy district attorney in the child support enforcement division of the District Court in Colorado Springs, Colorado. Immediately following law school, she served as a judicial court clerk and as a volunteer for pro bono cases for Pikes Peak Legal Services.

What are the communication challenges as a new lawyer?

EVELYN: One of the big things in communication is the set pattern and patterns of communication dictated by litigation and the court. This is a profession with established communication patterns and previously those have been male dominated. Old patterns are hard to die. Male and female litigants, bench and bar interactions, counselors and clients. . . . There is a great deal of misinterpretations based on gender. I believe this is true in the family law area more than in criminal or civil law.

Can you give an example?

EVELYN: Yes, many women use more qualifiers or less powerful language than their male counterparts who, in turn, interpret the female position as less established than it is. When the man is talking, the female may nod and exhibit nonverbal listening behaviors which are perceived as agreement rather than just listening. When the result is not agreement and the female attorney evidences a strong position, the male attorney often reacts that the female attorney was not dealing fairly.

What do you do when you see that happening?
EVELYN: I fall back to my basic communication training. Whenever I am uncomfortable with an interaction or believe there is discomfort on the other's part, I meta-communicate, I clarify, I ask: Am I understanding the following . . . ? We have to encourage people to do that.

Is it difficult for women to enter the legal profession?
EVELYN: There is a place for us all. There are difficulties for some. Some women integrate well, some have difficulty; some men do well, some have difficulty. It is up to all of us to bridge gaps and make our contributions to the profession.

How do you conceptualize your career and your success?
EVELYN: Not on money or the positions I have. To me I must measure my success by the contributions I make to bettering life situations. Then I can go home happy with my work. I must do something that brings satisfaction, not just develop an impressive resume.

What is the most difficult aspect for determining career success?
EVELYN: The perception that success is measured by old models. Colleagues expect the old models. Maintaining my own sense of myself and what I want success to be is the hardest part. [*Laughs*] I'm doing OK so far.

Based on your experiences, what advice would you give other people beginning their careers?
EVELYN: Set goals—set high goals—but be aware you need to diversify, not just set goals for where you think you are going in terms of job positions. Set a quality factor. Think about the quality of what you do as a goal. What are the steps to your own personal satisfaction? How are you going to ensure that satisfaction? Also, as you begin a career think about other areas of your life that should contribute to your satisfaction and meet your needs.

What would you do differently in terms of academic preparation?
EVELYN: I would have preferred to start younger. I started my undergraduate work at age 25. By the time I was in law school I had a tough time getting by on three or four hours sleep per night. I am happy with my undergraduate major and degree; I had the breadth I needed. I wish in law school I had explored more [of] the litigator track. I focused on corporate law. Corporate law is intellectually stimulating but litigation also is fun—getting people to tell the truth, a truth they are sometimes avoiding, having the facts. For me right now, [it's] helping the kids, getting dads and moms to pay the support their kids need.

What's next for Evelyn Hernandez Sullivan?

EVELYN: I like what I am doing for now. I'm going to try to keep an open mind.

YOUR ASSIGNMENT

1. From the interview, describe Evelyn's career values.
2. Gender bias still exists in many segments of our society. Based on communication theory and research, describe the underlying issues contributing to bias and develop strategies for female professionals entering new jobs.
3. What changes in current career models does Evelyn suggest?
4. Describe how organizational and professional values influence perceptions of career success.
5. Examine your own definitions of career success. What values are embedded in your definitions? What type of career model is suggested?

PART III

Organizational Change, Innovation, and Effectiveness

Commentary

ORGANIZING, INNOVATING, AND COMMUNICATING: CHALLENGES AND CHANGES

> The transformation of civilization through the fusion of computing and communications technologies has been predicted for at least 50 years. Now the revolution has truly begun. The impact will be as profound as was the shift from an agrarian to an industrial society.
>
> Michael L. Dertouzos, "Communications, Computers and Networks," *Scientific American,* September 1991

A top executive of a major company recently complained in the trade press he was sick and tired of hearing about all this change. Everyone was already convinced of change and there did not seem to be much point in continuing to belabor the issue.

This man is wrong, but he is not unlike others who believe that the present turbulence will pass and we will continue on with business as usual. There will be changes but nothing we cannot handle. These professional managers are making the mistake of believing their past experiences will continue to serve them well when, in fact, the challenges we face require us to find answers in the future not our past. If we are "to handle" change we have to shift our thinking from action and reaction to anticipatory action; we have to understand that an organizational revolution is on us with as much force as the political revolutions of recent years. We must continue to explore the shared realities of strong organizational cultures while seeking to understand how networked organizations with dissimilar values and beliefs generate joint actions. And we must come to understand that communication and the means of communication are both the processes and technologies fundamental to these changes.

Two interdependent factors—*globalization* and *information technology*—are generating powershifts that result in the organizational challenges of today and tomorrow. Toffler (1990) suggests that throughout history violence, wealth, and knowledge have been the ultimate sources of social power, and as we approach the twenty-first century, knowledge will be the ultimate source of power.

> Power, in the business of tomorrow, will flow to those who have the best information about the limits of information. . . . The new accelerated system for wealth creation is increasingly dependent on the exchange of data, information, and knowledge. It is "super-symbolic." No knowledge exchanged, no new wealth created. . . . Conventional factors of production . . . land, labor, raw materials, and capital—become less important as symbolic knowledge is substituted for them. (pp. 152, 238)

Japan and Germany have increasingly powerful economies forcing the once-dominant United States to share its international position in an ever-increasing "value-added" competition. The changes in Eastern Europe and Russia are yet to be fully understood, however, most agree these potential giants will influence the future as they move, along with China, to market economies. The European Economic Community and the Yen block influence policy in ways that only a few short years ago were the primary domain of the United States. Korea, Taiwan, Spain, and Singapore change the face of competition with their low-cost, high-quality products. Tom Peters (1990) contends, "Everybody talks about it. But what does it mean? For Americans— whether they run a multibillion-dollar, old-line manufacturing outfit or the corner mom-and-pop shop—it means that any remnants of isolationism must go" (p. 70). Information technologies support markets over hierarchies and provide real-time global linkages. The overall impact, according to Peters, is the realization of the global village first predicted by McLuhan some 40 years ago.

New industries will emerge and basic industries such as energy and banking will experience turbulence and change. Restructuring will be common and information jobs will increasingly dominate most environments, even manufacturing. Today over 300 of the Fortune 500 companies are experimenting with new organizational forms. These innovations will continue to proliferate as hierarchies are replaced by flat designs, the "middleless" organization. Networks of organizations will increase and most small companies will do business beyond traditional geographic boundaries. Subcontracting will be common and most will experience pressure to "beat the competition" in terms of speed, quality, customer satisfaction, and cost. Individuals will be affected by changing definitions of career success and the requirement for continual upgrading of skills and abilities.

Globalization and technology are interrelated with the control of technology, or access to information, a critical factor in organizational change. George Gilder (1991) describes the emergence of information *heterarchies,* a new organizational form based on decentralized control made possible with computer workstations. Using Brooktree (inventor of RAM-DAC and devices to convert digital video to analog) as an example, Gilder states,

> As new computer systems decentralize control and empower people all along the information chain, they dissolve conventions of ownership, design, manufacturing, executive style, and national identity. Brooktree is not a hierarchy but an information heterarchy, with multiple centers of power and hundreds of on-line multiple centers of power and hundred of on-line workstations around the globe. The company has no one factory of its own but links its process technology with any number of major chip fabs around the world. Its devices are made in Japan or the United States, packaged in Korea, and burned in and tested in San Diego. (p. 152)

The battle for control of information heats up around attempts to control standards that both propel and constrain technological innovation. The battles over computer operating systems have been obvious for some time and many are intrigued by attempts at collaboration for system compatibility among old rivals such as IBM and Apple. However, most agree that although the operating system wars (control of what goes on in computers) are important, they pale in significance to political attempts to control telecommunications standards or what goes on between computers. As data flows internationalize, these decisions increase in complexity. Wallenstein (1990) summarizes the standards issues:

> A new world power is in the making—not a superpower, but a true suprapower. Its realm is the transnational structure of standards. It has no sovereign territory, no capital city, no currency, no police or military force. Its leaders owe allegiance to regional or global organizations; their broad mandates provide only for coordination of the work of others, not line management authority. Decisions are made by autonomous committees, whose members fight internecine battles that end in peace agreements published as standards. This suprapower's diffused activities proceed far from public awareness, and farther still from critical debate in the media or government circles. Yet the published output has heavy economic and political significance. Many standards acquire the force of law worldwide or regionally. They control widely used products and services, and thereby the success or failure of major businesses. However, high-level managers, business elite's "decision-makers," have little influence on standards and must accept them as decided by people at lower levels of their own organizations. Indeed, both development and administration of standards is left to experts with little management responsibility. Coming together from competing companies and diverse countries, these standards-makers form a small, transnational subculture held together by technical expertise and a specialized language of their own making.
>
> Thus, the much hailed information age builds its own controlling structure that transcends the powers of national governments. (p.1)

Given this complexity, what are the challenges for organizing and communicating? At the risk and reality of oversimplification, I propose five primary challenges for today and tomorrow: restructuring and designing the new organization, facilitating technological change, developing flexibility for jobs and careers, providing creative training, and implementing improved organizational communication processes.

Organizational Design

Synchronous innovation, mutually supportive simultaneous changes in technology, organization, jobs, and people, is proposed as an action-oriented approach to organizational change. Introduced by Ettlie (1988), the approach suggests innovation will be most productive when matched by change in interacting systems within and without the organization. According to Ettlie, "The theory of synchronous innovation predicts that firms will be most successful when they match the degree of radicalness in their administrative experiment with the degree of radicalness in the technologies they adopt" (p. 51).

Currently, many different types of organizations in diverse industries are redistributing influence throughout the organization. Hierarchies are abandoned for flatter and more horizontal designs. Decision making is dispersed throughout the organization with self-managing teams assuming responsibilities previously reserved for managers in areas as diverse as planning, scheduling, work design, and rewards. The engineer/blue-collar team and cross-functional teams are common examples of organizational approaches to close coupling of top management with the line activities of the organization. Downsized and delayered organizations reject economies of scale for minimal inventories, subcontracting, fast changeovers, just-in-time manufacturing, and quick response. Toffler (1990) refers to the free-form organizational models of the future as "flex-firms." He explains,

> To grasp the "flex-firm" concept, it helps to remind ourselves that bureaucracy is only one of an almost infinite variety of ways of organizing human beings and information. We actually have an immense repertoire of organizational forms to draw on—from jazz combos to espionage networks, from tribes and clans and councils of elders to monasteries and soccer teams. Each is good at some things and bad at others. Each has its own unique ways of collecting and distributing information, and ways of allocating power. (p. 186)

Hitt, Hoskisson, and Harrison (1991) conclude strategic competitiveness will be based on restructuring organizations while cultivating an organizational culture based on entrepreneurial spirit, global focus, and high-quality products and services. Specifically, they suggest organizations should downscope and reduce diversification, divest of problem businesses, develop human capital, and renew commitment to innovation.

Technological Change

The introduction of technological innovations is high risk at best, with most estimates placing the rate of success during the first introduction at less than 25 percent. The challenge, then, to facilitating technological innovation is to increase the likelihood of acceptance while preparing the work force for maximal use. Flynn (1988) suggests, "Changes in skill requirements, training needs, the industrial and occupational mix of employment, and the spatial location of jobs are indicative of technological change and the dynamic character of production processes. These changes in turn affect employers' hiring and staffing patterns, workers' career paths, and economic growth and development'' (p. 141). Technological change influences information control and supports or dismantles hierarchical structures. It is related to powershifts within organizations and competition between organizations. It contributes to organizational networking and global interaction. Therefore, technological change becomes a critical factor in organizational design and restructuring.

Jobs and Careers

Toffler (1990) views the work force of the future as more autonomous with more open access to information and power than at any previous time in industrial history. More power, however, does not equate with more upward mobility or traditional definitions of career success. The collapse of middle management, the restructuring of most industries, and increased international competitiveness all change the nature of jobs and careers for almost everyone.

More of us will work in teams. We will be evaluated as a group with less attention to individual performance. Individual performance is more likely to be evaluated by our peers than by our manager, and peer support will be critical for upward mobility. We will be asked to be job flexible; most of us will change the substance of what we do numerous times in our careers. We will be viewed as human capital and compared globally for our cost and productivity. The challenge will be to live with uncertainty and define new career models for success.

Training

Skill deficits, changing technology, and new responsibilities all contribute to an increased need for training. Organizations currently curtail training budgets in an effort to reduce overhead. Yet, managers and employees alike voice concerns about the readiness of the work force to meet the demands of the current organizational revolution.

Some organizations are committed to retraining employees. Others prefer layoffs and hiring new and more highly skilled personnel. Internal training and partnerships with educational institutions focus on work force readiness. At the same time, thousands of jobs leave the United States annually to be performed by skilled foreign labor at lower costs. The term *life-long learning* no longer applies to the most highly educated among us; the concept applies to all segments of the work force. The challenge is to identify the future's training needs, understand the contribution of training to competitiveness, and balance the organizational responsibility for training with the individual's personal responsibility. The challenge also is to design and implement new and creative training, including both self-paced and group approaches.

Organizational Communication

Complex communication processes are embedded in all of the previously identified challenges. However, the challenges for both individual and organizationwide communication extend beyond structure, technology, jobs, and training. Globalization fundamentally changes our understanding of the world. When we interact regularly with an international business community, our multicultural communication competencies and processes are called into question. Communication strategies of the past have emerged from relatively homogeneous organizations. Strategies for the future will be based on diversity—of employee populations, customers and markets, values, approaches, and sociopolitical world views.

Team participation presents new challenges. Communicating effectively in groups has always been important, however, peer evaluations and responsibility for work planning predictably will result in conflicts requiring dedicated and effective resolution techniques. The rhetoric of criticism is more readily available to most than the rhetoric of resolution.

Decision making requires new and improved processes. More of us will work with technologically assisted decision tools; yet these processes are genuinely "artificial" intelligence and only well utilized when in the hands of capable human communicators. Furthermore, the sheer volume of information coupled with the disappearance of the time float and geographic barriers present new challenges.

Finally, the technology itself is a communications and communication challenge. Understanding how telemediated meanings are shaped and reshaped, merging video and computer literacy, and applying technology appropriately for effective and efficient information flow raises new issues for organizational communication.

The revolution is here. It is an exciting and difficult time. How we answer these challenges will determine whether we actually leave the information age behind and enter the knowledge age. Information abounds and power is shifting, but knowledge is more than information and power. Knowledge, in the organizational sense, is the application of information to problems of organizing, innovating, and communicating.

REFERENCES

Dertouzous, M. 1991. Communications, computers and networks. *Scientific American* 265 (3): 62–69.

Ettlie, J. 1988. *Taking Charge of Manufacturing* (San Francisco: Jossey-Bass).

Flynn, P. 1988. *Facilitating technological change: The human resource challenge.* Cambridge, MA: Ballinger.

Gilder, G. 1991. Into the telecosm. *Harvard Business Review* 69(2): 150–161.

Hitt, M., R. Hoskisson, and J. Harrison. 1991. Strategic competitiveness in the 1990s: Challenges and opportunities for U.S. executives. *The Executive* 5(2): 7–22.

Peters, T. 1990. Prometheus barely unbound. *The Executive* 4(4): 70–84.

Toffler, A. 1990. *Powershift.* New York: Bantam.

Wallenstein, G. 1990. *Setting global telecommunication standards.* Norwood, MA: Artech.

CHAPTER **8**

Communication and Technology

Tandem Industries: Managing by Electronic Adhocracy

Janice Mills had been pleased when her boss, Richard Hunt, agreed to reorganize the field sales support staff for Tandem's growing number of government contracts. Janice had argued long and hard for change to provide better customer service and more flexibility in utilizing personnel across contracts. After all, if Tandem expected to service over $30 million of business with only ten people she needed flexibility in coordination and deployment of both people and technical resources.

Janice had headed Tandem's field sales support staff for two years when she finally sold Hunt on investing in coordination-intensive information technologies. Traditionally, each member of the field sales support staff had a list of contracts that they serviced. Field staff called on clients regularly, troubleshooting technical problems and determining future needs related to contracts or potential new business for Tandem. Six staff members were geographically dispersed throughout the western United States, one lived in Germany, and the remaining three worked in Minneapolis where Janice was located. Janice contended this approach provided some customers with more service than they required while leaving others with inadequate support—particularly when serious technical problems needed fast solutions. She wanted the flexibility to combine the field sales support staff into account teams with the ability to shift team composition as needs changed or workload dictated.

Hunt agreed Mills should install a customer hotline to receive trouble calls. Two highly trained operators would record problems in a computer data base, notify an account head assigned to the contract, and provide Janice and the account head an electronically generated assessment of the problem based on similar problems stored in the data base. In addition, the system could provide Janice a daily analysis of work assignments and geographic locations of all sales support people in order to form the best and most available troubleshooting group for fast client response. Each member of the field staff was equipped with hand-held computers programmed to record work assignments, travel information, customer needs, and miscellaneous observations. Each night the stored information was to be transmitted to Minneapolis to a central computer. Each morning Janice could access a report on the previous day's activities as well as send updates to all field personnel. Janice also viewed the system as a means of gathering problem-solving ideas from all staff members. She told Hunt she intended to regularly use the system's electronic mail function to hold staff meetings designed to exchange information and innovate in field service.

When Janice introduced the system to the quarterly meeting of the field sales support staff, there were mixed reactions. Most agreed that increased networked communications could facilitate their work but there was skepticism about daily reporting and the potential of frequent assignment to new clients even though the team would be headed by a designated account person. Janice told the group it was important to think about more flexibility but she would listen to all concerns and monitor needed changes as the system was put in place.

SIX MONTHS LATER

Janice left the office fatigued and concerned. She reflected on a troubling conversation with Richard Hunt. He had praised her new communications system but also expressed concern because two senior members of her staff had complained directly to him about increased workload and the depersonalization of contact with Janice. Although they exchanged messages more frequently, it was not on the telephone or in person. Janice acknowledged this practice and reflected on the 125 electronic mail messages she had sent and received in the last eight hours in addition to her computer conference. She began to assess the strengths and weaknesses of managing by *adhocracy* (the dependence on many rapidly shifting project teams with an emphasis on lateral communication among relatively autonomous groups). Her daily reports verified customers were receiving faster response to problem situations and the cost to Tandem for response teams had decreased over the previous quarter. She had been pleased with the quality of input during her "electronic" staff meetings, although at times she wondered at the length and complexity of answers from several members of the field staff. She felt positively because at least these individuals were involved and concerned, and in the case of the person living in Germany, it was the most input anyone could remember receiving from this highly capable individual. Janice wondered what she should do. She agreed the workload had increased and showed no signs of letting up. Her system was involving more people and better utilizing their skills but could potentially drown everyone in a sea of communications.

YOUR ASSIGNMENT

1. What are the communication issues in this case? For the field staff? For customers? For training? For management?
2. Describe how this communications system influences daily decision making.
3. Describe the strengths and limitations of managing by electronic adhocracy.
4. Describe the human communication challenges in an organization structured for constant change. What are management challenges?
5. How would you advise Janice Wells?

The "Better Technology, More Complaints" Case

Megan Morris was pleased with the new computer and telephone system in the billing and accounts receivable department for Pennren Hospital. Pennren management had asked her to reduce her staff by seven people and the new technology made that possible. The system facilitated the mailing of more than 5,000 monthly patient statements as well as continual billings to insurance companies. Patient statements could be handled by two hourly clerks and insurance company billings were staffed with three level-one billing specialists. The billing department alone was reduced by five personnel. The voice-mail telephone system recorded patient inquiries, allowing Pennren management to reduce the return calls staff from four to two people. A recorded message told patients to specify their question, provide a daytime phone number where they could be reached, and expect a response within 40 working hours.

Megan and her supervisor, Jerry Schiller, carefully selected their best employees for training on the new systems. Accuracy in data entry was essential as was the ability to handle a large volume of work. Megan and Jerry saw little need for cross-training between patient and insurance billing systems although the telephone response team had to access information from both data bases. Sophisticated software was used to simultaneously post receipts to both patient and insurance ledgers. Jerry was responsible for resolving problems with little decision-making authority delegated to his staff.

Megan's initial reports to Pennren management were favorably received and preliminary productivity statistics were positive. Aging of receivables had been reduced by three days during the first four months of system use.

The year-end report was not as positive. Although staff costs were significantly reduced, statistics for collection of receivables indicated no difference in any category from the previous year. Both Megan and Jerry were puzzled. They were convinced their staff was well trained and Jerry, in particular, reported few problems requiring his attention. Megan was amazed when the president of Pennren called her to his office and confronted her with information from a recent patient survey—her department was rated as the most ineffective unit in the entire hospital. He handed her a letter and asked her to think about what her new systems had done to customer service.

August 21, 1991

5668 Ridge Brook Drive

Newport, Rhode Island 80918

Pennren Health Care Systems

P.O. Box 9470

Newport, Rhode Island 80907

Re: account no. 00567705-7940

I take care of all the billing for my mother, Liethe C. Stonegate. We have just received what you describe as your final notice for $108.12. I have talked with one representative from your office about this bill. Unfortunately, I did not retain her name. I asked if Mother's supplemental insurance payment had been received and further, why any balance was due since all her Medicare deductibles were met in January of this year. The woman indicated she would research the problem and call me back. She never did.

I received two additional statements. Both times, I called the numbers listed on the statements, left messages on your message machines, and received no phone calls from you. I, therefore, am not pleased to be told you are placing this account with a collection agency. I have in good faith attempted to deal with this bill and have not been met with the same attempts from your office.

My mother's supplemental insurance policy is Blue Cross/Shield High Option, subscriber number: 462-3205550, group number 9899.

I do not want a telephone call—my previous one was not successful. Please respond in writing. We want you to receive your money, however, the last time Liethe Stonegate wrote you a check you had to refund it because her insurance had paid the bill. We can easily afford the $108.12 and we want you paid but I believe you likely already have the money.

Sincerely,

Penny Stonegate

[The following note and statement were appended to the initial letter and sent by registered mail to the president.]

September 21, 1991

I have just opened the attached bill. Additional charges have been added, I have received no response to my letter of August 21, 1991. Again, we intend to pay our bills, however, we need clear and correct explanations. I have been patient, however, your lack of response is becoming extremely irritating. I will wait until October 21, 1991 to receive clarification. If not received by that time, I will consider the account paid in full.

Dr. Penny Stonegate

YOUR ASSIGNMENT

1. What are the organizational communication issues in this case?
2. Is this a technology, staffing, or training problem?
3. How would you advise Megan?
4. What can Penny Stonegate's letter tell Megan and Jerry about their problems?
5. What can we learn about technology and customer service from this example?

The "It Works So Well, Why Are We Falling Apart?" Case

Deanna Reinfield is supervisor of the Customer Service Division of Public Utilities of Akron, Virginia. As one of the most modern operations of its type, the customer service division handles more than 800 calls per day with operators initiating actions for new service hookups, dispatch for repairs, adjustments of billing errors, and payment schedules for past due accounts. The division has 12 experienced operators who average more than 60 calls each during an eight-hour daytime shift. The evening shift runs from 5 to 10 P.M. and is staffed with two operators.

During the past year the division has changed computer and telephone systems to enlarge its data base and increase the speed of data processing. The new system was designed to increase the numbers of calls each individual operator could take by decreasing the time necessary to access information and initiate orders and changes. Most operators were pleased to be trained for the new systems and Deanna believed management would soon see evidence of a positive return on their investment. She was not prepared for what Ruby Jenkins had to say. Ruby, who had been asked to accept responsibility for expressing the 12 operators' complaints about work pressures and job burnout, came to talk with Deanna on their behalf.

DEANNA: Ruby, I am amazed. All the reports look excellent. You are doing a fine job. During our first six months [*with the new system*] we have increased our numbers of calls handled per operator and decreased the length of time customers must be put on hold. The customer survey that went out in last month's billing statements came back with very favorable ratings for us. Help me understand what is wrong.

RUBY: Deanna, you can't imagine the pressure. For one thing, technology can help us manage more information but when you increase call volume you increase the number of "real" people we must work with per day. You know, you have been on the phones—that can be extremely tiring. People don't know what they want or need. Even ten more of them per day wears a person down.

DEANNA: I had not thought of it in that way. What else?

RUBY: We hate the new call waiting function. Before, we had an audio beep; now, the new timing device shows how many calls have bounced onto an individual line and the seconds or minutes each caller is waiting. You need to work the phones for an entire day. Watching three red lights each with counting time is enough to drive us crazy. I mean we all knew that when we were training but it seemed like a good idea. However. . . .

DEANNA: Ruby, I can see there are some problems we need to think about. Is there anything else the group wants me to know?

RUBY: Yes, we are not sure about how well the entire company is responding to our increased volume of orders. Several of us have noticed that we are getting repeat customer calls asking for what we had already put in the works, but nothing seems to be happening. Yesterday, for example, I called up an account [*on the computer screen*] when a lady called. She was asking for a heater inspection and she said she had been told someone would call her the next day to schedule. Sure enough, her account showed I had requested Service to call her on Friday to schedule. It was the following Thursday and she had not heard from anyone. Now, I know she could be at fault, maybe gone when they called, but several of us believe this is beginning to happen. I wonder if we can't overload the other divisions by speeding up beyond what Repair, Service, and Billing can handle. If we do that, in the long run, we are going to have more unhappy customers than before.

DEANNA: Ruby, I have noticed that we had a record number of sick leave hours last month. I just thought the flu was going round especially hard. Did people stay away because they were really sick or just upset?

RUBY: They were sick—you don't have those types of operators. But I think that too much pressure can make people sick. Deanna, I have been here for ten years and I have never seen it this bad. It seems hopeless after all the money that was spent on the new system and the training. The bottom line is, we are good at the job, but we hate the job.

DEANNA: Does the group have recommendations for me?

RUBY: No, I'm afraid not. It took some time to even decide to come talk to you. Not that we don't think we can, but everyone is counting on this new thing to work—so much money was spent. What can you do?

DEANNA: Ruby, I don't know but I obviously have to try.

Immediately following her meeting with Ruby, Deanna scheduled an appointment with her manager, Ruth Sturgeons. Ruth had been heavily involved in decisions to purchase the new system and was noted for her desire to innovate in customer service.

DEANNA: Ruth, I think I have a problem. Ruby Jackson came to see me yesterday on behalf of the operators. You know we have been so pleased with the statistics; I must admit I have apparently neglected an important part of my job—staying close to the people who work for me. They are feeling some considerable distress and feel caught because we have so much invested in this thing.

RUTH: Explain what you mean.

Deanna summarized Ruby's conversation and then added her own concerns about the potential backlog in other areas created by the increased work orders generated with the new system. Ruth responded:

Deanna, you are right. We have a problem. We can't lose the people we have, they are the backbone of this operation. We have to consider their concerns and deal with the issue. Let's call a meeting of the entire group. Pay overtime and ask everyone to come in on Saturday morning for one hour. We will hear their concerns and consider our options. In the meantime I will contact the design consultants who actually proposed the system and ask them if they have faced similar problems with any of their other clients. We may be expecting too much, or the group may need some other changes.

Prior to the meeting, Deanna had a visit from two operators who told her the system was not the only problem. Jill and George told Deanna interpersonal problems were at an all-time high among operators. In particular, Jim and Jerry were not switching their systems to pick up overload calls and assist the busiest operators. This had caused an argument among those with workstations nearest Jim. Jim and Jerry had become defensive and accused the group of trying to get rid of them. Jim and Jerry were not speaking to most of their peers and everyone was uncomfortable. Deanna could not remember a time when friction had been so intense.

During the operators' meeting, Ruth and Deanna heard most of the group express concern with the system. They liked its capability to make data more available but did not like the pressure from an increased call load, especially late in their shifts. Two longtime operators stated they were personally close to "flaming" (work-related stress, i.e., burnout) and their doctors had suggested rest or a change of job. One operator admitted applying for a job in another company based on her husband's concerns. The group expressed resignation and worry. They believed little could be done. Several members thanked Ruth and Deanna for their concern.

Ruth and Deanna talked with the consultants immediately after the operators' meeting. Both consultants were surprised at the intensity of the group's feeling and promised to study the problem and report back within two weeks. They asked Ruth and Deanna if they thought the group was truly motivated to tackle the added responsibility. Ruth assured them this was a good group and expressed her displeasure at their general lack of experience with assessing the impact of technology. Ruth also told Deanna she intended to contact the heads of the repair, service, and billing divisions to determine what their response statistics indicated.

Deanna called a meeting of her operators the following Tuesday. She asked them to make recommendations prior to the consultants' report. She also volunteered to schedule herself for regular relief shifts during the day. She would commit two hours daily to help extend break time for operators. Privately, she asked herself how she could have thought things were going so well.

YOUR ASSIGNMENT

1. What are the communication issues in this case?
2. How should an organization approach assessing the impact of technology on human performance?
3. Discuss the interrelationship between technical system capacities and human responses.
4. Discuss the statement, "System designers frequently understand technical capacity without understanding the dynamics of human technology use. This gap in understanding retards technological progress and increases human stress."
5. How would you advise Ruth and Deanna? The operators? The consultants?

The Fiber Management Team

Drake Industries, one of the nation's leading manufacturers of medical and hospital supplies, has four plants in three Florida cities: Orlando, Miami, and Daytona Beach. The corporate office is in the Orlando plant but all four plants have their own division management running day-to-day operations. The relationships among the four plants have frequently been confrontational. The two Miami and Daytona Beach management teams believe Orlando plant management has an advantage in shaping policy through more frequent contact with corporate managers.

When the corporate information systems (IS) vice-president approached the four division managers with a proposal to link all plants with a fiber optic network capable of video, voice, and data traffic, the Miami and Daytona Beach managers were most receptive. The Orlando general manager expressed some reservations but conceded that voice and data savings alone might justify the fiber link. The Orlando plant is the site of central data processing and the site of most management meetings. Data and telephone transmission costs, therefore, are important overhead items only for Miami and Daytona Beach. The Daytona Beach general manager was spending $75,000 per year on telephone and data links to Orlando, or approximately 40 percent of the proposed annual lease of the fiber system. After several months of discussion, the four plant managers agreed with the IS vice-president to proceed with the networking of the four plants.

A fiber system committee was established to develop policy and to stimulate use of the system. Each general manager appointed one individual from his staff to join corporate management in support of the project. The Fiber System Committee elected to have their meetings "on the fiber" using its teleconference capabilities.

The committee met weekly during the first year the system was in place. Committee members were frustrated by the plants' limited use of video conferencing or training capabilities. A technical subcommittee, established to get voice and data on the system, made somewhat more progress in establishing specifications for equipment necessary to transfer information to the fiber. The information systems people in the Orlando plant were the most resistant because they believed their budgets and system control would be lessened with more active involvement from the other plants.

The general manager from Daytona Beach agreed with the IS vice-president that he should chair the Fiber System Committee as its second year began. Most committee participants believed more direct information to top management would stimulate use of the system. The Daytona Beach general manager could potentially achieve the most cost and time savings if the system experienced extensive use.

The president of Drake Industries refused to hold general management meetings on the system. He wanted all his top managers physically present when he conducted business. The finance and research support groups in Orlando refused to participate in system training claiming video conferencing and video training were substandard methods of communicating information.

During the latter half of the second year of the fiber lease, voice and data linkages were established among the plants. Costs transferred from commercial providers to the system paid for approximately 80 percent of the lease. Use of the fiber for administrative meetings and training was virtually nonexistent. Only the Fiber System Committee regularly utilized video conferencing and the communications managers were the sole group to provide training via the system.

At the end of the second year, the Daytona Beach general manager proposed communications managers for each plant be asked to formalize a plan to increase system usage. The head of communications for Miami Central was asked to coordinate the group. Members of the Fiber System Committee privately agreed interorganizational politics were retarding system use, as was the fear of introducing new technologies for decision making. The IS vice-president in particular stressed the need for new strategies to encourage familiarity and use as he saw the potential for training hospital clients via fiber and satellite hook-ups.

The communications managers were enthusiastic about their assignment. Jill Majors, the Miami Central manager, believed the group would cooperate and knew that Dan Johnson was one of a few Orlando managers who saw long-term potential in the technology. As Jill convened the first meeting she had high expectations of the group.

JILL: I am pleased we could all meet today. I believe that most of our meetings should be on the fiber [*a reference to video conferencing*] but I wanted us all to be together to talk about the goals of this group and our strategy.

NORM: [*Daytona Beach*] I agree, we have a lot to do in a short period of time.

DAN: [*Orlando*] Jill, I agree we are the right ones to put this proposal together. But I want to know what the chances are for its adoption. This entire system has gotten too political for me and at a time of budget constraints the thought of talking to people about new ways to do things is difficult.

JILL: Dan, I asked the question about what would happen to our proposal before I ever agreed to chair the committee. Well, I was given assurances that something would happen. We have already put over $250,000 into this system and we have transferred overhead costs from commercial carriers to our own lease.

MARY: [*Miami Main*] I am glad we are doing this. Everyone else would mess it up.

JILL: How do you see our responsibilities?

The group discusses its understanding of the goals for a proposal and generally agrees specific proposals to increase system use should be developed, beginning with customer service programs.

JILL: Well, if we are all in general agreement, how do we see the problems, I mean, the reason we are here?

DAN: There is simply resistance to using video conferencing. People have been in face-to-face meetings all of their lives. They don't know how to deal with the distance, the lack of some nonverbal cues, the appearance on camera. Also, it eliminates back-door agreements. It is hard to step out of the room during a video conference. No bathroom breaks. [*Laughs*] One-on-one decision making is tough.

MARY: Dan, you have hit it right on the head. This new technology shifts power arrangements. And we have people in all of the plants who like to control through this back-channel stuff.

NORM: I also think there is a fear factor. Many people cannot stand to see themselves. Our quad-split screen means you not only talk and contribute but see yourself. Of course, we could modify that and may want to do so.

JILL: Norm, I think the fear factor is in training. Most people think of themselves as if they were on television. They don't believe they have that expertise, even our best trainers. I had to laugh, the other day one of our computer trainers told me she could not possibly train on the system because she would have to be too prepared. Well, I thought to myself—prepared?—aren't you prepared now when you train our people?

MARY: The big opportunity may be in training. Many of our customers would like real-time interactive training on our new equipment. Also, this type of system is being used with a satellite up-link to troubleshoot problems with machines in crisis situations. Marshall [*a prime competitor of Drake*] just used this approach in Anchorage with a customer who had a failure. They had that machine up within minutes. They were visually directing a repair group on the Anchorage end. Pretty exciting stuff, not for the faint of heart.

JILL: So far we are saying politics and fear—or concern about being on television. What can we propose?

DAN: I think experience and exposure are the only real solutions. We don't have options about attendance at other types of meetings. Why should this be any different?

MARY: Are you suggesting that we need to get everyone some mandatory exposure?

DAN: Yes, I think I am.

NORM: Dan, how can we get our own president involved? If he won't play, then how can you require others?

JILL: Norm is right. We will have an uprising if we require others to do what John won't. I don't think management would take such a proposal.

DAN: You may be right, but maybe we should target specific departments and try to develop a plan to assist their customers.

MARY: Or better yet, why not survey our customers to determine the types of needs we might be able to meet with this technology? We could then go to selected groups and show them how to solve a problem.

JILL: Now we are on to something.

The meeting continues. . . .

YOUR ASSIGNMENT

1. The Drake Industries case illustrates resistance to innovation. Describe the various resistance factors the communications managers should consider.
2. Video conferencing and training using an interactive (audio and video) fiber and/or satellite system are feared by many who consider themselves to be capable communicators. Identify concerns people have when approaching these technologies. Describe how video technologies influence meetings and training or educational settings.
3. How would you approach the assignment the communications managers have received?
4. How do complex communications technologies influence organizational power distributions?
5. Many companies require computer literacy from their work force. Should video literacy be required as well? Discuss.

WHAT HAPPENED NEXT?

The communications managers invited sales and marketing directors from each plant to join them in an effort to understand better how interactive video, data, and voice on a fiber system with satellite up-link and down-link capabilities could assist customers in receiving training to repair Drake products. The response was mixed and ranged from specific suggestions on how to provide customer service support with the technologies to outright rejection of the idea. The group decided to propose a limited number of pilot projects for interested customers. Communications managers would assist marketing and sales support staff in developing and presenting training programs to be evaluated at the end of a 12-month period. Only then would a decision be made as to whether to expand the service to others.

Initially the Daytona Beach general manager and the IS vice-president believed the group had not made comprehensive recommendations. Jill argued resistance was so great, including the president of Drake, the group believed field success was the most likely way to stimulate interest. She contended positive evaluations from customers would potentially make it difficult to continue to resist or to suggest technology was substandard for training and customer service.

The pilot programs were well received by customers and during the same time period two additional Drake competitors began use of fiber systems. At the end of the 12-month experiment, the Fiber System Committee and the communications managers presented results to Drake's president asking him to reconsider his personal position and proposing expanded customer services. The president conceded he was retarding progress by refusing to participate. He agreed to hold quarterly management meetings on the system with his weekly meetings remaining in the face-to- face mode. He circulated a memo encouraging other departments to follow his lead. Marketing and sales groups were allocated a one-time training budget to familiarize key personnel with system potential.

Five years after the lease was initiated, Drake now utilizes the system at about 40 percent of capacity. The IS vice-president and others contend the coming years will see Drake a leader in the field with state-of-the-art customer support. Detractors contend the company will waste another $300,000 during the current year on a system few really support. The Daytona Beach and Miami plant managers have not reduced their overall overhead costs but believe the expanded capacity makes their return more than worth the costs. The Orlando plant manager frequently misses video conferences held on the system. The communications managers see the system as somewhat effective but remain discouraged about moving Drake into the twenty-first century.

Science Is Not All That Objective: The Mitchell Laboratories Case

Mitchell Laboratories, a subsidiary of Newton Pharmaceutical, has long attracted to its labs some of the nation's top scientists in biology and chemistry. Known for pioneering in biochemistry, Mitchell researchers actively generate new product and process developments for Newton while contributing through publications basic knowledge to the field. The lab manager, Mary Simmons, was shocked to receive notice from Martin Kerrs's attorney of his law suit against the lab based on age and salary discrimination. Kerrs, a longtime member of the biochemistry staff, alleged Sandra Denton, the head of biochemistry, had evaluated him unfairly by recommending no salary increases for the past three years. Furthermore, Kerrs charged that Denton provided adequate research resources only to those department members who agreed with her interests in molecular biology. The researchers receiving the largest amount of support dollars all were junior in seniority and age to Kerrs.

The attorneys for Mitchell recommended that Mary review Kerrs's file and discuss the situation with Sandra Denton prior to determining how to respond. Contents of the file surfaced a long-standing dispute between Denton and Kerrs, based initially on disagreements about research direction and in later years on salary and resource issues. Mary learned Kerrs had not received salary increases for three years and, indeed, had the least amount of money for project support of any department member. A memo from Denton to Mary's predecessor, Samuel Boston, charged Kerrs was making no significant contributions to the department and cited his refusal to redirect his research program and retool in molecular biology. The memo contained references to Kerrs's age, 59 at the time, and the need to provide younger and more productive staff with salary incentives and research support. A letter from Kerrs to both Denton and Boston revealed he was unaware of the memo until two years after it was written. Kerrs filed a formal complaint with Mitchell's human resource department demanding the removal of the letter from his file and asking that Denton and Boston be reprimanded for withholding evaluations of his work. The head of human resources wrote letters of reprimand to both Denton and Boston but declined to remove the letter from the file. Kerrs was asked by human resources to provide support for his claim of scientific productivity and to add any other relevant information to the file. Kerrs provided six of his journal publications and three letters from colleagues at Newton. The file also revealed that Denton had suggested—three months prior to the attorney's notice of suit—that Kerrs should either take early retirement or a leave of absence that would allow him to become more familiar with trends in molecular biology. Kerrs had responded the direction of the lab was in question and refused to either redirect his efforts or retire.

When Mary interviewed Sandra Denton her concern for Mitchell's legal position increased. Sandra was vague about details and angered Martin Kerrs could challenge her authority. Sandra contended Kerrs was stubborn and would not realistically evaluate where the lab's research efforts might leverage the most new products and processes for Newton. Sandra admitted Kerrs was competent but in an area of biochemistry that contributed little to Mitchell. Sandra defended her poor evaluations and the decision to cap his salary at its present level. She dismissed any charge that age was a factor. It was coincidental that those receiving more support were younger. Sandra admitted the dispute had been going on since the day she came to Mitchell, some 17 years ago. She told Mary no attempts had been made to resolve the conflict. Mary referred to the letter from human resources recommending mediation. Sandra said nothing ever came of it.

Mary advised the attorneys that Mitchell was in a difficult position. Written records favored Kerrs's position and the scientific merits of Sandra's decisions would be difficult to support.

Mitchell attorneys scheduled a meeting with Kerrs, his attorney, and Mary. They were prepared to negotiate a salary increase with research support or to offer a financially desirable retirement package with continued access to laboratory space and limited funding for ongoing projects. Kerrs would be evaluated directly by Mary should he choose to continue his employment at Mitchell. Kerrs's attorney was pleased with the offers. Kerrs, however, stormed out of the meeting stating he would see them in court.

YOUR ASSIGNMENT

1. Describe the organizational communication issues in this case.
2. What types of communication processes or procedures should the lab use to determine scientific direction or evaluate the viability of a particular line of research?

3. Discuss the possibility that the issue is age discrimination. Discuss the possibility that the issue is scientific disagreement. Discuss the possibility that the issue is interpersonal conflict between Denton and Kerrs. Discuss the possibility that the issue is a combination of the three.
4. How can Mary Simmons advise Sandra Denton?
5. How can lab management prevent this type of situation from occurring in the future?

WHAT HAPPENED NEXT?

Kerrs's attorney convinced Martin to take one of the two offers. He reasoned the company had admitted liability and to go to court was a lengthy and expensive process without guaranteed outcome. Kerrs deliberated for three months before making a decision. He took the salary increase and lab support but refused to report directly to Mary Simmons. He claimed he wanted to be an active part of the biochemistry section and recognized by Sandra Denton for his efforts. Mary Simmons met with Sandra and explained the legal situation. Sandra was outraged and refused to cooperate. Mary then scheduled a meeting with Sandra and Mitchell's attorneys. Sandra again refused and asked for a severance package to be established for her attorney to review. Mary was concerned about Mitchell's reputation and what the loss of Sandra might mean to the researchers with whom she had a positive working relationship. Mary decided to risk losing Sandra and refused to support the severance package. Although this angered Sandra, she was pleased that Mary did not want her to leave. Mary suspected Sandra felt threatened yet wanted to remain with Mitchell. At the end of six weeks of negotiation, Sandra decided to stay with Mitchell and supervise Martin Kerrs. Mary asked to be included in all future meetings with Kerrs. She also requested that an outside consultant from a major university be hired to consider directions for research support and to make recommendations about how to best utilize Martin's skills and provide Mitchell with a better return on its investment. Mary wondered why her predecessor had ignored this problem for so long.

CHAPTER **9**

Creativity, Effectiveness, and Communication

The National Aerospace Propulsion Agency Reorganization

The Herbert Walker Propulsion Center (HWPC), one of six divisions of the National Aerospace Propulsion Agency (NAPA), has just been notified that it will participate in a massive management reorganization designed to provide better coordination among all NAPA divisions. Located in Minot, North Dakota, HWPC is responsible for research and development in the field of aerospace propulsion. The reorganization directive has come from NAPA's new director, James Minkin. Minkin's notice asked the six division directors who report directly to him to submit a plan for reorganizing their management functions based on specified guidelines, including: (1) reduction in overall management personnel; (2) coordinated responsibilities at various functional levels; and (3) reassignment of personnel to NAPA's Washington, D.C., staff.

The HWPC division reorganization will be more extensive than other NAPA divisions because Minkin's directive specifically requests that Hal Roberts, division director of HWPC, join Minkin's staff in Washington, D.C. Sources close to Minkin believe Roberts's move is designed to quell the HWPC director's frequent criticism of the Washington office and to block Roberts from his somewhat independent operation of HWPC.

HWPC at Minot is divided into three large sections with a work force of 2,500. The research section is charged with testing the strength of new alloys to be utilized in propulsion and is staffed with approximately 500 engineers. The development section is responsible for the practical application of the new alloys to engines and engine designs and is staffed with 300 engineers. Both development and research are headed by separate section chiefs and assistant section chiefs.

An additional 1,700 personnel are located in the support section, which is responsible for computer services, including development of both hardware and software; fabrication; library services, including editorial style and translation; finance, both in-house and for contract purchases of equipment and work; contracts; secretarial services; mechanical services such as mechanical and electrical instrumentation for research projects; and buildings and grounds. Development section funding is on a project basis directly approved by the Washington staff of NAPA. Research section activities are funded through block appropriations from Congress. The support section also receives block appropriations, although special equipment purchases are submitted annually as line-item requests.

Section chiefs and assistant chiefs report directly to Hal Roberts. Development section projects are reviewed quarterly with Roberts, who prepares appropriate reports for NAPA headquarters. Research section projects have not been reviewed on a regular schedule. New or controversial projects have been reviewed by project engineers and the HWPC division director. Historically, communication has been limited among the six NAPA divisions with coordination of assignments coming from the Washington management team.

HWPC has enjoyed an excellent record of achievement since its inception in 1957. Top engineers and scientists from other NAPA divisions frequently have requested transfers to HWPC. From 1957 to the present, either scientists or engineers have held the top management positions there. Hal Roberts is an engineer by training and has two scientists and one engineer reporting directly to him.

Roberts worked for 15 years in the research section prior to his appointment as division director. He was known as a brilliant engineer who was responsible for many of the early advancements in the utilization of new alloys. His technical competence was responsible for his promotion to the position of section chief for research. When Dave Andrews, division director since the founding of HWPC, retired, Hal was named to take his place. Shortly thereafter, the charter of the National Aerospace Propulsion Agency was changed to include a development section. Roberts, with his strong technical background, insisted on very direct contact with both development and research management and projects. During the early years of his leadership, he closely reviewed projects in both sections.

Hal Roberts is confident of his knowledge of most technical aspects of aerospace propulsion and his concrete accomplishments support his perceptions. He is a man who demands close adherence to his direction and is known to be rudely critical of incomplete efforts or hesitancy of engineers to undertake an effort beyond present capabilities. Industry contractors find him the most critical of the NAPA division directors.

In early 1985, Roberts created the position of associate director for HWPC in order to relieve some of his technical workload. He selected Jim Henderson to fill that position. Jim had worked with Hal when Hal was section chief for research. Although Roberts had confidence in Henderson, he only substituted for Roberts on rare occasions. An assistant director, Tom Mannes, was responsible for all activities relating to personnel and the support section.

Dave Andrews had named Alan Smith to replace Roberts as research section chief. Roberts had disagreed with the choice but did not want to disturb the retiring director. Smith is a quiet man who is well liked by both his peers and subordinates. He is known to be technically competent and hardworking.

Hal Roberts believes the reorganization directive from Minkin is implied criticism of the way he runs HWPC. He is aware the expanding private sector aerospace propulsion industry is attracting many good engineers from the Minot facility. Roberts believes the long-term outstanding record of HWPC is directly related to the freedom of the division from overall NAPA management. He is convinced the drain of engineers to the private sector will correct itself with the upcoming NAPA budget expansion.

Roberts does not respect James Minkin. Minkin, an attorney, is the first nontechnical director of the agency. He has an outstanding record in government reorganization and is well liked by many influential people in Washington. Minkin has been charged with expanding the scope of NAPA with a possible charter revision to allow the agency to undertake energy research. He is aware Roberts has considerable influence throughout NAPA because of his technical capability and previous successes. Members of Minkin's staff believe Roberts thinks he is technically superior to anyone in the agency. Minkin worries Roberts's reputation for technical competence could cause him trouble in Washington.

Roberts considers the possible criticisms Minkin might have for his reorganization proposal. Roberts believes transfering to the Washington office will enable him to have broader influence over NAPA activities. He knows influence can come from his unequaled technical ability, however, he would also like to reorganize HWPC for continued responsiveness to his direction.

Tom Mannes and Jim Henderson are key individuals in the reorganization planning. Roberts is hesitant to recommend either man for HWPC director because he believes neither has the necessary technical ability for the job. Roberts has discounted Minkin's suggestions that both men are capable in personnel management.

Roberts knows the other divisions are creating a position of associate director of liaison relations. The only man Roberts can trust in that position is Jim Henderson. Roberts considers making an argument for the expansion of Henderson's present role to include the liaison function. Roberts remains concerned about a recommendation for the division director position. Tom Mannes, although an engineer, has worked for the last ten years in the support section. Roberts does not find him qualified to head HWPC. In addition, Roberts is concerned Minkin regards Mannes too highly. The remaining possibility for division director is Alan Smith, section chief of research. Roberts finds Smith totally unacceptable.

Roberts knows his reorganization proposal must appear to support Minkin's philosophy if his influence is to grow in Washington. The plan, however, must not relinquish his control. Roberts decides he will approach the reorganization as he would a tough new research project. As the deadline for plan submission draws near, Hal Roberts makes a list of the data he needs and the variables he can and cannot control.

YOUR ASSIGNMENT

1. What are the organizational change issues in this case?
2. HWPC has a successful record. Describe how communication may have contributed to that success. Describe Roberts's leadership approach.
3. HWPC is expected to change. How might these changes influence effectiveness?
4. Describe Hal Roberts's approach to influence.
5. What are potential communication problems when Roberts goes to Washington? Describe potential problems for Roberts and potential problems for Minkin.

The Individual Contributor

This account is an accurate description of Sue James's career. Names and places have been changed to assure the privacy of those involved. The case is about communication, risk, change, survival, and effectiveness. As you follow Sue's career and decisions, think about organizational communication and the life influences for this almost 30-year span.

1964

Sue James has just graduated first in a class of 3,000 from a major midwestern university. A communication major, Sue is excited about applying for jobs and beginning a career. She is in no way prepared for what is about to happen.

Norton Industries, an electronics company with substantial government contracts, is looking for a management trainee in its marketing communications department. Norton advertises the position in regional newspapers and asks for written applications. Sue is chosen from among approximately 50 other applicants to come to Houston for testing and management interviews. Sue takes written tests for two days and then endures five hours of interviews with various Norton executives. Sue scores higher than the other candidates and the managers with whom she interviews are impressed. The director of marketing communications offers Sue the job two days later. Sue accepts and begins preparations to move to Houston.

Sue is surprised when two days after accepting the job the director calls again. She can hardly believe his comments. Top management had reviewed the offer and has decided they do not want a woman in their management training program. Norton will honor Sue's offer and train her as the highest paid administrative assistant in the company. Sue immediately refuses the job. She is shaken because she has stopped interviewing and turned down other offers for the Norton position. Her anger is quiet but real.

1965

Sue James goes to work for Roth Corbridge Advertising as an account executive in training. Corbridge, a small advertising and public relations company, is run by a brilliant and creative man known to pay scant attention to business details.

Sue's university advisor tries to talk her out of taking the job because he is worried about Corbridge's reported financial instability. Sue is discouraged by larger companies and likes Roth Corbridge's approach during her interview. At this point she just wants to go to work and put the last three months behind her.

Sue likes the people at Corbridge Advertising. Everyone is reasonably new to the industry and wants to learn as much as possible. Roth is a good teacher who encourages people to try all aspects of the business. Within a year, Sue is buying media time, planning promotions, and producing television spots. Roth sends her to Washington, D.C., to work on political accounts. She scarcely realizes she is working 60- to 80-hour weeks. Sue loves the business.

Corbridge Advertising owes the bank money and several clients do not pay bills promptly. Sue asks Roth if she can help. During her second year with Corbridge, she begins collecting receivables and working with clients to bring their accounts up to date. She succeeds in helping Roth reduce his bank indebtedness and he promotes her to senior account executive. She is 22 years old. Sue worked for Roth for another three years before a new offer came in late 1969.

1969

The president of Uniresource, Inc., calls Sue and asks to talk with her about an opportunity. Uniresource, Inc., is a new advertising agency in Dallas run by people who have excellent prior experience with major southwest agencies. The president, a longtime friend of Roth Corbridge and an acquaintance of Sue, offers her the management of Uniresource. Uniresource is losing money and investors want someone to come in and attempt to manage for recovery. Although the president and all the staff will remain, they agree that a new, aggressive manager is what they need. Sue cannot believe what she is hearing—five years in the industry and she is offered a management job at twice her existing salary.

Sue takes the job with one condition. If she successfully returns investors' money she wants to obtain majority ownership of Uniresource. Sue hates to leave Corbridge but helps him understand her desire to have an opportunity of her own. Sue rationalizes her fears by remembering she did not lose the investors' money and she is young enough to get another job if Uniresource goes under. Furthermore, she has few personal financial liabilities.

1973

By 1973 Uniresource billings exceed $1 million annually and investor debt service is on schedule. One client, a national retailer, accounts for approximately 60 percent of the billings. When Mervin Retailers is bought by Dayton Stores of Chicago, Uniresource is threatened with substantial loss of business. Sue goes to Chicago to negotiate. Dayton Stores owns its own agency and intends to move the Mervin business to Chicago. Sue persuades Dayton executives to retain Uniresource for local coordination and media support. Even so, the loss of billing is substantial.

Sue is discouraged. Her staff of 15 will have to be reduced unless billings are significantly increased. Operating flexibility is minimal due to the demanding debt service schedule. Sue consults with her senior staff as to their alternatives. Most feel they should reduce overhead and consider other business options. Sue is tired; she has worked long hours for more than eight years.

1974

Robert Nelson, a senior member of her staff, has always wanted his own production studio. He offers to buy the production part of the agency, retain all production personnel, and free Sue to pursue her other consulting interests. Sue was unaware that Robert came from a wealthy family with the resources to make such a purchase.

Sue experiences mixed emotions but decides to sell the production equipment and clients to Robert. The sale permits her to retire the investors' debt and obtain sole ownership of Uniresource, including all accounts receivable. There is one catch—Sue cannot do competitive business with Robert for a period of three years.

1975

Sue moves to San Francisco and begins to think about her future. Her Uniresource administrative assistant, Sarah Mitchell, stays in Dallas to administer the details of the sale and transfer of business. She and Sue maintain frequent contact and talk about opening a new type of business using the corporate structure of Uniresource but not competing with Robert Nelson.

By the end of 1975, Sue decides to actively pursue a consulting practice in corporate communications. Her San Francisco and Washington, D.C., contacts convince her there is business to be had and someone of her experience will find opportunities. Sue has considered other options, including a lucrative offer from Dayton Stores. In the end she rejects working for others, in some ways still stung by the Norton rejection.

1976

Sue and Sarah define the initial types of services the revived Uniresource will offer. Sue will seek business and Sarah will handle all administrative details. Within six months, Sue has sufficient work to think about new ways of supporting the expanding business.

Sue and Sarah make an unusual decision. Sue realizes she is tired of "selling" to support a large overhead. She opts for a new organizational structure that has both strengths and weaknesses. Sue and Sarah decide to hire the best people they can find on a project basis. These individuals will not be asked to work for Uniresource on a full-time basis but will be highly paid for project work. The flexibility of this approach potentially will service a more diverse client base while effectively managing overhead. The problem, of course, is finding enough talented people who are attracted by this arrangement.

1977

Sue and Sarah have ten associates working with them and billings are increasing. Sue decides to return to school and pursue a Ph.D. in organizational communication. Her consulting interests are broadening beyond marketing and advertising to organizational diagnosis and change. She believes additional study and credentials are necessary. (Sue obtained an M.A. in communication while working for Roth Corbridge.)

1980

Sue completes her Ph.D. and expands her work to high technology firms. She begins to travel extensively, working primarily with research and development laboratories. Sue develops a model to audit communication performance in high-tech work groups, implement communication processes to address identified issues, and monitor progress. Sarah continues to live in Dallas and the revived Uniresource is highly profitable.

1981–1990

Sue and Sarah are financially successful with clients in 15 states. They continue to refine their model of hiring people for project work. By now many of their project employees have worked with them for more than ten years. Sue works for some of these talented individuals on their own special projects.

1991

Sue decides it is time to change again. The company is profitable and she now accepts business only by referral. She has begun to question the effectiveness of much of her work. She knows it has been helpful but believes she also must change in changing times. Sue interviews several new people with corporate and academic experience in organizational development. She associates with foreign professionals seeking to work with Americans in joint consulting ventures. Still she is dissatisfied.

Sue Talks About Herself

SUE: I can be a good team player. In fact, most describe me as an excellent team player. I know, however, I have rarely really played on any team although I am loyal to others and value their opinions. I have never been outgoing. You know, I read once that people who can get up and give good presentations often dread cocktail parties. Well, that is me. I'm afraid of conflict at times but I have had to deal with a lot of it. I'm somewhat driven, and a lot of that comes from the beginning. I just couldn't believe the unfair rejection. It was a pivotal experience. Am I successful? I don't know. I think success is a process. I have made plenty of money, I meet interesting people, I do work I like, but successful, I'm not sure.

YOUR ASSIGNMENT

1. Is Sue James successful? What is your definition?
2. What are the organizational communication issues in this case? The career issues? Does this case reflect an early experience with the "glass ceiling"? Why? Why not?
3. What are the strengths and weaknesses of the organizational structure of the current Uniresource?
4. Is Sue James a risk taker? Why? Why not?
5. Is Sue James effective, creative, or what? Why? Why not?

Overload or Innovation

The following discussions are within three separate departments of ITT, one of the largest of the new hotel chain giants. ITT has grown rapidly within the last 18 months, acquiring six smaller hotel chains and adding over 5,000 personnel. Growth has put pressure on a number of typically centralized functions such as international reservations and group telemarketing. ITT management must make important decisions about new reservations systems and expanded group telemarketing efforts. ITT's information systems department is in the process of designing new software to regionalize reservations and support an expanded centralized telemarketing function. ITT's human resource department is reviewing data on work-related medical claims. Although their conversations differ, all three groups are concerned with information overload and innovation.

ITT MANAGEMENT MEETING

Henry Hopper, vice-president for reservations and telemarketing, is meeting with his senior staff to discuss needs for new reservations systems and expanded telemarketing efforts. Henry is concerned that present systems cannot handle ITT's growth and is impatient with information systems management, who tell him a redesigned system could take as much as 20 months to bring on-line.

HENRY: I have just reviewed last month's data. Advance reservations are holding their own in our older properties but have declined by as much as 27 percent in the new acquisitions. I believe the key here is that our people [*reservations personnel staffing 800 telephone numbers for the computer reservations system*] are on the phone longer than ever before. Calls back up; no one really has all the data readily available on the newer properties. We quote wrong rates and show full when we have considerable space left.

SALLY: Henry, you have to expect that each call will extend by 20–30 seconds based on the increased data the system is handling. I too am concerned that we have an increase in numbers of customers bumping onto the recording when they first call. We do have somewhat of a problem in that area. Our daily call load per operator is up about 12 percent. I think, as I said in our last meeting, we need to hire about ten more experienced reservations people and expand the equipment on our present system. That doesn't solve, of course, the problem you say exists with wrong rates and inaccurate space counts.

GEORGE: Why would we get wrong rates and occupancy data? Has anyone in IS [*information systems*] been able to explain?

HENRY: The best explanation I can get is that we aren't getting the right data for input. I just don't believe that. Mark Haynes [*head of information systems for ITT*] and I had a real knock-down drag-out over this issue. Mark claims it is not the technology but that we have too many people working with the new property data. He could be right but I doubt it.

SALLY: Shouldn't we attempt to find out? I agree we need to make some quick changes. A new system must be several months away. Remember when we brought this one on-line? I will never forget overbooking those Pennsylvania properties for five straight days before the bugs were cleared. I thought we were going to have managers in our office with shotguns. [*Laughs*]

HENRY: Sally, this is no laughing matter. I want to get a handle on IS's decentralization proposal. In some ways it makes sense but I'm not sure. Can they really save money and keep us networked with telemarketing? Again, when I talk with Haynes he argues for comprehensive planning and taking our time. But who has 20 months? Besides his software design folks usually take a lot longer than he says. Twenty months could become 3 years.

GEORGE: Henry, I think we need to consider Haynes's proposal. There would certainly be facilities savings associated with a decentralized approach. I think we have to believe he knows what he is doing with the decentralization idea.

HENRY: I'm not against change, but it is a massive investment in new technologies. We will also have considerable additional training costs. I need to know about the basic return on our investments. In the meantime, I have a system going down with overload. We can't have customers backed up for so many months.

SALLY: Henry, we need to take things in order. First, we have to troubleshoot the problem with wrong data. I don't care who is right or wrong; we have to get it fixed. Next, we need to develop a short-term strategy, and then we need to meet with Mark and his people and really get to the bottom of what they are proposing. If we don't decide, it for sure won't be on-line in 20 months.

The meeting continues. . . .

ITT INFORMATION SYSTEMS MEETING

Mark Haynes, head of information systems, is meeting with his two software engineers in charge of reservations and telemarketing projects.

MARK: I am really taking the heat over this reservations system. Henry is angry when I tell him you guys can't possibly get a system in place for 20 months. And when I say 20 months to him my ulcer acts up. I know very good and well it could take 30 or more to really get us up and running. If we decentralize that will take more time even if it is the right answer.

JIM: Mark, lighten up a little. Sure you take the heat but the right thing is to use the new approach with decentralized systems networked to telemarketing. I thought we all agreed?

MITCHELL: I think we just go ahead. The system will really be late if we keep waiting. What do we need to do to get the go ahead?

MARK: I want to make sure our planning is solid. The old system created some really tremendous headaches when we brought it on-line.

JIM: You keep telling us. . . . But that is history and today is today.

MARK: Well Jim, we are building software pretty much the same way we did 15 years ago. I wish writing code were more of a science. I sometimes think we treat it more like an art—based on what you guys want to do.

MITCHELL: [*Somewhat heatedly*] Don't blame us. If people can't explain what they want it is tough for us to do our jobs.

JIM: Isn't that really the problem? We need more up-front planning. I need to know more about where the business is headed to create the best possible system. Technically this is expensive, yes, but not beyond the realm of our capabilities. We can subcontract much of the routine work and Mitch and I can lead the integration effort that is the most complex and important.

MARK: By the way, Henry is on my back about wrong data for the new properties. Is it even conceivable that the additions we made to the program are the problem? I have him almost convinced it is data entry, but I don't want egg on my face.

JIM: Sure, it could be the code. We had to put those revisions in with little to no planning. I don't think it is the code but it could be. Do you want me to run some tests to make sure?

MARK: Yes, and the sooner the better.

JIM: Mark, you need to let us know when there are problems. This won't help our credibility on the new system if we have screwed up the new properties and don't even know it.

MARK: Jim, I know you are right. But I have a lot to think about with this new proposal. I need you guys to tell me how we can bring this thing on-line in less than 20 months. Even if it costs more money.

MITCHELL: Mark, money is important, but it isn't always money. It is planning, it is complexity, it is the art of this thing. We need time to bring about the best possible system.

JIM: Mark, remember when our payroll department actually refused the upgrades we proposed? They said it would cost too much down time to retrain people. They didn't think there was enough value added with our changes. We can't have that kind of thinking again. Let's meet with Henry and his people. Let's try to get this thing off to a good start. Otherwise there is going to be resistance every step of the way.

The meeting continues. . . .

ITT HUMAN RESOURCE DEPARTMENT MEETING

Charles Clemmons is meeting with his benefits staff to review worker claims for the past 12 months. He is concerned about a trend in stress-related claims that began approximately 3 years ago.

CHARLES: The data don't look good to me. Over a 5-year period we are up approximately 600 percent in stress-related claims while our accident claims are down 12 percent We are in a service industry, our accident claims decline more than the industry average but the stress claims go through the roof. How do you account for that?

MARY: Charles, we have good safety training for our managers. They know how to train employees at the direct service level. And that program is working. We are better than the industry with that program and we know it. But the stress thing. Let me put it in perspective. In California last year, stress claims were up across all industries more than 700 percent. Our competitors are seeing much the same types of increases we are. I think we need to address it but I don't see us as unusual.

HERB: Mary is right. We have done another analysis. The stress claims are disproportionately coming from our management ranks. I think that helps us identify the problem. We have so much change and new ways of doing things that hardly anyone can keep up. We are so flexible that we can't stand up in a strong wind.

MARY: What about targeting a group going through change and see if we can come up with a program to help? We could pay for the program if we only slightly reduce these claims. [*ITT is a self-insured company.*]

CHARLES: That's an excellent idea. I believe reservations is ideal. If there were ever a group needing to make significant decisions it's reservations and telemarketing. They are considering an entirely new system plus decentralization. I don't know if Henry would be receptive, but I am certain some of his staff would be.

HERB: Then we meet with his staff first and develop a proposal.

MARY: [*Laughing*] I think we need to get this a little more concrete here first. How about talking with our training people?

CHARLES: Yes, of course, but I'm excited. I can't just sit by and see this thing get worse without attempting some new thinking. Besides, what works for other departments might help us as well. I see our claims are up as well, although certainly not like the others.

The meeting continues. . . .

YOUR ASSIGNMENT

1. What are the communication issues in this case?
2. How is information overload contributing to problems in each of the three departments?
3. Describe innovation processes at ITT.
4. What are the barriers to innovation?
5. How would you advise each of the managers?

Reengineering—A New Organization for Hockaday

Over the past 25 years, Hockaday Engineering has been one of the most successful of the instrument and computer giants. Riding the wave of industry expansion, Hockaday grew from 100 people in 1965 to its current worldwide size of 87,000 employees. Hockaday's founders have prided themselves on building a company where loyalty to employees and customers has paid handsome dividends.

During the late 1980s, Hockaday began to experience pressure from foreign competition along with the maturing of their traditional markets. Increased competition and slow market growth as combined factors contributed to the first sales decline in company history. Profits stalled and Wall Street watched for signs of management's response. At first it was slow in coming. By the early 1990s, however, management was aggressively involved in reengineering the organization with dramatically reduced hierarchy, increased spans of control, and centralization of key worldwide services. In addition, Hockaday targeted a 10,000-person reduction in worldwide employment by announcing plans for retirement incentives, voluntary severance incentives, and hiring freezes.

Financial services was one of the first functions to be slated for Hockaday's organization of the future. A financial service group historically operated as an autonomous unit in each of Hockaday's eight regions, and typically handled accounts payable, accounts receivable, payroll, benefits administration, travel, and expense accounts for all divisions in a given region. Hockaday management concluded this approach created unnecessary duplication of processes and equipment and required far too many personnel for cost-effective operation. During 1992, Jim Franklin was given the responsibility to put together a plan to merge the eight regional groups into one consolidated organization to be located in Phoenix, Arizona. Jim previously headed the corporate accounting division.

Jim Franklin knew he had enormous opportunities and challenges. His managers would give him two years to bring the new organization on-line, at which time regional functions would cease to operate and employees would be placed in other jobs or encouraged to participate in the variety of severance incentives already in place. Only selected individuals would be given the opportunity to transfer to Phoenix to become part of the new team. Jim and his managers targeted the new financial service operation at 500 employees, a 380-employee reduction from the regional centers' combined staffs.

The first challenge Jim faced was recruiting a team of senior managers willing to risk designing an entirely new organization with worldwide responsibility for financial services. Jim and his managers concluded the organization needed a strong process design group, technology experts, and at least two senior managers to work with supervisors and assist teams of people assigned to the various financial service operations.

Before leaving Hockaday's Boston headquarters for Phoenix, Jim selected the four individuals who would become his staff. Sue Cartwright was appointed process manager, Clarence Hines became technology manager, and George Green and Dora Hernandez were selected as team managers.

During their first weeks in Phoenix the new financial services group worked long hours to establish a time line for developing processes and acquiring technologies to assist each function of the group. Budgets, vendors, and industrial space analysts met with every team member. At the end of the first two months, Jim was pleased with the initial planning and believed it was time to tackle the major challenge—the reengineering of the organization.

Jim assigned George and Dora responsibility for reviewing business and academic literature to determine what others were doing in establishing high-performance teams. Jim personally contacted other Hockaday managers who were quasi-experimenting with new organizational structures and processes. Jim, George, and Dora concluded they should request the assistance of a consultant to help them identify the parameters of the organization and develop a training and implementation plan.

Jim, George, and Dora reviewed several proposals before selecting Pam Johnson of CCI as the person and company with whom they wished to work. Pam's fact-finding meeting with the group had raised important questions, and the process she recommended included continuous evaluation and adjustment, a factor missing in other proposals. Jim distributed a shortened version of her proposal to Sue and Clarence and asked his entire staff to prepare for a meeting with Pam to determine how they should proceed.

THE PROPOSAL

Dear Mr. Williams:

The following proposal for the new financial services function is based on our conversations and my meeting with Dora Hernandez. I believe further refinement is desirable, however, suggest you review the following as a recommended process to achieve the goals that both you and Ms. Hernandez outlined. The proposal suggests a team-building training, describes a process to establish implementation plans for the training of teams to be hired within the next two years, and provides approximate costs of training design and training delivery for teams to be hired beginning approximately June, 1993.

[Cost figures are not included in this case by request from CCI. Hockaday management determined CCI costs were competitive with other vendors.]

Step One: Team-Building for Management

Team-building for top management serves two functions: (1) facilitates management performing as a self-managing or high-performance team; and (2) enables management to develop a successful implementation plan for establishing self-managing or high-performance teams throughout the organization. Additionally, team-building for top management provides an opportunity for managers to experience the information to which all organizational members will be exposed. This experience and opportunity for evaluation assists in refining the final training design for all new organizational members.

The initial team-building training would include the following general modules:

Working with Diversity
  Awareness of personal style
  Understanding individual differences
  Moving from individual to group to team
  Appreciating work force diversity

Group Processes
  Establishing vision, focus, and goals
  Identifying roles, relationships, responsibilities
  Productively dealing with conflict and consensus

Meeting Effectiveness
  Planning and organizing
  Sharing leadership
  Task orientation
  Maintenance orientation
  Monitoring team effectiveness—the Team Management Process

Work Planning
  Job assignments
  Roles and responsibilities
  Time management
  Total quality control

Problem Solving and Innovation
  Approaches to problem solving
  Making decisions

Implementing decisions
Evaluating decisions
Persuading others

Interpersonal Skills
Communicating with clarity
Giving and receiving feedback (constructive, positive, corrective)
Active listening
Sharing leadership
Leadership and power

The modules outlined above help team members identify team purpose and build critical relationships both internal and external to the team. Individual performance issues are addressed as well as team performance. Special emphasis is given to conflict resolution, trust, and problem solving.

These modules can be presented in a four-day training or in several half-day segments. Half-day segments are preferred with work application objectives established for each segment. For this group, work objectives would center on the definition and implementation of a team plan for the entire organization. Issues of organizational structure, reward systems, individual and team recognition, responsibility, and training would be assigned to the management team. The management team's application of training principles would in effect be an application of team-building principles to the design of the organization. Additionally, the management team would evaluate the training design to determine its' fit to the organization they envision. Alterations would be expected once vision and focus are established by the management group.

Step Two: Evaluation of Training Design and Establishment of Implementation Plan

Top management involved in the initial training would meet with the consulting team to evaluate the effectiveness of the initial training design and make refinements for broad implementation.

Step Three: Implementation of Team Training

Quarterly training schedules will be established. Following each training module or modules work objectives will be set for each team. De-briefing sessions will be scheduled at appropriate intervals for all teams in order to evaluate the application of learning to practice and provide additional information as needed. De-briefing sessions can be accomplished in regularly scheduled brown-bag lunch meetings.

Step Four: Periodic Assessment

Annually, or at specified intervals during the initial 2–3 years of the project, team effectiveness audits would establish success of the project and identify additional needs or adjustments necessary for success.

Mr. Williams, we at CCI are excited about the potential of this project and would like to contribute to both training and implementation planning. I look forward to talking with you about the approach in this proposal.

Sincerely,

Pam Johnson

President, CCI

THE PLANNING MEETING

Jim Williams reserved an afternoon for the meeting with Pam Johnson. Sue, Clarence, George, and Dora were all pleased to be involved.

JIM: Pam, we like your proposal and want to figure out how we should get started. What do you think the issues are?

PAM: Jim, I'm glad you found the proposal interesting. We want to do the work because it is an exciting opportunity to be in on the ground floor of an organization. Usually, people like us get called in when problems occur and often it is too late to have the most influence. You asked me about the issues. Well, I think there are several but maybe most important is the reward and performance evaluation system you structure. You can want high-performance teams but if the reward system remains individually oriented you get a very different result. Have you worked out how you can approach this issue?

JIM: Dora and George have been looking at this issue. What do you think?

DORA: Well, the literature we have looked at is mixed. We are considering peer evaluation but some of the results are good and some are not. Also, we have to work through corporate if we were to base compensation on team versus individual metrics.

GEORGE: One thing Dora and I have discussed is having a compensation plan where teams receive x amount of merit increase for meeting their goals and then have x amount which they divide among themselves based on individual contributions to efforts. And they assess those efforts themselves.

PAM: Have you considered that some organizations just replace individual competition with team competition? One of the important things to consider is the structure of the reward and recognition system to encourage the sharing of innovation. You don't want to replace individual problems with team problems.

JIM: Pam, how would you propose we make these decisions?

PAM: Jim, I think our proposal is designed to help do that. We envision your team's training—essentially the five of you—to be an introduction to key concepts and then the application of those concepts to the design of this organization. Additionally, we will need to gather all of the potential alternatives you have for what Hockaday will actually let you do, I mean in terms of pay, performance evaluation, and development. You may want to consider adding a key HR [human resource] decision maker to your planning team. Would that work in this environment?

SUE: I think that's a good idea. If one of the VP's for HR really understood what we are attempting to do we might get more help. Jim, could we ask Diane Dugins? I think she is really willing to take risks and innovate.

JIM: I agree and I think Diane is just the right person. I will make a note to give her a call and see if we can get her on board.

PAM: Jim, in your budget planning, how many supervisors are you considering and how many people per team?

JIM: Well, I think George or Dora can best answer that. The processes vary somewhat but what would you say? Five to 9 people per team?

GEORGE: Yes, we only have two processes that will require 9 people. I wanted to keep the teams relatively small. Pam, the organization will have a technical group—Clarence will head about 25 folks in that area and Sue will have another 25. We are talking about 50–55 process teams when we have them all up and running. Dora and I will split them by process and function and then we each will have 4 supervisors working for us—8 in total. In the old days we would have at least 30 and more like 40 supervisors for this span of control.

PAM: It occurs to me you really won't have supervisors, not in any traditional sense. They will have to be more like content or process experts and coaches or facilitators. Do you agree?

GEORGE: You bet I do. You can't control anything with that number of people, and we have to be cost competitive. I think that is the excitement—letting go of that old traditional control and holding teams accountable for their own supervision. You wouldn't take away the technical support. In fact, what I said about Sue and Clarence—they will actually give us more support than before, and we will need it. Some of this new technology is complicated.

PAM: It is almost like the supervisors are going to become process consultants. That really makes this reward and performance evaluation thing critical. But just as importantly will be how all of this is consistently and clearly communicated. It will take commitment to strong communication planning.

PAM: Clarence, how much training is going to be required on the processes and technology—for the average new hire?

CLARENCE: We estimate six weeks per process. That is why we intend our hiring plan to bring on teams of people working on similar processes. We will phase in the various functions, run parallel processes with the regions for about six months, and then phase out the regions. We will start with accounts payable—I wouldn't start with payroll on a bet. People can only sue us [*Laughs*] if we get behind on payables.

PAM: We are proposing a phased training on the team-building side. I think it is going to be important to have the follow-up sessions to see where problems are or other needs emerge. You know you aren't going to get a lot of people who have worked this way. I also want to consider involving people who have been through training and are working in the processes in helping newer hires understand the culture and how this new organization works. Credibility comes from people doing the job, not just from trainers. Communication planning will include people in all types of jobs—that is probably the only way to make this flat organization work.

JIM: I know, and we want to design an assessment of some sort for our hiring process to determine if certain people are more likely to succeed in this type of environment. What do you think?

PAM: I think that is a good and tough question. What types of predispositions do you need? We can tackle that in your group's training and work.

CLARENCE: I also think we are going to have to consider how you do recognize the individual contributor. What type of career mobility do these people need and what can they expect? I know the days of upward mobility are over, but you can't sit and do the same thing forever. Not that I am really worried, the way things change around here nobody gets to stand still.

JIM: Pam, I want us to begin. When can we schedule our training.

[*Logistics are discussed and Pam agrees to provide dates to the group. She will also provide a pretraining set of questions and issues to be considered.*]

PAM: I want to be flexible with the time but am convinced the HR piece is critical and needs to be in place. Because, one thing for sure, if you start hiring before these changes are in place you will have the old hierarchical organization—a much harder thing to change.

The meeting concludes with enthusiasm and a sense of the magnitude of the task ahead.

YOUR ASSIGNMENT

1. Describe the change factors in this case (at the organizational level, the interpersonal level, the management level, and the technology level).
2. Where are likely barriers to innovation?
3. What are principal resistances to self-management or high-performance teams?
4. What predispositions and experiences contribute to an individual's productivity and satisfaction in this type of organization?
5. How would you advise Jim and his staff. Do you think a new organizational structure can be created? Why? Why not?

Joint Organizational Development Visions and Ventures: Russian and U.S. Collaboration

GAYNELLE WINOGRAD PH.D.

Conversations in a Russian hotel and a coffee house during the spring of 1990 gave birth to a new vision. Together, three U.S. and two Russian consultants began to share mutual hopes and dreams. They wanted to form a collaborative venture between Russian and U.S. consultants in organizational development (OD). Two of these futurists, Sergei Lebedev and Tantiana Kramtchenkova, were from Saint Petersburg, Russia, and represented the consulting firm, "Project." Three others—Chris Kloth, Julie Harmon, and Bob Rehm—were from the United States and comprised the consulting firm, "Changeworks."

As Bob Rehm recounted: "It started in March of 1990 when we were on the ODN Soviet Study tour. Julie, Chris, and I were part of a group of about 30 consultants who travelled to the [former] Soviet Union under the sponsorship of the Organization Development Network (ODN) for about three and a half weeks." Although they met many specialists in organizational theory, they only encountered two people, "who were truly experiencing organizational development the way we knew it." In fact, they were not even part of the tour. Bob commented, "It was just happenstance."

Prior to their visit, a professional friend and colleague, Carolyn Lukensmeyer, chief of staff for Richard Celeste, Governor of Ohio, told Chris and Julie about Tanya and Sergei, whom she had met on a trip to Russia. "Right away," Bob related, "she knew that she had uncovered a priceless gem." As a result, this team of U.S. consultants arrived in Russia with Tanya and Sergei's telephone number.

Continuing his story, Bob commented: "So very early in our tour the three of us—Julie, Chris, and I—were sitting in the hotel and decided to give it a shot to see what would happen. We didn't know Russian, the phones seldom worked. . . . Nothing works over there. But Chris picked up the phone, dialed the number, and said, 'This is Chris Kloth, and I'm looking for Sergei Lebedev.' It was Sergei and it was a beginning."

Subsequently, they arranged a meeting; Sergei and Tanya brought an interpreter because they were nervous about their ability to speak English fluently. As it turned out, they were very proficient with the English language. Their first meeting lasted for two-and-one-half hours. When recalling the conversation, Bob exclaimed: "It was the most wonderful exchange! That's when we first learned about their vision. It was amazing. As we talked back and forth, it became clear to us that we were talking to people who were doing OD work, and that was the first, and only, time we had that experience over there."

During the interchange, these innovative Russians described their team-building sessions and their model of how to change organizations. With each anecdote about their work, the Americans became even more excited. When it became time to go, Sergei asked: "When will you be in Moscow?" When the Americans reported their itinerary, he responded: "I'll meet you in Moscow. I'll find a way to get there."

To pick up on Bob's narrative again: "So a week and a half later, we found each other in Moscow, which was another adventure. Successful, fortunately, and we ended up in a little coffee shop somewhere for another three-hour meeting. That's when we really got down to the specifics about how we could invite him over and to start working together. What [Sergei] really wanted to do was make a connection with American consultants. His vision of the future was very clear and made so much sense to us from the very beginning."

Following these events Tanya and Sergei visited the United States for almost two months in the summer of 1991.

After the Russian visit, I interviewed two of the American host consultants. The following questions raise insights as to the communication challenges ahead for such cross-cultural ventures. As you will discover, even in the face of many inhibitors, the positive forces propelling these OD adventurers are still, if not more, strong.

What is your vision for your OD joint venture between Russian ("Project") and American ("Changeworks") consultants?

BOB: "In order for perestroika and transformation to be successful in Russian business environments, it will take some joint ventures between Western and Russian companies and enterprises. Sergei had been watching how joint ventures were going and said there were two reasons so many were failing. One is the lack of convertible currency. The other problem is the differences in culture.

So Sergei thought: "What if American and Russian consultants could joint venture themselves and prove it could work . . . that they could cooperate, get to know one another, work together successfully, and then provide a bridge to organizations coming together to facilitate the cross-cultural communication and business planning."

We listened to that idea and thought it made good sense. It was an attractive concept. So we started to talk about forming our own joint venture to support companies and enterprises coming together. We agreed the first step was for consultants to spend as much time in each other's culture as possible to soak it up and understand it, and have a deeper appreciation for the differences. We invited Sergei and Tanya to the United States to initiate this process.

The other part of Sergei and Tanya's vision is to see organization development as a field spread in Russia, starting in St. Petersburg. They told us there is education in organizational theory, including psychology and the social sciences, but little practical application to organizational settings. It's all in their heads. The present emphasis is on research and study. Sergei and Tanya would like to see their colleagues educated in American OD practices. So our joint venture would start by creating a conference or workshops on organization development in St. Petersburg.

CHRIS: My vision of our venture includes three primary dimensions: (1) an organization development learning community in Russia; (2) a model joint venture; and (3) a resource for Russian–American joint ventures—particularly those operating primarily in Russia.

While all three are important to me, my primary focus is the first. The core values of Changeworks have always included client empowerment through technology transfer. More simply put, to the most practical degree possible, a part of our client services includes learning to do what we do so they become less reliant on outside consultants.

My fantasy related to this part of the vision involves an organizational structure and training approach comparable to NTL (National Training Laboratory) or the Gestalt Institute. The Russians we have talked with who have studied management and organizations seem very analytical and rational. While they are very aware of the resistance of others to change, they do not seem to be in touch with their own feelings of resistance. They have very few effective strategies or skills for responding to resistance. Therefore, a strongly experiential approach will be critical.

The theoretical base for organization development is in applied behavioral sciences. Until recently these were considered false sciences in the former Soviet Union. Thus, there has been little opportunity for Russians and other Soviets to learn about organization development—much less practice it.

For Russians to rely on outsiders risks much. During our 1990 trip to Russia some of my OD colleagues had preconceived ideas on what paradigms, strategies, techniques, values, and approaches would "work" in the USSR. As the trip proceeded, these people worked hard enough at creating a force-fit that "confirmed" their beliefs. Other colleagues seemed overwhelmed and confused by what they experienced, throwing up their hands in frustration. Feedback from Soviets we talked with, including Sergei and Tanya, suggests that these two responses are common among American business, government and management consultants. Neither approach is of value.

Whereas the first part of the vision has my focus because my rational side understands it and considers it doable, my heart is more responsive to building a model joint venture. On a personal level, this part of the vision allows me to anticipate a deeper level of intimacy with Sergei and Tanya. It also offers the most challenging personal and professional risks and learning. It is also the part of the vision which I seem to fear most.

What are the major communication challenges in achieving this vision?

BOB: When I think about communication challenges, the first thing that comes to mind are the cultural biases we carry around. One of the things I learned from my visit to Russia is that we have a tendency to want everyone to be the same or to see everyone as the same.

As we travelled around the country our general response was: "When it comes down to it, we're all the same." I never believed this was true. It didn't make sense to me. Sure, on one level we are all human beings with common experiences, stories, archetypes, and mythologies. But on some other level, I realized there were things about the Russian people I really did not understand.

Whenever I talked to a Russian, at some point in the conversation, the Russian would say: "Well, this is very complex." No matter what the subject was, the Russian would always try to help me understand the complexity of the situation in Russia. It wasn't until I returned home and met Steven Rhinesmith, a scholar and consultant on Russian culture, that I understood our group's reaction and what it meant for future communications between the countries. Rhinesmith's model of cross-cultural complexity goes something like this. In the first place, when a person first visits Russia, the reaction is what we experienced.

"Isn't it wonderful; we're all the same. Unity—it's all one universe." The second phase is a little different. "We are all the same, but something is different and I am not sure what it is." That describes me on my first trip. Then, the third phase hits home when people say: "This is really complex."

Another word that comes to mind when I think about communication and the cultural differences between Americans and Russians is "paradox". The Russian people I met are comfortable with paradox. In American business we talk about the value of paradox in creativity and the importance for managers to be more comfortable with ambiguity and uncertainty in a turbulent world. We encourage our managers to be able to hold up different points of view as a way of finding creative solutions. But we have a hard time with this because it does not come naturally to Americans. In Russia it's different. One of my first questions to Sergei when we met in the St. Petersburg hotel was this: "What are your thoughts about the changes in the Soviet Union? Are you hopeful? are you pessimistic? Is it all going to fall apart?"

Typical of many Russians, Sergei's answer took about 15 minutes. Sergei reviewed a long litany of all the things going wrong in his country, all the things that are failing, all the reasons perestroika was doomed. It went on for 10 minutes, or so it seemed. I was getting depressed just listening to him and watching him sink lower in the chair. Then, at the end, Sergei smiled, sat up, and said: "And of course, I'm optimistic." This is a good example of how Russians look at their world through paradoxical eyes. "Yes, things are terrible, *and,* we are moving to a better future."

Sergei and Tanya, like most Russians we talked to, do not expect things to change or improve quickly. If the coup succeeded, for instance, they do not believe that event would stop the larger movement toward democracy. They see themselves on a generational path. The changes they want are not expected to occur in the next three quarters, the way we tend to see things in this country. It took Moses 40 years in the desert with the Israelites, and so too, in Russia, people believe generations will come and go before their transformation is complete.

This comfort with paradox came home to me when Sergei, Tanya, and I would disagree or argue about certain points. For instance, one day the three of us sat around the table with a notebook. We took turns drawing and describing models of change and development. After one person would draw and explain a model, we would discuss and argue about the model. Then we moved on to another model and then another. We never came to resolution on any of the models, nor did Sergei or Tanya think that was important. The differences were OK with them. Conflict resolution did not occur to them at all.

As I think about communication issues and organization development in Russia, the American concept of facilitation comes to mind. Organization Development grew up in democratic societies and facilitation is one of its main tools. Steven Rhinesmith told me one day: "Facilitation is a profoundly democratic concept." Facilitation is alien in nondemocratic environments, which may describe why it is so difficult to introduce into American companies. Facilitation is middle ground between the extremes of open freedom and chaos on the one hand and totalitarian control. The Russians I talked to see those two extremes but have no experience with the middle ground. On the ODN Study Tour, we facilitated many meetings and the Russians' reactions were interesting to watch. In one meeting, three of us led a discussion with a group of Soviet entrepreneurs. We asked each person to write down their reactions to a question we asked. Then, in a nominal group technique format, we asked each person to share their point so it could be recorded on flip chart paper. We had simultaneous translators helping with the facilitation. One of them actually wrote the answers in Russian on one page while an American wrote in English on another page. The experience was awkward for the group at first.

The Russians were expecting either a free for all or a highly controlled lecture, not something this alien and unusual. And the idea of seeing their words written for all to see was especially unnerving. What could be more dangerous in a totalitarian environment than having your words in public for all to see. But we did it, and they started to enjoy it. We were surprised to realize that flip chart paper could be such a revolutionary innovation.

So, in the end we began to realize that, of course, we are all one, but there are complex differences between Russians and Americans that joint ventures need to come to grips with. At this point in the development of our relationship with Sergei and Tanya it is clear to me that we are still at the tip of the iceberg of human understanding. And, if that's true, maybe our consulting joint venture can pave the way for companies struggling with the same issues.

CHRIS: We anticipate a number of communication challenges. While Sergei and Tanya speak very good English, the fact that our Russian language is so weak means that Tanya and Sergei consistently have to be responsible for clarifying communication. Bob, Julie, and I have improved our ability to understand the structure and nuances of the Russian language, but we have a long way to go.

One example of this difficulty is the name of their enterprise. On their business cards, and in their pronunciation, the company is called, "Project." When we were discussing the names we could use for our joint venture, I expressed a concern that "project" in English sounds like a short-term effort or a tangent, something extra, something that we work on for a limited period of time. However, the Russian pronunciation for "project" is more similar to our word combination "proact" or "proactive." Their pronunciation sounds like "proact." The more we discussed their pronunciation, the more it became clear that their understanding of the word is very closely related to our word "proactive," which seemed like a very appropriate name for the activity we envision.

Another difficulty we face is in the realm of symbolic communication. The symbols and metaphors in the Russian language are quite different from those in English. In fact, there seems to be more of an emphasis on symbol and metaphor in the Russian language as we've experienced it so far.

One phrase which I have been challenged by in our discussions has been Sergei's frequent reference to "destroying" organizations. His understanding of how Russians change is based on the notion that, before someone can move on to a new way of working or thinking, the old ways must be completely destroyed. . . . Over time, I began to realize that his understanding of what they do in this phase of dealing with change is much more humane than it sounded to me. However, this is in contrast with American expressions which focus more on creating new visions and moving toward them.

Communication of feelings will also be challenging. Most of our communication will be by mail, telephone, and fax making it hard to sense feelings. Attending to nuance will be difficult. Furthermore in the rare circumstances when we talk on the telephone, the equipment in Russia makes it very difficult to hear very clearly.

Another element related to communicating feelings has to do with the immediacy and urgency which Tanya and Sergei feel most of the time about the change process in the Soviet Union. This is obviously quite natural. Their lives are directly affected on a daily basis. The fact that we are in the United States makes it difficult for us to have the same feelings.

One of the interesting communication dilemmas we've faced already is translating English to Russian. In addition to the colloquial and idiomatic expressions which make up a significant portion of both languages, the field of organization development has its own unique language. Some of our phrases, such as "capturing learnings," "visioning," "appreciative inquiry," "empowerment," "sociotechnical systems," and others, just don't translate very well.

Cross-cultural communication presents other challenges. Several experiences come to mind, and one in particular is worth sharing. Early in their trip to the United States, Tanya and Sergei had indicated to Bob that conducting "negotiations" during meals, particularly in restaurants, was very difficult.

Later, in Ohio, we had what Julie and I considered a lunch meeting to "get to know" some people from the Foreign Trade Office of the Columbus Chamber of Commerce. On the way home, Sergei said it was very difficult to conduct negotiations during such a lunch meeting. I was startled since I had not noticed any "negotiating" going on. We learned that, for Sergei, any business communication, including serious rapport-building . . . was a "negotiation."

The learning was not over. After traveling together on a whale watch off the shore of Cape Cod, we had dinner near the wharf. While we were waiting for dinner, we had continued to talk very seriously about our joint venture agreement and were conducting what I considered negotiations. Sergei had been persistent in his efforts to assure that these negotiations were finished before we left Cape Cod.

Shortly after our dinner arrived, I noticed Sergei's face looking extremely distant and disengaged from our conversation, which had continued to be on the subject of our agreement. I finally said, "Sergei, you look very distant." After a hesitant silence, Sergei and Tanya finally explained that discussing business during a meal is considered extremely rude and impolite. On a much deeper level than the distractions and the lack of privacy, which were both real concerns to them, there was this deep cultural aversion to behaving in this way during meals. They were only comfortable mentioning their concern after we had spent much time together. My primary learning from this experience is the importance of sensitivity to cultural behavior which operates at a deeper level than verbal communication.

Developing trust and rapport is essential to communicating cross-culturally. In this example it took two months of building rapport before the real values issue surfaced. The early stages of rapport-building, characterized by politeness, limited the depth of our early communication.

How has your vision changed since the historic events of August 1991?

BOB: The vision has not changed. As time passes we become more aware of the level of persistence and patience it will take to stay with it long term. The only down turn for me is that getting joint ventures going in the next few years is difficult. American companies are understandably leery of investing in Russian companies because of the lack of social stability. And of course this is when they need it most.

CHRIS: The essential elements of the vision for our joint venture as I see it have not changed in any way as the result of the coup. If there is any change in the vision, it has more to do with the sense of urgency that I feel about moving ahead. The difficulty is that financial circumstances as well as structural issues in the Soviet Union make it difficult to act on this sense of urgency, therefore, at this stage, I also feel a higher degree of frustration.

YOUR ASSIGNMENT

1. Using intercultural/international communication theory as a guide, identify the numerous communication issues presented in the interview narratives.
2. Describe the strengths of this type of joint venture? The weaknesses? How would you advise both the U.S. and Russian consultants as they begin to work together?
3. Using this case as a basis, develop a model for intercultural/international communication to be utilized by those engaged in joint ventures.
4. Describe the multiple innovations described in this case.
5. Identify cultural differences and similarities as evidenced in the case. Discuss the Russian concept of complexity. How does complexity relate to organizational communication theory?

CHAPTER 10

Organizational Communication in the Twenty-first Century

The Educational Revolution

> The physicist Murray Gell-Mann has remarked that education in the twentieth century is like being taken to the world's greatest restaurant and being fed the menu. He meant that representations of ideas have replaced the ideas themselves; students are taught superficially about great discoveries instead of being helped to learn deeply for themselves.
>
> Alan C. Kay, "Computers, Networks and Education,"
> *Scientific American,* September 1991

The Date: September 2002

The Settings: Three classrooms equipped with powerful computers networked to resources throughout the world. (One is a ninth-grade classroom in a public school; another is the training room of a major corporation; and the third is a public access multimedia lab in a local library.) The computers are fitted to all senses—there are displays for vision; pointing devices and keyboards for responding to gesture; speakers, piano-type keyboards and microphones for sound; television cameras for recording and playback as well as prerecorded review. Alan Kay, as long ago as 1991, outlined the potential benefits of this technology: (1) greater interactivity; (2) the capability of computers to become any and all types of media—print, visual, or musical; (3) information presented from multiple perspectives; (4) the use of simulation; (5) model-building capabilities designed with reflective flexibility; and (6) networked computers providing a universal library.

The Assignments: The ninth-grade students are studying the judicial process; the corporate employees are preparing for upcoming foreign assignments; and a group of individuals visiting the local library is using the library's new career assessment program.

Your Assignments: Using Alan Kay's potential benefits of advanced computer technologies, describe how each group of students might use the computer and communications technologies available to them. What are their opportunities, challenges, and potential problems? What communication competencies are they required to possess to utilize these approaches to learning? What do your answers imply for the concept of communications literacy?

Next review the following positions (synthesized from published quotes) and consider their implications for human communication and educational organizations of 2002.

The cost of advanced learning technologies is enormous. We are creating a two-class educational system—we must either invest heavily in achieving parity across educational systems or we will pay the price of increasing illiteracy.

> The parent of an inner-city school child

If the personally owned book was one of the main shapers of the Renaissance notion of the individual, then the pervasively networked computer of the future should shape humans who are healthy skeptics from an early age. Any argument can be tested against the arguments of others and by appeal to simulation. Philip Morrison, a learned physicist, has a fine vision of a skeptical world: ''Genuine trust implies the opportunity of checking wherever it may be wanted. . . . That is why it is the evidence, the experience itself and the argument that gives it order, that we need to share with one another, and not just the unsupported final claim.''

> Alan Kay, fellow of Apple Computer, a
> founder and fellow of the Xerox Palo Alto
> Research Center, chief scientist of Atari,
> in *Scientific American,* September, 1991

Advanced technologies can engage students in a more active process of thinking and problem solving, however, open-ended subjects such as moral philosophy, religion, historical interpretation, literary criticism, or social theory may not be benefited as much because they cannot be reduced to formal rules and procedures.

> Derek Bok, President of Harvard
> in *Harvard* magazine, 1986

The sheer volume of our options and the explosion of information has dulled our senses, challenged us yes, and caused us to retreat to more primary experiences.

> Corporate Research and Development Manager.

Our technological development outstrips our human development. They should go hand in hand but they don't.

> Graduate student, 1991

YOUR ASSIGNMENT

1. What are the implications of an educational revolution for human communication and organizational structures?
2. Describe the communications literary of the year 2000 and beyond.
3. What does the term *life-long learning* mean for communication and for organizations engaged in teaching and learning?
4. How can an organization foster a learning environment?
5. Describe your own vision of the classrooms of 2002.

Organizing and Communicating: Changing Processes

> The most profound technologies are those that disappear. They weave themselves into the fabric of everyday life until they are indistinguishable from it. . . . We are therefore trying to conceive a new way of thinking about computers, one that takes into account the human world and allows the computers themselves to vanish into the background. . . . Some of us use the term "embodied virtuality" to refer to the process of drawing computers out of their electronic shells. The "virtuality" of computer-readable data—all the different ways in which they can be altered, processed and analyzed—is brought into the physical world.
>
> Mark Weiser, "The Computer in the 21st Century," *Scientific American*, September 1991

The Year: 2020

The Setting: A leadership, participation, and management symposium in Aspen, Colorado, U.S.A.

The Subject: The changing processes of leadership and management.

The Participants: Businesspeople from ten nations, academics who study organizational communication and management, and undergraduate and graduate students from universities in the ten participating countries. The countries represented are: England, Italy, the United States, the Association of Soviet Republics, Germany, Ghana, France, Canada, Mexico, and Japan. Participants are divided into issue groups, each having access to a vast array of information technologies to support their pursuits.

Your Role: Identify yourself as a businessperson, academic, or student. Select your country of origin. Consider the implications of the following issues for organizing, communicating, and leadership and management. Attempt to determine how your role identification influenced your thinking.

The Issues: Over 4 million middle management jobs have disappeared worldwide during the last 25 years. Information technologies have reduced the need for human coordination of work while increasing the amount of actual coordination. Organizations have less well-defined boundaries, are flatter, and more fluid. What are the leadership, participation, management, and communication implications of these changes?

Those who formally aspired to management positions now seek responsibility for special projects. It is not uncommon to lead 10 to 15 projects within the course of a ten-year career span. New services are continually created and product life-cycles are shortened with products increasingly specialized to particular markets. What are the leadership, participation, management, and communication implications of these changes?

In manufacturing, companies all along the production chain are linked to respond quickly to customer demands while dramatically reducing inventories. Sales in a given market electronically trigger orders, shipping, and production activities through a multiorganizational structure. The reductions in inventory costs alone have more than paid for the required technologies. Competitors in a given industry frequently are technologically linked to expand market potential and share information and resources necessary to maximize individual profits. Orders get shifted from an overloaded organization to another with excess capacity. Companies are smaller than they were in the late twentieth century and rewards are closely linked to group performance. What are the leadership, participation, management, and communication implications of these changes?

Power is not as centralized in management hierarchies as in previous times. Decision making occurs throughout the organization. Organizational chaos has occurred at times when individual interests subvert the larger organizational good. Some contend this has been a problem for over 200 years; others blame new information technologies and adhocracy. What are the leadership, participation, management, and communication implications of these changes?

More people work at home than at any time since before the industrial revolution. It is common for task groups to be geographically and internationally diverse. People commonly belong to problem-solving groups several years following formal retirement and part-time and job-sharing assignments are common. What are the leadership, participation, management, and communication implications of these changes?

Professional loyalty and affiliation is more important than organization-specific ties. People frequently change organizational affiliations and corporate management seeks better and more innovative reward structures to retain talented people. What are the leadership, participation, management, and communication implications of these changes?

Managers often are responsible for work assignments to individuals they have not met in face-to-face interactions. Teleconferencing, electronic mail, and computer conferencing have replaced much corporate travel. Most people report confidence in information exchanges but note a general deficiency in interactions contributing to individual development. What are the leadership, participation, management, and communication implications of these changes?

YOUR ASSIGNMENT

1. Describe the human communication issues in the environments described in our Aspen symposium.
2. Describe leadership and participation responsibilities and competencies necessary for the new environments of the twenty-first century.
3. What are the strengths of these new organizing and communicating processes? The weaknesses?
4. Will information technology interactions replace face-to-face interactions for decision making? If so, what are the implications? If not, why?
5. How can the student of today prepare for an information-intensive future?

The New Communications Literacy

Harold wanted to be manager of the field sales team for Minkin Industries' frozen food lines. Harold, John, and Diane had worked together in product development and later in marketing for the frozen food lines. All three were considered top contributors, which made them highly competitive for the management position.

Harold was surprised that John and Diane had not applied for the manager's job. The three of them had worked together for over five years and promotional opportunities were rare. Although Harold wanted the job he knew both John and Diane were highly qualified. He determined he would ask them as soon as the selection process was over.

The successful manager applicant would be responsible for a sales team located in 15 states and 5 foreign countries. Product sales and competitor data were compiled daily through the company's computer network, pricing changes were made several times per week, and the group met monthly by video tele-conference. In addition, the manager used compressed video technology to have face-to-face discussions with individual salespeople experiencing problems or opening new accounts. Minkin planned to expand into 20 new states and 2 foreign countries over the next five years. The new manager would be expected to use video technology to interview, hire, and train new sales personnel. The company anticipated creating two assistant sales manager positions to support the expansion. Harold believed this was his dream job.

Harold invited John and Diane to have lunch with him to celebrate the news of his promotion. Both responded favorably and early conversation recalled their days in product development and marketing. John and Diane both seemed genuinely pleased by the announcement. Eventually Harold was compelled to ask why they had not applied. The silence that followed was telling. Finally, Diane revealed what Harold wanted to know.

Neither John nor Diane believed they could motivate a sales staff without face-to-face interaction. Although both were comfortable enough in participating in teleconferences, they expressed serious concerns about interviewing, hiring, and training in such a manner. John knew the approach was cost competitive and futuristic but doubted his own ability to use the new media as the leader of a large group. John and Diane were comfortable with interactive computer technologies but the merged approaches that supported audio and video interactivity were another story. Harold reminded them that for more than 20 years the company had supported distance education using these same technologies. He was surprised they doubted their abilities to be effective leaders using similar approaches. Harold hoped they would reconsider their positions and think about becoming his new assistants. John and Diane thanked Harold for his support but made no commitments to reconsider.

YOUR ASSIGNMENT

1. What challenges does video interactivity pose for human communication? For motivation?
2. How does video interactivity differ from traditional computer interactivity? How is it similar? What are potential strengths? Weaknesses?
3. What communication competencies are particularly important for video interactivity?
4. How would you advise Diane and John? What is the potential impact of their decisions on their career futures? What would you tell Harold?
5. Describe the concept of a new communications literacy.

The New Organizational Control: Knowledge Masters

> Knowledge itself, therefore, turns out to be not only the source of the highest-quality power, but also the most important ingredient of force and wealth. Put differently, knowledge has gone from being an adjunct of money power and muscle power, to being their very essence. It is, in fact, the ultimate amplifier. This is the key to the *powershift* that lies ahead, and it explains why the battle for control of knowledge and the means of communication is heating up all over the world.
>
> Alvin Toffler, in *Powershift,*
> Bantam Books, New York, 1990

The executive committee of Hudson Retail Supply is meeting in emergency session prior to the annual board of directors meeting slated for January 14, 2002. Les Hedrin, CEO of Hudson, has learned the president of the board, Mary Watson, intends to demand a reorganization strategy from the executive committee in response to declining profits during the past four consecutive quarters. Mary, a tough-minded businessperson, believes Hudson has not kept pace with changes in the industry and that Les Hedrin, in particular, is resistant to change.

Hedrin opens the executive committee meeting by describing his call from Jack Miller, vice-president of the board, alerting him to Mary Watson's intentions. Les reports Jack believes there will be considerable support for Mary's proposal. Present at the meeting are Tim Watson, marketing vice-president; Joan Grieder, chief information officer; Roy Stanley, vice-president for finance; John Hernandez, vice-president for operations; and Rhonda Hunt, vice-president for product development and acquisition. Missing from the meeting is Roger Davis, vice-president for sales.

Hudson Retail Supply has been in business for over 75 years; it grew from modest beginnings as a regional appliance wholesaler in upper New York State to a $200 million supplier of major appliances to discount retailers. Over the past 10 years Hudson has developed a direct-order business for individual customers by utilizing excess capacity on its advanced computer order, manufacturing, and delivery system. Hudson does business in all 50 states plus Canada and Mexico, and is known for quality, affordable products; good customer service for both retail and direct accounts; and steady if somewhat sluggish growth. Les Hedrin has been CEO of Hudson for 8 years and has come up through the ranks of both sales and product development and acquisition. All but one member of his executive committee are experienced Hudson people; Joan Grieder joined Hudson 3 years ago to head the acquisition of extensive computer networks to manage sales, manufacturing, service, and delivery functions. Joan is considered an expert in communications and information systems and has been welcomed by most members of the executive committee.

Executive committee members know Mary Watson believes the Hudson hierarchy results in bureaucratic decision making. Les, in particular, believes Hudson's long-term success is a result of continuing central coordination even though some of his staff and many consultants suggest the demands of changing markets and new technologies make central coordination and control obsolete. Les asks the committee for their evaluation of the current situation.

ROY: Les, we can't ignore that we have stalled. We are experiencing losses, but the market is not stagnant—we are. I think we should consider a reorganization.

JOAN: Roy is right. We have too many layers of management and don't let people with the immediate hands-on information make the decisions at the sales or account level.

RHONDA: I know, everything you read and hear, everything the consultants tell us—change, flat, smaller, more responsibility at the individual level—but I don't quite see how that works. What about accountability and responsibility? Who controls that?

JOAN: Well, an executive committee can get more information than ever. Our systems don't really support the chaos you are describing; the thing is really, how do you free people to make decisions? Let them go. We will get the results immediately. Now we don't make some of the decisions in a timely fashion. For example, our data on sales inquiries from the direct customer business suggest that we need a new line of kitchen computers; we haven't even decided to go into the investigation stage much less act on this increasing market. Johnson products announced yesterday they will have a new line of kitchen computing and control devices ready for Christmas 2002. We can't get there before 2003 unless we act today. We have had the information about feature sets from our customer requests but we can't seem to move.

TIM: I agree with Joan. We should preempt Mary Watson and propose a reorganization strategy for the board to consider. We could shift many of our middle managers to special projects and organize smaller field sales groups to manage their own sales, manufacturing, and service units by product lines.

LES: Wait a minute, how can you say we should uproot everything that has worked for so many years. Sure we all hear bureaucracy is dead, but no one can tell me what really replaces it.

JOHN: Les, information and communication strategies replace our old top-heavy systems. We have got to let smaller groups of people make fast decisions and then implement. It takes letting go because they can have the information in their hands the same day a shift in the market takes place. That has been happening for several years now. We need to let them go. We can monitor daily as we have been doing. It doesn't give us less power, it shifts power to the appropriate level and lets us take it back if necessary. I don't think we need to run all the basic innovation from this level.

TIM: Les, has one point. People have the information but have not been used to that type of responsibility. I am afraid a lot of our people are not ready for that type of leadership. They are good folks but they are used to management layers making most of the decisions. It would take an entirely different reward structure and a belief that failing once in a while will not only be tolerated but encouraged.

LES: I can't quite get behind "failing is encouraged."

JOAN: Well, Les, we are failing right now. I don't think you want to get behind that either.

RHONDA: We have to make some changes. I have a report here on international competition that is heating up. If we are struggling with domestic folks just wait two or three more years. Les, we love you, but . . .

LES: But, you are telling me Mary Watson is right. I agree, but it will take such effort to make the changes, and I feel unsure of where we are headed.

TIM: Les, we are all unsure of the result, but we are sure Hudson goes down the tubes if we don't change.

JOAN: Les, we need to begin to draw some plans and evaluate how to become more flexible. We have good people working for Hudson, we can enhance their abilities and careers with some creative but sound moves. Putting decision making and innovation with smaller units does not cubbyhole information. We will have all the information we can handle. That's the problem. We aren't dealing with what we have in a timely fashion. We have to experiment.

LES: I know, I really do know. The question is, where do we begin?

YOUR ASSIGNMENT

1. Describe your conception of the statement, "Knowledge is the most important form of power in organizations of the twenty-first century."
2. How would you advise Les Hedrin? The members of the executive committee? Is Hedrin correct that many people don't want increased decision responsibility? Support your answer.
3. What types of organizational structures seem likely as information becomes increasingly available and "democraticized" and power distributions change throughout organizations?
4. What are the advantages of new organizational structures? The disadvantages?
5. How will new forms of organizing and organizations impact organizational communication?

Individuals and Organizations in the Twenty-first Century: Changing Roles and Relationships

During the last decade of the twentieth century most were aware of a technology revolution that was reshaping organizations into the first decades of the next century. Some called it the knowledge revolution—beyond the information age—an age where the expansion of knowledge and technical interactivity were interdependent. The prime technologies of the information age—television, computers, telephones, and stereos—had been successfully merged by the turn of the twenty-first century. An array of multimedia hybrids provided incentives to build high-capacity, fiber-optic communications systems that crossed and connected countries in much the same way as the old transportation systems of the nineteenth and twentieth centuries.

The year is 2010. Commercial and home applications of multimedia technologies mix video, sound, text, and graphics; this allows users to interact, customizing information to all types of needs and tastes. Television sets have high definition clarity and average 400 to 600 channels. Sets serve as home computers, compact-disc players, telephones, and libraries. Interactivity is advanced; shopping, banking, working, consulting with doctors and attorneys, and going to school via technology all are common.

You are about to meet individuals in four different families: Marv and Sally Fuller, Dee and Donald Tiffin, Arlene Kulick, and George Reynolds. All live in Minneapolis and all illustrate different types of interactions with the organizations of the twenty-first century.

Marv Fuller is a salesperson for a large multimedia technology manufacturer. Marv is comfortable with the technology, and spends at least one-third of his work week communicating with customers from his home. Using his fully networked equipment, Marv makes sales calls, send proposals to customers, generates reports for his boss, and processes what used to be called paperwork. Marv's children are technology literate and are studying two foreign languages with a miniature version of his system, called the home entertainment unit. Marv's wife, Sally, is an attorney who works at her home office approximately 35 hours per week. Sally spends less than 2 hours per week in the courtroom and only rarely has face-to-face client meetings. She and several other attorneys share an electronically equipped conference office, one of the new trends among professionals desiring to reduce office overhead. Marv and Sally enjoy an affluent standard of living. They are highly educated and expect their children to spend increasing amounts of time in distance education programs, working with home technology. Marv and Sally believe the evolving technology is excellent in almost all respects. They are concerned, however, that adequate safeguards for privacy of individual information may not be present in some systems. Sally particularly is concerned about the growing capability of many retailers to profile individual buyers through extensive analysis of purchasing patterns.

Dee and Donald Tiffin are not as pleased with the progress of the last 10 years. Dee, a production worker for a major computer company, has been unemployed for the past 11 months. Robotics and new artificial intelligence programs have contributed to layoffs in her industry and in numerous plant closures, including the one where Dee had worked for 17 years. Dee has a high school degree and extensive experience with manufacturing processes using computers and statistical quality control. She can hardly believe her skill level is now considered marginal. She does not know where to turn. Donald's job appears steady but his earnings alone are insufficient to send their two children to college. Donald works as manager for the food services department of a local hospital. Dee is afraid to consider leaving Minneapolis because of Donald's work. Dee and Donald have a home computer and a small inexpensive multimedia unit. They have limited interactivity and neither have worked at home. Dee believes all this progress has hurt many people. She is fond of saying, "The rich get rich and the poor get poorer."

Arlene Kulick is a widow and sole support of her aging mother. Arlene works for a local bank and employs home care for her mother during work hours. Arlene spends most of her 40-hour work week solving problems customers encounter with the myriad of electronic banking services. Arlene believes at least one-half of the bank's customers do not understand the available interactive programs for reconciling account balances. Arlene gets tired of explaining processes she contends should be easy for people to understand. Arlene cannot afford a home multimedia system. Her mother dislikes the technologies and criticizes Arlene for saving money to purchase a home unit. And Arlene resents not being able to use public access systems at night and on weekends because she must care for her mother. Sometimes Arlene considers participating in the bank's new telecommuting work force. She hesitates, however, largely because she is not sure she can stay at home all day even if someone is present to care for her mother.

George Reynolds is 19 years old and has never held a job. He dropped out of high school in the tenth grade, and tried to join the military when he turned 18. George tested for several positions and was refused based on his inability to exhibit any type of communications or technical literacy. George is bitter. He lives with his parents and spends most of his days hanging around the neighborhood playing computer games with his friends. George rarely wins anymore and some of his friends believe he is doing drugs on an infrequent basis. George does not have a bank account, does not own a car, and no one in his neighborhood has any of the new home multimedia systems. George has been offered an opportunity by an old friend to join her at night GED classes. George has refused because the instructor reportedly will force all the students to learn to use computers.

All very different stories. Yet these individuals and families all face changing roles and relationships with contemporary organizations based in part on advanced technologies. And, to some extent, markets for the technologies of the middle and late twenty-first century will be shaped by the relationships these individuals in 2010 forge with the organizations of the knowledge age.

YOUR ASSIGNMENT

1. Describe how technology influences individual relationships to organizational life. Discuss all of the different relationships identified in the profiles.
2. How will ready access to highly specialized and individualized information alter our common understanding of events or processes? Or will it? Argue your position.
3. Many are concerned about a growing polarization between "technology haves" and "technology have nots." Discuss the implications of this concern.
4. Describe how multimedia technology will influence power distributions in organizations, in education, in political processes, and in family relationships.
5. With increased specialization of information comes the potential for "information fragmentation." In the 1990s we have been concerned about common understanding, shared realities, and how organizational cultures emerge and are maintained. Given the technologies of 2010, predict how we will describe organizational culture and communication processes.

Conversations

The final set of conversations are in response to three basic questions: (1) What are the technical telecommunications trends for the next several years? (2) As we approach the twenty-first century, what do you see as the major issues for educational use of telecommunications? (3) What are the emergent issues in organizational communication?

The Industrial Edge Lies in Telecommunications

WITH NEIL JOHNSON, TECHNICAL CONSULTANT, U.S. WEST COMMUNICATIONS

What are the technical telecommunications trends for the next several years?

JOHNSON: The world is indeed in a state of change technologically. Here at U.S. West Communications change is happening in order to meet the demand that our customers require, sometimes on a daily basis. Some of those changes are:

More and more customers are wanting larger bandwidths for data communications. Individual data circuits from 1,200 Kbps to 56 Kbps are quickly becoming too slow for customers' increased demand for data transport. Even 1.544 MBPS (our T-1 carrier rate) is quickly becoming too small for some of the larger customers, which require DS-3 rate fiber optics (45 MBPS) to accommodate the Enterprise Networks being established.

Video teleconferencing is beginning to be used in more than just the corporate world. Schools are now using distance learning applications to broaden the horizons of their district by remote access to collegiate courses. Health sciences are using video teleconferencing for tele-radiology and universities are using video teleconferencing to keep teachers current with their recertification classes.

Bandwidths of up to 45 MBPS are still too narrow for some futuristic thinkers. Plans are in development to prepare us for the future with SMDS [Switched Multi-megabit Data Services, Frame Relay], FDDI [Fiber Distributed Data Interface], B-ISDN [Broadband Integrated Services Digital Network], [and] SONET [Synchronous Optical Network]. These services, as standards and equipment are developed and deployed, bring us into the future with up to gigabits of information per second.

The Educational Edge Lies in Telecommunications

WITH SHELLY WEINSTEIN, PRESIDENT, EDSAT INSTITUTE

As we approach the twenty-first century, what do you see as the major issues for educational use of telecommunications?

WEINSTEIN: There is no doubt in my mind that it will be the extent to which this nation integrates telecommunications, in all of its forms in teaching and learning in schools, colleges, universities, and libraries.

Today, as in past eras of democratic social reform, change is taking place because of society's disillusionment with government's performance—in this case, the performance of America's schools, rapid transformation in every sector of our lives which has been brought about by technology, and the capacity of telecommunications to empower the individual. By necessity this change must be deep and systemic if the economy and society of the United States are to meet the global challenges of our "information age."

What are the current problems?

WEINSTEIN: There is a well-documented crisis in American education. Although public education is a constitutional responsibility of the states, commonwealths, and territories, the consequences of a failed education system affect the nation as a whole. Not only is the quality of American education generally substandard, there are also significant differences from one community to another in the quality of educational opportunities available.

Another piece of the problem is that, at a time when the nation's students are testing close to or at the bottom of national and international standards in math, sciences, and languages, the U.S. Chamber of Commerce estimates that 42 percent of the work force (49.5 million people) will need retraining over the next 10 years to keep pace with employers skill demands. Not included in this number are the approximately 37 million workers who will need entry-level training. Additionally, the nation's governors have adopted a set of education goals for the Year 2000. They would have every adult literate, possess the knowledge and skills necessary to compete in a global economy, and exercise effectively their rights of citizenship.

As the nation pursues these seemingly herculean challenges while facing barriers of teacher shortages, retraining needs, budget deficits, mounting problems for youth at risk, and increasing costs of delivering programs for the unserved and underserved, there can be no question that the states must make the most cost-beneficial use of public resources and teachers if they are to succeed in improving the quality and productivity of America's schools.

Where does telecommunications fit this picture?
WEINSTEIN: Unquestionably, an integrated satellite-based telecommunications system linked with existing cable and telephone lines holds a part of the promise to provide quality educational opportunity which is equitable and affordable for all youths and adults, regardless of the wealth of their school, their geographical location, or the density of their population.

How do America's educational institutions measure up in their access and utilization of telecommunications for the delivery of instructional programming, teaching, and educational resources? How is the nation measuring up in its investment in educational access and use of telecommunications?
WEINSTEIN: International standards and measures closely tie a nation's economic development and productivity to telecommunications development, i.e., telephones, radios, television sets, computers, and other equipment. If these standards were to be applied to America's telecommunications infrastructure dedicated to education, in my view, we would find that the education sector roughly resembles that of a developing nation. Today, the U.S. invests only about $100 per student in education in computers and capital investment compared to $50,000 per worker in private industry, and $100,000 per worker in high-tech companies. While the rest of America created a $20 billion-a-year industry by putting 45 million personal computers into use during the last 10 years, United States schools acquired anywhere from 2 to 2.5 million computers, worth about $2 billion.

What are the benefits of increased use of telecommunications?
WEINSTEIN: Universal, equitable access to the rich education resources of the nation is possible—in part—through telecommunications. Although telecommunications has turned the world into a "global village," America's schools, for the most part, have remained relatively isolated enterprises. The encouraging news is that this situation is changing rapidly. My organization, the EdSat Institute, released a report entitled, "An Analysis of a Proposal for an Education Satellite," on February 26, 1991. It found that individual states are beginning to invest heavily in telecommunications technology as one approach to sharing educational resources.

The communications technologies through which these programs are delivered at the local level include optical fiber, co-axial cable, microwave and fixed-based broadcast television, as well as the receivers of satellite transmissions.

All land-based technologies are essential to a complete telecommunications infrastructure and currently satellites are the best means by which to distribute multiple education programs simultaneously to every part of a state and the nation at a relatively low unit cost.

There are at least 55,000 educational sites receiving telecommunications programming across the country. Sixteen percent of the nation's school districts have satellite dishes and 23 percent of the schools within these districts have dishes. There are at least 111 providers of satellite-based educational programming. The economics of the communications revolution and the needs of the education sector make it imperative that the states, education institutions, the private sector, and the Congress must join together to make telecommunications in all forms, available in the classrooms of the nation.

What does all this mean to you?

WEINSTEIN: As a people, Americans have a long history of "looking forward," always striving to make things better. As a nation, we have learned that "transportation infrastructures" are effective and economical when they provide access to and for increasingly greater numbers of users; and when the primary systems link and interconnect through multiple secondary transportation systems, both those existing and those still to be built. America's interstate highway transportation system gave the American family access to employment, housing, education opportunities, and other social benefits which far exceeded our greatest expectations and dreams.

For those of us who share this vision for the "information age," there is no doubt that even greater economic and social benefits will accrue from an integrated telecommunications system that transports America's rich and abundant educational resources to all children and adults regardless of wealth and geographic location.

Governor Wallace Wilkinson of the commonwealth of Kentucky reminds us that we already know how to make some schools better; what we need to do now is to make all schools better. We must begin to build a telecommunications highway dedicated to deliver education resources for the education sector to be competitive and effective well into the twenty-first century.

Emergent Issues in Organizational Communication

WITH GARY L. KREPS, PH.D.

What do you see as the emergent issues in organizational communication as we approach the twenty-first century?

KREPS: Modern organizational life is rife with uncertainty and equivocality, seriously challenging organizational actors to make sense and take charge of their organizational destinies. In the future I suspect that organizational life will grow increasingly complex and challenging as a result of many uncertainties wrought by rapidly changing organizational environments. The ever-increasing complexity of modern organizational life will subject organizational actors to a wide array of new challenges and constraints. Changes in international competition and interdependency, technologies, markets, work-loads, socio-economic trends, as well as changing systems of organizational oppression and dominance will increase the equivocality of modern life, making the following six issues increasingly salient for organizational communication inquiry:

1. How can communication be used to help organizational actors cope with increasing levels of stress? Individual stress levels will inevitably increase as the difficulties organizational actors have in coping with complexity increase. The emergent nature of organizing will force strategies for responding to these situations, predict outcomes of actions taken, and make far-reaching strategic decisions about future organizational activities, often with limited information. Future organizational communication inquiry will examine the central role of human communication in interpreting equivocality and helping to maintain optimal levels of stress in organizational life.

2. How can communication be used to promote ethical behavior in organizational life? There are serious ethical improprieties in modern organizational life, where people are lied to, treated unfairly, denied employment, sexually harassed, and given unfair advantages in business, professional, government, human service, educational, and even religious organizations (which further exacerbates the stresses felt by organizational actors). The ways organization members communicate with one another demonstrates relative levels of respect, honesty, integrity, equity, and responsibility that underlay organizational ethics. Since ethical dimensions of organizational life are inextricably tied to organizational communication processes, where communication patterns express the moral character of organizational life, an important trend in organizational communication inquiry will be to examine ethical issues and develop strategies for promoting ethical behavior in organizational life.

3. How can communication be used to enhance personal satisfaction and growth in organizational life? The quality of interpersonal communication in organizations has a major influence on the development of meaning-ful and satisfying organizational relationships. The provision of social support and the use of therapeutic communication in organizations can help organizational actors make sense of organizational life and strategically direct behaviors to accomplish personal and organizational goals. An important trend in organizational communication inquiry will be to examine the ways interpersonal communication can be used to humanize organizational life.

4. How can communication be used to promote effective multicultural relations within organizations and within interorganizational fields? The

role of communication in promoting cultural sensitivity between organizational actors from different national, ethnic, racial, and gender orientations will be increasingly important in the future. Not only is the future work force becoming more culturally diverse, but widespread development and adoption of advanced communication technologies will decrease the functional distance between peoples and nations. This will transform the world into a "global village" with a high level of international interdependency, where there will be a dire need for coordination and cooperation among members of international inter-organizational fields. An important trend in organizational communication inquiry will be to examine intercultural and international organizational communication, increasing sensitivity to cultural differences and similarities, and developing strategies for establishing meaningful intercultural and international relationships.

5. How will new communication technologies influence organizational communication? As new communication technologies are developed and adopted they will inevitably change the way organizational actors communicate and accomplish organizational activities. Future organizational communication inquiry will examine the influences of new technologies on organizational life and develop strategies for effectively implementing and using these technologies to enhance organizational communication.

6. How is communication used to establish systems of domination and control in organizational life? Human communication is used to establish the emergent political structures of social organization by expressing changing patterns of influence among organizational actors. Future organizational communication inquiry will examine the use of communication to overtly and covertly express power and political influence in organizations.

Researching and Reporting Case Studies

Cases are examples or illustrations of organizational problems to which we apply the theory we study in an effort to determine the best solution. A case gives information about the organization, its people, and its performance. The case study approach to organizational communication provides an opportunity to blend theory, analysis, and practice in our efforts to better understand how communication processes create and shape organizational events. Case studies provide rich opportunities to apply theory to organizational practice. They bridge the gap between reading about organizations and theory and knowing what to do in actual organizational situations. They also expand our analytical and critical capabilities as we examine dynamic and complex events for their impact on organizational behavior. And they help us develop strategies and approaches for application to real organizational problems. The primary purpose of the case study approach is to develop our abilities to both understand a variety of organizational circumstances and problems and develop strategies for productively addressing complex situations.

The case study method uses prepared cases, such as those provided in this book, and provides opportunities for the development of original cases based on our personal experiences or from interviews and observation of organizational members who can identify interesting communication problems. This method requires research, development, and presentation of cases so that others can understand the central issues of concern and how these issues or concerns can be addressed or understood within an organizational setting. Cases are usually presented (either orally or in writing) in story or narrative forms with enough clarification so others can contrast their solutions to ours or generate original solutions. Proposed solutions are presented with reference to identified problems and the theory-based reasoning for the solutions.

THE BASIS OF CASE ANALYSIS

The case study method is based on a systematic search of the case for the complex processes, events, or factors that have contributed to the presented problems, issues, or circumstances. Case analysis requires that we develop an understanding of a variety of research-based theories, propositions, and positions, which can then be used to explain the behaviors we see exhibited in a particular organization. These theories, propositions, and positions are also used to support the types of decisions and actions we propose as case solutions. In other words, case study analysis can be both explanatory and prescriptive. Analysis aims to provide theory-based explanations of events as opposed to anecdotal or conventional wisdom explanations. (In many cases, of course, theory-based and conventional wisdom explanations are the same.) Prescriptions are recommended courses of action based on an examination of options and theory-based reasoning for recommended decisions. Most cases lend themselves to an outline of description, analysis, and proposed solutions. Researching and reporting case studies can be accomplished in a three-step process: identify and describe the situation or problem; develop alternatives and test the "reality" of possible solutions; and propose solutions and suggest implementation plans.

IDENTIFY AND DESCRIBE THE SITUATION OR PROBLEM

The following list of questions will assist you in identifying and describing case situations and problems. The list is not exhaustive and is provided to help you begin a systematic search of the case.

What is factual information about this organization, its people, and their problems?

What is assumptive or inferential information?

What are the major and minor problems in the case?

What communication theories apply to these problems?

What organizational theories or perspectives are apparent?

How do environmental factors influence this situation?

What information is missing?

Are technological factors important?

Are formal organizational factors important?

Are individual behavior factors an issue?

Are group behavior factors an issue?

Who or what appears to be most responsible for the communication problems?

What are the "shared realities" of the organization?

Are the principal individuals good communicators? If not, what are their limitations?

Are the principals in the case assuming responsibility for their communication behaviors?

What are the major organizational strengths? Weaknesses?

What skills do the case principals exhibit? What is needed?

What is important or valuable to the individuals involved?

Do the principals share similar values?

How would you describe the culture of the organization?

Are individual and organizational goals compatible?

Case analysis requires that we not only identify answers to these questions but that we search for theory-based explanations of our answers. The annotated bibliography of this book provides a beginning. A review of the citations will help you identify theory that applies to cases in each chapter. Of course, this bibliography is not intended to be comprehensive to all potential theoretical explanations nor would it necessarily apply to original case material you develop. However, it will help you begin your search. The theories you select will add important analysis questions.

Often you will find that you lack important information for analysis. If the case does not provide information you believe to be important, state your need and make reasonable assumptions based on what is both present and missing. Be sure to identify any assumptions you make based on missing information. Moreover, watch for problem/symptom confusion. Many times organizational issues or concerns are symptoms of basic problems rather than the problems themselves. Continually ask "why" of identified symptoms and look for underlying causes or problems.

DEVELOP ALTERNATIVES AND TEST THE "REALITY" OF POSSIBLE SOLUTIONS

What should be done based on your analysis?

What can be done?

How many alternatives for decisions/behaviors/changes/ can you identify?

What are the strengths and weaknesses of each alternative?

Can alternatives be combined?

Are the people involved willing to change?

Which theories, propositions, or positions support your choices?

What is the cost of your possible solutions?

Do your alternatives address the problem at its present state or represent an approach that would have prevented the problem? (Many case presentations address problems at their beginning rather than from the present situation. It is important to analyze a problem from its present state rather than just stating how it could have been prevented in the first place.)

PROPOSE SOLUTIONS AND SUGGEST IMPLEMENTATION PLAN

Explain your theory-based reasoning for solution selection. Link solution selection to problem analysis.

Identify who is responsible for what.

Determine a timetable for implementation.

Suggest how your solutions might be evaluated.

If applicable, predict what will happen.

PREPARING THE ORIGINAL CASE

Original cases can be developed from a variety of organizational experiences. If you choose to develop a case in which you were personally involved, you will need to assess objectively your own involvement or develop the case with a definite statement of your potential bias. Cases can also be developed through interviews with organizational members, review of written materials, and observation. Cases in this book, as well as others, can serve as examples for writing styles and approaches. When developing the original case you will want to be concerned with issues of confidentiality and permission to use names and specific information. It is common—as with most cases in this book—for such accounts to be fact-based, with names changed to protect the identity of specific individuals and organizations.

Bibliography

The following bibliography contains articles and books related to the subject matter of cases in each chapter. The bibliography is not intended to be inclusive but reviews recent literature in organizational communication and related fields. These references, along with other significant works, provide information important for analysis, discussion, and problem solving.

CHAPTER 1: UNDERSTANDING ORGANIZATIONAL COMMUNICATION

Adizes, I. 1988. *Corporate lifecycles: How and why corporations grow and die and what to do about it.* Englewood Cliffs, N.J.: Prentice-Hall.

Baum, J., and C. Oliver. 1991. Institutional linkages and organizational mortality. *Administrative Science Quarterly* 36(2): 187–218.
The effects of direct and regularized relationships between organizations and government or community constituents are evaluated.

Bettinger, C. 1990. *High performance in the 90s: Leading the strategic and cultural revolution in banking.* Homewood, Ill.: Business One Irwin.

Bullis, C. A., and P. K. Tompkins. 1989. The forest ranger revisited: The study of control practices and identification. *Communication Monographs* 56(4): 287–306.
Implications for cultural influences are made as a result of observing through comparison study a shift to a more direct or obtrusive form of control within the forest service.

Buona, A. F., and J. L. Bowditch. 1989. *The human side of mergers and acquisitions: Managing collisions between people, cultures, and organizations.* San Francisco: Jossey-Bass.

Cameron, K. S., R. I. Sutton, and D. A. Whetten, eds. 1988. *Readings in organizational decline: Frameworks, research, and prescriptions.* Cambridge, Mass.: Ballinger.

Corman, S. R., S. P. Banks, C. R. Bantz, and M. E. Mayer, eds. 1990. *Foundations of organizational communication: A reader.* White Plains, N.Y.: Longman.

Davidson, W. H. 1991. The role of global scanning in business planning. *Organizational Dynamics* 19(3): 5–16.
Development of effective global scanning, analysis, and planning capabilities is a critical challenge for all firms. Events, trends, and situations are connected by rationales of the effects on the organization.

Deetz, S. A. 1992. *Democracy in an age of corporate colonization: Developments in communication and the politics of everyday life.* Ithaca, N.Y.: State University of New York Press.

Goldhaber, G. M., and G. A. Barnett, eds. 1988. *Handbook of organizational communication.* Norwood, N.J.: Ablex.

Jablin, F. M., L. L. Putnam, K. H. Roberts, and L. W. Porter, eds. 1987. *Handbook of organizational communication.* Newbury Park, Calif.: Sage.

Kreps, G. L. 1990. *Organizational communication.* 2d ed. White Plains, N.Y.: Longman.

LaPalombara, J. 1987. *Democracy Italian style.* New Haven, Conn.: Yale University Press.

Lei, D., J. Slocum, Jr., and R. Slater. 1990. Global strategy and reward systems: The key roles of management development and corporate culture. *Organizational Dynamics* 19(2): 27–41.
The ultimate global fight will be one of getting and retaining high-quality people. Analysis of several multinational corporations identifies their global strategies and shows the competitive advantage resulting from management development, cultural development, and performance reward systems.

Lei, D., and J. Slocum, Jr. 1991. Global strategic alliances: Payoffs and pitfalls. *Organizational Dynamics* 19(3): 44–62.
Companies form global strategic alliances to help outflank competitors. Focusing on licensing arrangements, joint ventures, and consortia, examination is made of rationales for formation, benefits and costs, factors critical for success, and human resource management.

Morrison, A., D. Ricks, and K. Roth. 1991. Globalization versus regionalization: Which way for the multinational? *Organizational Dynamics* 19(3): 17–29.
This study indicates globalization is no panacea. Companies are finding implementation of global strategies is prohibitively costly in terms of morale, internal opposition, and lost opportunities to exploit key subsidiary strengths.

Rosenzweig, P. M., and J. V. Singh. 1991. Organizational environments and the multinational enterprise. *The Academy of Management Review* 16(2): 340–361.
Hypotheses are examined regarding the relative impact of the pressure for isomorphism with the local environment and the pressure for internal consistency.

Ruch, W. V. 1989. *International handbook of corporate communication.* Jefferson, N.C.: McFarland.

Shockley-Zalabak, P. 1991. *Fundamentals of organizational communication.* 2d ed. White Plains, N.Y.: Longman.

Troester, R. 1991. The corporate spokesperson in external organizational communication: What we know and what we need to know. *Management Communication Quarterly* 4(4): 528–540.

The communicator of the organizations' message to the community. A literature review summarizes normal organizational–media relationships, corporate crises, and issue management efforts. Suggestions are made for future research.

CHAPTER 2: CULTURE AND COMMUNICATION

Boje, D. M. 1991. The storytelling organization: A study of story performance in an office supply firm. *Administrative Science Quarterly* 36(1): 106–126.
Storytelling is the key to organizational member sense making. Support for a theory of organization as a collective storytelling system in which the performance of stories is a key part of members' sense making.

Caropreso, F. 1991. *Managing globally: Key perspectives.* New York: Conference Board.

Cascio, W. F., and M. G. Serapio, Jr. 1991. Human resources systems in an international alliance: The undoing of a done deal? *Organizational Dynamics* 19(3): 63–74.
In a global alliance, people with different cultures, career goals, compensation systems, and other human relations differences often must work together. Unless utilized appropriately, these people factors can halt alliances' progress, sometimes permanently.

Denison, D. R. 1990. *Corporate culture and organizational effectiveness.* New York: Wiley.

Dulek, R. E., J. S. Fielden, and J. S. Hill. 1991. International communication: An executive primer. *Business Horizons* 34(1): 20–25.
Recognize the type of culture when engaging in international business, and then apply the correct principles in dealing with foreign nationals. The utility of division into high and low context cultures is described in the framework of conversation, presentation, and written principles.

Garland, S. B. 1991. Were civil rights laws meant to travel? *Business Week,* January 21, 36.
The U.S. Supreme Court will decide if antibias laws apply to U.S. companies abroad. The debate over who regulates conduct in a foreign country will likely continue.

Glover, M. K. 1990. Do's and taboos: Cultural aspects of international business. *Business America* 111(15): 2–8.
Understanding and heeding cultural variables can mean the difference between success and failure in international business.

Goodall, H. L. 1989. *Casing a promised land: The autobiography of an organizational detective as cultural ethnographer.* Carbondale: Southern Illinois University Press.

Onkvisit, S., and J. Shaw. 1991. Myopic management: The hollow strength of American competitiveness. *Business Horizons* 34(1): 13–19.
U.S. firms would be wise to avoid imposing their own cultural values on foreign customers. Self-critical examination of practices of U.S. corporations shows ways in which competitive edge may be restored.

Rizzo, A., and C. Mendez. 1990. *The integration of women in management: A guide for human resources and management development specialists.* New York: Quorum Books.

Schneider, B., ed. 1990. *Organizational climate and culture.* San Francisco: Jossey-Bass.

Sullivan, J., N. Kameda, and T. Nobu. 1991. Bypassing in managerial communication. *Business Horizons* 34(1): 71–80.
Words must be defined in context and across cultures; misunderstandings can lead to dire consequences. Many examples are given along with suggestions for successful communication.

Tung, R. L. 1991. Handshakes across the sea: Cross-cultural negotiating for business success. *Organizational Dynamics* 19 (3): 30–40.
Negotiating a global alliance across widely divergent cultures is difficult at best. Key elements of successful business negotiations with Koreans are identified.

CHAPTER 3: INDIVIDUALS IN ORGANIZATIONS

Albrecht, T., and B. Hall. 1991. Relational and content differences between elites and outsiders in innovative networks. *Human Communication Research* 17(4): 535–561.
Innovative behavior contributes more power and influence to individuals displaying the behavior. Central elite groups are characterized by dense communication linkages and tend to form around the concept of acceptance of new ideas.

Cohen, A. R., and D. L. Bradford. 1990. *Influence without authority.* New York: Wiley.

Downs, T. M. 1990. Predictors of communication satisfaction during performance appraisal interviews. *Management Communication Quarterly* 3(3): 334–354.
Effective communication is the key to successful performance appraisals. Discusses measures of communication satisfaction, perceived communication behaviors, and effect of communication training.

Fishman, D., and C. Cherniss, eds. 1990. *The human side of corporate competitiveness.* Newbury Park, Calif.: Sage.

Gorden, W. I., and D. A. Infante. 1991. Test of a communication model of organizational commitment. *Communication Quarterly* 39(2): 144–155.
The model is based on the idea of individual freedom to communicate.

Jones, M. O., M. D. Moore, and R. C. Snyder, eds. 1988. *Inside organizations: Understanding the human dimension.* Newbury Park, Calif.: Sage.

CHAPTER 4: GROUPS AND PROBLEM-SOLVING COMMUNICATION

Barker, D. B. 1991. The behavioral analysis of interpersonal intimacy in group development. *Small Group Research* 22 (1): 76–91.
More effective groups revealed behavioral occurrences of intimate relations for enhanced awareness.

Bettenhausen, K. L., and J. K. Murnighan. 1991. The development of an intragroup norm and the effects of inter-personal and structural challenges. *Administrative Science Quarterly* 36(1): 20–35.
The intragroup norm formation process: A guide for group member behaviors.

Bollen, K. A., and R. H. Hoyle. 1990. Perceived cohesion: A conceptual and empirical examination. *Social Forces* 69(2): 479–504.
Group members' perceptions of cohesion are important for the behavior of the individual as well as the group as a whole. A sense of belonging and feelings of morale are the two dimensions tested for determining the individual's perception of cohesion.

Crott, H., K. Szilvas, and J. Zuber. 1991. Group decision, choice shift, and polarization in consulting, political, and local political scenarios: An experimental investigation and theoretical analysis. *Organizational Behavior and Human Decision Processes* 49(1): 22–41.

The process of decision making in groups. A test of predictive capability of several decision-making theories.

Gemmill, G., and C. Wynkoop. 1991. The psychodynamics of small group transformation. *Small Group Research* 22(1): 4–23.
The overt and covert intellectual and emotional forces restraining and driving group transformation.

Larson, C. E., and F. M. LaFasto. 1989. *Teamwork.* Newbury Park, Calif.: Sage.

Mannix, E. A. 1991. Resource dilemmas and discount rates in decision making groups. *Journal of Experimental Social Psychology* 27(4): 379–391.
Coalition formation and resource disposition as a function of the value placed on the future state. Energetic or benevolent coalitions may benefit sluggish or poorly motivated group members.

McGrath, J. E. 1991. Time, interaction, and performance (TIP): A theory of groups. *Small Group Research* 22(2): 147–174.
Emphasis on temporal processes in group interaction and task performance. An attempt to conceptualize groups and group activity at a level of complexity that reflects the nature of groups in everyday activity.

Mullen, B. 1991. Group composition, salience, and cognitive representations: The phenomenology of being in a group. *Journal of Experimental Social Psychology* 27(4): 297–323.
Proportionate sizes of in-groups and out-groups are shown to predict a variety of effects at the interface between social cognition and group processes.

Olshan, M. A. 1990. The old order Amish steering committee: A case study in organizational evolution. *Social Forces* 69(2): 603–616.
Differences in value systems between a collective and an organization structured around government standards provides an environmental driving force for an organization antithetical to central authority.

Parker, G. M. 1990. *Team players and teamwork: The new competitive business strategy.* San Francisco: Jossey-Bass.

Powell, J. L. 1991. An attempt at increasing decision rule use in a judgement task. *Organizational Behavior and Human Decision Processes* 48(1): 89–99.
Investigates the decision rule as a decision aid. If the formula is known to work its use is enhanced, which reiterates the use of formal learning as a substitute for experience.

Raudsepp, E. 1991. Overcoming barriers to effective problem-solving. *Supervision* 52(2): 14–16.
Suggestions on how to improve your solutions to problems, how to innovate.

Sainfort, F., D. Gustafson, K. Bosworth, and R. Hawkins. 1990. Decision support systems effectiveness: Conceptual framework and empirical evaluation. *Organizational Behavior and Human Decision Processes* 45(2): 232–252.
Videotape training for conflict resolution is compared to results from computerized resolution.

Storey, D. 1991. History and homogeneity: Effects of perceptions of membership groups on interpersonal communication. *Communication Research* 18(2): 199–221.
Greater homogeneity and history contribute to greater intimacy between group members.

Williams, J., and J. Nelson. 1990. Striking oil in decision support. *Datamation* 36(6): 83–86.
Decision support systems (DSS) should be flexible and tailored to the information problem. Rationales for the use of DSS by two petroleum companies.

CHAPTER 5: LEADERSHIP AND MANAGEMENT

Anderson, L., and J. Tolson. 1991. Leaders' upward influence in the organization: Replication and extensions of the Pelz effect to include group support and self-monitoring. *Small Group Research* 22 (1): 59–75.
When the leader has significant upward influence in the organization, group members have an enhanced feeling of a sense of control.

Barge, J. K., and D. W. Schlueter. 1991. Leadership as organizing: A critique of leadership instruments. *Management Communication Quarterly* 4(4): 541–570.
A review and critique of four recent instruments to measure organizational leadership.

Connor, P. E., and L. K. Lake. 1988. *Managing organizational change.* New York: Praeger.

Dalziel, M. M., and S. C. Schoonover. 1988. *Changing ways: A practical tool for implementing change in organizations.* New York: American Management Association.

Emshoff, J. R., with T. E. Denlinger. 1991. *The new rules of the game: The four keys experienced managers must have to thrive in the non-hierarchal 90s and beyond.* New York: Harper Business.

Fairhurst, G. T., and T. A. Chandler. 1989. Social structure in leader-member interaction. *Communication Monographs* 56(3): 215–239.
Discusses leader–member exchange and how word forms convey power, social similarity, and social distance.

Flamholtz, E., with Y. Randle. 1990. *Growing pains: How to make the transition from an entrepreneurship to a professionally managed firm.* San Francisco: Jossey-Bass.

Fletcher, B. R. 1990. *Organizational transformation theorists and practitioners: Profiles and themes.* New York: Praeger.

Gunz, H. 1989. *Careers and corporate cultures: Managerial mobility in large corporations.* Oxford, England: Blackwell.

Hackman, M. Z., and C. E. Johnson. 1991. *Leadership.* Prospect Heights, Ill.: Waveland.

Hickman, C. R. 1990. *Mind of a manager, soul of a leader.* New York: Wiley.

Hirokawa, R. Y., R. A. Kodama, and N. L. Harper. 1990. Impact of managerial power on persuasive strategy selection by female and male managers. *Management Communication Quarterly* 4(1): 30–50.
The amount of power a manager possesses impacts the choice of persuasive strategies a manager uses. Gender of manager is not a factor.

Jackson, D. E. 1988. *Interpersonal communication for technically trained managers: A guide to skills and techniques.* New York: Quorum Books.

Levitt, T. 1991. *Thinking about management.* New York: Free Press, Maxwell Macmillan International.

Limerick, D. C. 1990. Managers of meaning: From Bob Geldof's band aid to Australian CEOs. *Organizational Dynamics* 18(4): 22–33.
A study of Australian business and government organizations shows their leadership approach to be appropriate for current demands. In a study of 50 Australian CEOs, they were found to face the tasks of cutting across loosely coupled groups (often successful in their own right) and of getting them to collaborate for new common goals.

Morley, D., and P. Shockley-Zalabak. 1991. Setting the rules: An examination of the influences of organizational founders' values. *Management Communication Quarterly* 4(4): 422–449.

Description of the influence of organizational founders' values on member values and communication rule emergence.

Peters, T. 1987. *Thriving on chaos.* New York: Knopf.

Puffer, S. M., and J. B. Weintrop. 1991. Corporate performance and CEO turnover: The role of performance expectations. *Administrative Science Quarterly* 36(1): 1–19.
Corporate performance and CEO turnover. Disappointing annual earnings communicate the need for change of CEO.

Russ, G. S., R. L. Daft, and R. H. Lengel. 1990. Media selection and managerial characteristics in organizational communications. *Management Communication Quarterly* 4(2): 151–175.
Discusses media selection and how effective managers fit the medium to the message.

Schein, L. 1989. *A managers guide to corporate culture.* New York: Conference Board.

Suchan, J., and R. Dulek. 1990. A reassessment of clarity in written managerial communications. *Management Communication Quarterly* 4(1): 87–99.
A commentary arguing for systematic evaluation of the complex role of communication in organizations.

CHAPTER 6: CONFLICT AND COMMUNICATION

Burrell, N., W. Donohue, and M. Allen. 1990. The impact of disputants' expectations on mediation: Testing an interventionist model. *Human Communication Research* 17(1): 104–139.
The mediation process as characterized by highly participative mediators: expectations have little effect.

Conrad, C. 1991. Communication in conflict: Styles-strategy relationships. *Communication Monographs* 58(2): 135–155.
Supervisors eventually change communication styles as conflict intensifies.

DeWine, S., A. Nicotera, and D. Parry. 1991. Argumentativeness and aggressiveness: The flip side of gentle persuasion. *Management Communication Quarterly* 4(3): 386–411.
Argumentativeness and verbal aggressiveness scales are two popular communication instruments.

Morris, G. H., S. C. Gaveras, W. L. Baker, and M. L. Coursey. 1990. Aligning actions at work: How managers confront problems of employee performance. *Management Communication Quarterly* 3(3): 303–333.
Employee performance as the constant challenge for managers. Enhancement of alignment between managers and employees is examined in three broad categories: alternatives to confrontation, investigative action, and fault finding.

Mumby, D. 1988. *Communication and power in organizations: Discourse, ideology, and domination.* Norwood, N.J.: Ablex.

Pascale, R. T. 1990. *Managing on the edge: How the smartest companies use conflict to stay ahead.* New York: Simon and Schuster.

Prunty, A., D. Klopf, and S. Ishii. 1990. Argumentativeness: Japanese and American tendencies to approach and avoid conflict. *Communication Research Reports* 7(1): 75–79.
Argumentativeness as a Western practice.

Sutton, R. I. 1991. Maintaining norms about expressed emotions: The case of bill collectors. *Administrative Science Quarterly* 36(2): 245–268.
A qualitative study of a collection agency is used to further develop understanding of emotion in organizations.

Witteman, H. 1991. Group member satisfaction: A conflict-related account. *Small Group Research* 22(1): 24–58.
Measures of member satisfaction, perceptions of three conflict-management styles, and motivation to work for the group and group-member satisfaction.

CHAPTER 7: VALUES, ETHICS, AND ORGANIZATIONAL COMMUNICATION

Bassiry, G. R. 1990. Business ethics and the United Nations: A code of conduct. *Advanced Management Journal* 55(4): 38–41.
A draft code is summarized, critiqued, and discussed. Recent developments require changes during final adoption stage.

Bavaria, S. 1991. Corporate ethics should start in the boardroom. *Business Horizons* 34(1): 9–12.
Corporate ethics as a discipline is so new that its scope is undefined. Issues raised have not been examined closely from an ethical perspective. Ethics codes that are not a part of boardroom behaviors fail to affect major decisions about corporate strategy and executive compensation.

Bhide, A., and H. Stevenson. 1990. Why be honest if honesty doesn't pay. *Harvard Business Review* 68(5): 121–129.
Examples of success in the business world where strict adherence to morality would have resulted in failure.

Cullen, J., B. Victor, and C. Stephens. 1989. An ethical weather report: Assessing the organization's ethical climate. *Organizational Dynamics* 18(2): 50–62.
The organization's ethical climate helps to determine how employees at all levels make ethical decisions. Employee response to a questionnaire helps identify the climate and provides management the information needed to strengthen and change the ethical climate.

Delaney, J., and D. Sockell. 1990. Ethics in the trenches. *Across the Board* 27(10): 15–26.
Business behavior and ethical behavior are not always synonymous. Four case studies with responses by persons prominent in business, academic, and public life.

Delaney, J., and D. Sockell. 1990. Ethics in the trenches. *Across the Board* 27(11): 31–33, 35–39.
Blue-ribbon panel tackles three more ethical dilemmas drawn from real life.

Falsey, T. A. 1989. *Corporate philosophies and mission statements: A survey and guide for corporate communicators and management.* New York: Quorum Books.

Hosmer, L. T. 1991. Managerial responsibilities on micro level. *Business Horizons* 34(4): 49–55.
To get managers to act ethically, we must hold them accountable on an ethical level of management. Development of the argument that the ethics is the top-most of managerial responsibilities.

Lee, S., S. Yoo, and T. Lee. 1991. Korean chaebols: Corporate values and strategies. *Organizational Dynamics* 19(4): 36–50.

Chaebols, the conglomerate groups responsible for South Korea's widely admired economic growth, possess unique corporate values. Along with their distinct diversification strategies they are examined with regard to need for change.

Scott, W. G., and D. K. Hart. 1989. *Organizational values in America.* New Brunswick, N.J.: Transaction Publishers.

Shames, L. 1991. Profiting from principles. *Best of Business* 13(1): 43.
Capitalism with a conscience may be the image-building gimmick of the 1990s, but this skeptic doesn't buy it.

CHAPTER 8: COMMUNICATION AND TECHNOLOGY

Ajami, R. 1990. Global trans-border data flows: Concerns and options. *International Journal of Technology Management* 5(5): 589–604.
Emerging communication technologies allow the free flow of data across national boundaries.

Allen, G. 1989. What's hot in corporate TV? *Communication World* 6(10): 16–19.
Corporate television as an excellent medium for employee, stockholder, and customer communication.

Buchner, B. J. 1988. Social control and the diffusion of modern telecommunications technologies: A cross-national study. *American Sociological Review* 53(3): 446–453.
Relative growth of telephone and television technologies in Marxist nations versus non-Marxist nations.

Fulk, J., and B. Boyd. 1991. Emerging theories of communication in organizations. *Journal of Management* (Special issue—yearly review of management) 17(2): 407–446.
Recent theoretical developments in organizational communication that deal with information processing: communication media choice, computer-supported group decision making, communication technology and organizational design, and communication networks.

Fulk, J., E. Rogers, and M. Von Glinow. 1988. Managing change through communication technologies in third world countries. *Journal of Organizational Change Management* 1(2): 21–37.
A critical examination of three related models of the diffusion process in the introduction and adoption of new technologies into third-world countries.

Gattiker, U. E. 1990. *Technology management in organizations.* Newbury Park, Calif.: Sage.

Gilder, G. 1991. Into the telecosm. *Harvard Business Review* 69(2): 150–161.
In the next decade or so telecomputers will accept inputs from voices, microphones, cameras, remote sensors, vision systems, and graphics processors display outputs in high-resolution video and sound or even in three-dimensional images.

Goodrich, J. N. 1990. Telecommuting in America. *Business Horizons* 33(4): 31–37.
Some of the key issues facing managers based on a national sample.

Hurt, H., and R. Hibbard. 1989. The systematic measurement of the perceived characteristics of information technologies I: Microcomputers as innovations. *Communication Quarterly* 37(3): 214–222.
A test is developed to measure the perceived characteristics of microcomputers as innovators.

Huseman, R. C., and E. W. Miles. 1988. Organizational communication in the information age: Implications of computer-based systems. *Journal of Management* 14(2): 181–204.
Introducing the integrative model of information systems and organizational communication and the implications of four computer-based systems.

Komsky, S. H. 1991. A profile of users of electronic mail in a university: Frequent versus occasional use. *Management Communication Quarterly* 4(3): 310–340.
Characteristics in the nonstudent population are evaluated to provide insights for encouraging use of electronic mail.

Kraut, R. E. 1989. Telecommuting: The trade-offs of home work. *Journal of Communication* 39(3): 19–47.
Employees balance need for flexibility against need for supplemental income. Employers balance need for interpersonal contact for required work against possible low pay for equivalent work.

Orman, L. V. 1989. Public information systems. *Information Society* 6(12): 69–76.
The impact of public information systems on society.

Papa, M. J. 1990. Communication network patterns and employee performance with new technology. *Communication Research* 17(3): 344–368.
The positive relationship between new technology and employee productivity.

Reinsch, N., Jr., C. Steele, P. Lewis, M. Stano, and R. Beswick. 1990. Measuring telephone apprehension. *Management Communication Quarterly* 4(2): 198–221.
Results of studies leading to a reliable self-report instrument, which predicts telephone use among practicing managers.

Rice, R., and C. Aydin. 1991. Attitudes toward new organizational technology: Network proximity as a mechanism for social information processing. *Administrative Science Quarterly* 36(2): 219–244.
User attitudes are critical to the successful implementation of organizational information systems. Development is investigated.

Ritchie, L. D. 1991. Another turn of the information revolution: Relevance, technology, and the information society. *Communication Research* 18(3): 412–427.
As communication shifts from a technology of control by people toward a technology of control over people, the result is a weakening of the relevance relations by which persons establish their identities and understand their social environments.

Scientific American. September 1991.
A special issue devoted to communications, computers, and networks. How to live, work, play, and thrive in cyberspace.

Scott Morton, M. S., ed. 1991. *The corporation of the 1990s: Information technology and organizational transformation*. New York: Oxford University Press.

Sikes, A. C. 1991. National communications: Seeking a consensus. *Vital Speeches* 57(9): 266–268.
FCC proposals to redistribute the electromagnetic communications spectrum.

Sproull, L., and S. Kiesler. 1991. *Connections: New ways of working in the networked organization*. Cambridge, Mass.: MIT Press.

Sugimoto, T., and S. Burleson. 1990. Kinder, gentler computer technology. *Business and Economic Review* 36(3): 43–45.
The computer with its technological changes is becoming a true bearer of knowledge leading to enhanced human productivity.

CHAPTER 9: CREATIVITY, EFFECTIVENESS, AND COMMUNICATION

Argyris, C. 1990. *Overcoming organizational defenses: Facilitating organizational learning.* Wellesley, Mass.: Allyn and Bacon.

Bach, B. W. 1989. The effect of multiplex relationships upon innovation adoption: A reconsideration of Rogers' model. *Communication Monographs* 56(2): 133–150.
Shared communication links as related to the process of organizational innovation. The failure of support for the hypothesis provided suggestions for change and further testing.

Bandrowski, J. F. 1990. *Corporate imagination plus: Five steps to translating innovative strategies into action.* New York: Free Press.

Belasco, J. A. 1990. *Teaching the elephant to dance: Empowering change in your organization.* New York: Crown.

Benton, P. 1990. *Riding the whirlwind: Benton on managing turbulence.* Cambridge, Mass.: Blackwell.

Best, M. H. 1990. *The new competition: Institutions of industrial restructuring.* Cambridge: Harvard University Press.

Caropreso, F. 1990. *Restructuring and managing change.* New York: Conference Board.

Golembiewski, R. T. 1989. *Organizational Development: Ideas and issues.* New Brunswick, N.J.: Transaction Publishers.

Golembiewski, R. T. 1990. *Ironies in organizational development.* New Brunswick, N.J.: Transaction Publishers.

Gomez-Mejia, L. R., D. B. Balkin, and G. T. Milkovich. 1990. Rethinking rewards for technical employees. *Organizational Dynamics* 18(4): 62–75.
In high-tech organizations, retaining key innovators can mean gaining a competitive edge. Although the pay system is a crucial element it is only one part of the total picture.

Heckscher, C. C. 1988. *The new unionism: Employee involvement in the changing corporation.* New York: Basic Books.

Howell, J. M., and C. A. Higgins. 1990. Champions of change: Identifying, understanding, and supporting champions of technological innovation. *Organizational Dynamics* 19(1): 40–55.
Characteristics of champions are described, then ways for management to support them are discussed.

Kanter, R. M. 1991. Transcending business boundaries: 12,000 world managers view change. *Harvard Business Review* 69(3): 151–164.
A global survey of business leaders showed change is everywhere—regardless of country, culture, or corporation. The idea of a corporate global village, where a common culture of management unifies the practice of business, is more dream than reality.

Kennedy, C. 1990. The road to the new millennium. *Director,* January: 32–36.
Pinpoints key issues of the 1990s: the wise use of information technology, Japanese competition, and the recruiting of top employees.

Kilmann, R., I. Kilmann, and associates, eds. 1991. *Making organizations competitive: Enhancing networks and relationships across traditional boundaries.* San Francisco: Jossey-Bass.

Knauft, E., R. Berger, and S. Gray. 1991. *Profiles of excellence: Achieving success in the nonprofit sector.* San Francisco: Jossey-Bass.

Lundberg, C. C. 1990. Towards mapping the communication targets of organisational change. *Journal of Organizational Change Management* 3(3): 6–13.
Mapping the role of communication in the four frames of organizational structure during change.

Massarik, F., ed. 1990. *Advances in organizational development.* Norwood, N.J.: Ablex.

Mitroff, I. I. 1988. *Break-away thinking: How to challenge your business assumptions (and why you should).* New York: Wiley.

Pascale, R. T. 1991. The two faces of learning. *Modern Office Technology* 36(2): 14, 16.
Organizational vitality and adaptiveness depend on learning. General Motors and Honda are compared.

Peters, T. 1991. Get innovative or get dead: Part two. *California Management Review* 33(2): 9–23.
Innovation, the key to organizational longevity. Radical approaches for putting innovation at the top of the corporate agenda.

Reardon, K., and B. Enis. 1990. Establishing a companywide customer orientation through persuasive internal marketing. *Management Communication Quarterly* 3(3): 376–387.
Persuasive internal marketing encourages employees to accept changes in company philosophy or policy and can facilitate the adoption of a greater customer orientation.

West, M., and J. Farr, eds. 1990. *Innovation and creativity at work: Psychological and organizational strategies.* New York: Wiley.

CHAPTER 10: ORGANIZATIONAL COMMUNICATION IN THE TWENTY-FIRST CENTURY

DeLisi, P. S. 1990. Lessons from the steel axe: Culture, technology, and organizational change. *Sloan Management Review* 32(1): 83–93.
The challenge of the future. When working closely with customers on information technology, the importance and centrality of organizational culture becomes obvious.

Feldman, D. C. 1990. Risky business: The socialisation of managers in the 21st century. *Journal of Organizational Change Management* 3(2): 16–29.
The declining work force with adequate skills for new jobs requires corporations to develop innovative ways to recruit, select, train, and develop new employees.

Goldstein, I. L., and H. W. Goldstein. 1990. Training as an approach for organisations to the challenges of human resource issues in the year 2000. *Journal of Organizational Change Management* 3(2): 30–43.
Training is an increasingly necessary and positive force for both the individual and the organization. Addressed are questions of why training is needed, what is needed, and how training may be provided.

Gordon, J. 1991. The skilling of America. *Training* 28(3): 27–35.
Redesigning jobs, training, and retraining may well be the most important economic challenge facing this country for the next decade.

Haas, E. B. 1990. *When knowledge is power: Three models of change in international organizations.* Berkeley: University of California Press.

Johnston, W. B. 1991. Global work force 2000: The new world labor market. *Harvard Business Review* 69(2): 115–127.
Tomorrow we will talk about a world market for labor. Human resources on a worldwide basis can be a source of competitive advantage.

Oddou, G. R., and M. E. Mendenhall. 1991. Succession planning for the 21st century: How well are we grooming our future business leaders? *Business Horizons* 34(1): 26–34. Companies say they want international experience for their top executives; but once they return these expatriate managers are not regarded so highly within their companies. Based on survey results some recommendations are made to improve the handling of returning managers and to utilize the important skills they have learned.

Toffler, A. 1990. *Powershift*. New York: Bantam Books.

Index

Note: This index contains fictitious as well as actual names of persons and organizations.

Abbott Hospital, 12–21
Acquisition of Abbott Hospital, 12–21
Allen, Anne Murray, 80
Americans for Indian Opportunity
    (AIO), 114
Ames, A. Gary, 45
Anderson, Bob, 38–40
Andrews, Dave, 219
Apple Computer Inc., 40–42, 197
Arambulo, Hector, 66–74
Arnold, Ron, 97
Atkins, Angela, 94–96
Atkinson, Lora, 89–92
Auditing, cases discussing, 141–148,
    169–173

Barnes, Ralph, 108, 109
Bennis, Warren, 83
Berger, Arnie, 120, 121
Better Technology, More Complaints''
    Case, The, 205–207
Bok, Derek, 244
Boston, Samuel, 214–215
Bradley, Connie, 182–183
Bradley, Nancy, 176–179
Bradley, Nick, 100–101
Bridges, Harry, 142–144, 146, 148
Britton, Jim, 160–163

Can This Ethical Manager Survive, or
    Should She?, 176–179
Careers
  cases discussing, 34–36, 97–98,
    160–163, 179–181, 182–183,
    220–224
  conversations discussing, 51–54,
    187–189, 189–191, 191–193
  future trends in, 200
Carson Products' Management Team
    Disaster, 105–107
Cartwright, Dora, 136–137
Case study method, 261–264
Celeste, Richard, 235
Cesaria, Ruggero, 54–55, 57–59, 66
Chandler, Robert, 25–27, 30–31
Change
  cases discussing, 9–11, 12–21, 34–36,
    138–141, 141–148, 155–157,
    158–159, 160–163, 165–167,
    181–182, 203–205, 207–210,
    214–216, 217–220, 224–228,
    228–234, 245–247, 251–253
  in methods of communication,
    195–198
  types of, 57
Change Is Ruining Our Company,
    155–157

Chase, Tom, 80
China, 196
Clemmons, Charles, 227–228
Communication. *See also*
    Organizational communication
    as cornerstone of human relations
        approach, 4–5
    perspectives in, 258–260
    as process of shared realities, 2
Communications literacy
    cases discussing, 243–245, 247–248
    conversations discussing, 256–258
Conceptual materialism, 4
Conflict, cases discussing, 89–93,
        93–96, 98–100, 135–136,
        138–141, 155–157, 157–158,
        158–159, 160–163, 163–165,
        169–173, 176–179
Consulting
    cases discussing, 31–34, 93–96,
        141–148, 169–173, 234–241
    conversations discussing, 65–75,
        75–80
Continental Plastics, 160–163
Corbet, Myra, 182–183
Coronado YERS Case, The, 93–96
Coswell, Tom, 155, 156
Cross-cultural issues
    cases discussing, 31–34, 101–103,
        234–241
    conversations discussing, 51–54,
        63–65, 65–75, 75–80,
        185–187
Cultural diversity
    cases discussing, 42–45, 45–46,
        101–103, 113–120
    conversations discussing, 51–54
Culture sensitivity, 59
Culture Shock: The Russian
    Entrepreneurial Revolution,
    46–49
Customer satisfaction, case discussing,
    205–207

Davis, George, 165–167
Davis, Joan, 163–165
Davis, John, 181–182
Davis, Jordan, 109–113
Davis, Paul, 187–189
Deakins, Harold, 28

Decision making
    cases discussing, 9–11, 105–107,
        108–109, 109–113, 113–120,
        150–153
    communication and, 58
    future trends in, 201
    self-managing teams involved in,
        199
Decisions, No Decisions, More
    Decisions, 109–113
Dennis, Mark, 109
Denton, Sandra, 214, 215
Dertouzos, Michael, 195
Describing Our Changing Culture,
    60–63
Dillard, James, 45, 46
Dillard Electronics, 141–148
Diversity. *See* Cultural diversity
"Do My Values Fit?" Case, The, 182–183
Donald, Jerry, 175–176
"Don't Rock the Boat Around Here"
    Case, The, 165–167
Dora Cartwright's Leadership
    Dilemma, 136–137
Douglas, Jean, 34–36
Downsizing
    cases discussing, 34–36, 155–157
    results of, 83, 85
    trends in, 199
Drake Computer Corporation—A
    Lesson in Designing an
    Organizational Culture, 37–40
Drake Industries, 210–214
Duke, Lynne, 45
Duncan, Dave, 161

Eastern Europe, 196
Educational Edge Lies in
    Telecommunications, The,
    256–258
Educational Revolution, The, 243–245
Effectiveness, cases discussing,
        120–133, 217–220, 220–224,
        224–228, 228–234
Elliot, Jim, 170, 171
Ellis, Jan, 105–107
Emergent Issues in Organizational
    Communication, 258–260
Entering the Profession: An Attorney
    Begins Her Career, 191–193

Entrepreneurial culture, case
    discussing, 46–49
Ethics
    cases discussing, 12–21, 93–96,
        169–173, 173–176, 176–179,
        179–181, 181–182, 182–183
    conversation discussing, 189–191
    of personal advantage, 86–87
Ettlie, J., 198–199
European Common Market, 55, 58
European Economic Community, 196

Fast-Track Executive, 179–181
Fiber Management Team, The,
    210–214
Findley, Dan, 38, 39
Fired for Bending the Rules, 189–191
Fisher, B. A., 4
Flynn, P., 199–200
Forbes, John, 107
Foster Retailers, 89
Frankel, Glenn, 148, 149
Frazier, Mike, 181
Future
    case discussing, 243–245, 245–247,
        247–248, 248–251, 251–253,
        256–258
    conversations discussing, 255–256,
        258–260

Gassee, Jean-Louis, 41
General systems theory, 5
Germany, 196
Gerstner, W. C., 23, 25
Getting Beyond Monologues: A
    Cross-Cultural Meeting of
    Organizational Consultants,
    65–75
Gilder, George, 197
Globalization, 196–198, 201
Gomez, Adelina M., 51
Granite City, 9–11
Grant, Charles, 89–92
Grant, Madeline, 163–165
Group processes, cases discussing,
    109–113, 113–120, 120–133,
    133–134, 150–153

Hackman, Michael, 185–187
Hansell, W., 85

Harmon, Julie, 75–78, 80, 235
Harris, LaDonna, 113–114
Harrison, J., 199
Haynes, Mark, 226–227
Henderson, Jim, 219
Herbert Walker Propulsion Center
    (HWPC), 217–219
Hertz, Linda, 120
Hewett, Don, 29, 31
Hewlett-Pakard Company, 120–133
Hillis, Bill, 95
Hitt, M., 199
Hockaday Engineering, 228–234
Hopper, Henry, 224–226
Hoskisson, R., 199
Hudson, Harvey, 150–152
Hudson Graphics, 150–152
Hudson Retail Supply, 247–250
Human relations approach, 4–5
Hunt, Richard, 203, 204

IBM and Apple: Contrasting Cultures
    Working Together, 40–42
Illinois Power and "60 Minutes":
    Communicating About the
    Communications, 21–31
Individual Contributor, The, 220–224
Individuals and Organizations in the
    Twenty-first Century: Changing
    Roles and Relationships, 251–253
Industrial Edge Lies in
    Telecommunications, The,
    255–256
Information heterarchies, 197
Information technology, 196–198
Innovation, cases discussing, 207–210,
    210–214, 224–228, 228–234,
    234–241
Institute for Industrial Reconstruction
    (IRI) Group, 31–33, 54–59, 66
Institute for Management Research
    and Development (IFAP),
    31–33, 54
Internal change, 57
International business
    cases discussing, 31–34, 46–49,
        54–59, 101–103, 234–241
    conversations discussing, 185–187
International Business Machines (IBM),
    40–42, 197

Interpretive-symbolic-culture
approach, 6
Intex, Dave, 158
Intex Advertising, 158–159
Italy
cases discussing, 31–34
conversations discussing, 54–59,
65–75
ITT, 224–228
"It Works So Well, Why Are We
Falling Apart?" Case, The,
207–210

Jablin, J. M., 4–6
Jackson, Jerry, 155, 156
James, Doug, 89–92
James, Sue, 220–224
Japan, 196
Jean Douglas—The Former Quality
Assurance Manager, 34–36
Jenkins, Connie, 66–74
Jenkins, Ruby, 207–209
Jobs, Stephen P., 41
Johnson, Lee, 142–148
Johnson, Merv, 100–101
Johnson, Neil, 255
Johnson, Tom, 155, 156
Joint Organizational Development
Visions and Ventures: Russian
and U.S. Collaboration,
234–241
Joint ventures
cases discussing, 40–42, 234–241
conversations discussing, 75–80
Jones-Belew Brokerage, 155–156
Jost, Jim, 120, 121

Karen Rhodes—On Becoming a
Manager, 98–100
Kay, Alan C., 243, 244
Kelley, Joan, 160–163
Kelley, Wendell, 25–28
Kerrs, Martin, 214–215
Kloth, Chris, 75–78, 80, 235,
236–237, 239–241
Kola, Andrea, 158
Koperski, Larry, 120
Korea, 196
Kourman, Jack, 158
Kozak, Bill, 179–181

Kramchentkova, Tanya, 66, 75–80,
235
Kreps, Gary L., 5–6, 258
Krone, K. J., 4–6

LaFasto, F., 83–84, 86
LaPalombara, Joseph, 32–34
Larson, C., 83–84, 86
Lea Pearlman's Ethical Dilemma,
169–173
Leaders
managers vs., 82–83
principled, 83–84
Leadership
cases discussing, 12–21, 97–98,
98–100, 105–107, 135–136,
136–137, 138–141, 141–148,
148–150, 158–159, 163–165,
176–179
characteristics of effective, 84
conversation discussing, 187–189
management and, 82–83
Leadership: Margaret Thatcher, the
Iron Lady, 148–150
Leadership Takes on a
Nonmanagement Look,
150–153
Lebedev, Sergei, 66, 75–80, 235
Life-long learning, 200–201
Living and Learning: A Professor Goes
Abroad, 185–187
Loewenwarter, Paul, 22, 24
Lukensmeyer, Carolyn, 76

McAllister, Rick, 101, 102
McCain, Barbara, 63, 138
Managers
change in responsibilities of, 84–85
leaders vs., 82–83
Managing Cultural Diversity, 45–46
Managing at Dillard Electronics,
141–148
Managing the Self-Management Team,
133–134
Managing Your Manager, 100–101
Manatel, George, 155, 156
Mannes, Tom, 218, 219
Manz, C., 84
Mark Waite's Disappointed Staff,
135–136

Mary Theresa, Sister, 12–16
Mechanistic approach, 3–4
Media relations, 21–31, 173–176
Mergers, case discussing, 12–21
Middlesex Insurance, 165–167
Middleton Association for Retarded
    Citizens (MARC), 138–141
Miller, Pam, 89, 91–92
Mills, Janice, 203–204
Minkin, James, 217, 219
Minorities in the Work Force: How
    Satisfied?, 51–54
Mitchell, Sarah, 222, 223
Mitchell, T. R., 86
Mitchell Laboratories, 214–216
Morgan, G., 85
Morris, Megan, 205
Morrison Manufacturing, 169
Morton, Janice, 109–112
Motivation, cases discussing, 37–40,
    155–157
Moving Toward the Year 2000—An
    Italian Perspective, 54–59
Moyer, Alan, 157
Mt. Mercy Hospital, 12–21
Multicultural organizations, 6–7
Multinational organizations, 6–7
Murphy, Linda, 158
My Japanese Counterparts, 101–103
My Style Is My Style: Like It or Leave
    Me Alone, 89–93

Nanus, Bert, 83
National Achievement Organization
    (NAO), 163–165
National Aerospace Propulsion Agency
    (NAPA), 217–219
National Aerospace Propulsion Agency
    Reorganization, The, 217–220
Native Americans, 113–120
New Communications Literacy, The,
    247–248
New Organizational Control: Knowledge
    Masters, The, 248–251
New Zealand, 185–187
Nichols, Chris, 170–173
Nighthorse, Charlie, 45, 46
Nighthorse, Joan, 142–144, 146, 148
Nissan, 59
Norton Industries, 220

Organizational change, 57
Organizational communication. *See
    also* Communication
    commentary on processes and
        behaviors of, 81–87
    emerging perspectives in, 6–7
    explanation of, 2–3
    future trends in, 201
    human relations approach to, 4–5
    interpretive-symbolic-culture
        approach to, 6
    mechanistic approach to, 3–4
    systems-interaction approach to,
        5–6
Organizational Communication: Italian
    Style, 31–34
Organizational culture
    cases discussing, 31–34, 34–36,
        37–40, 40–42, 101–103,
        141–148
    conversations discussing, 54–59,
        60–63
Organizational design, 198–199
Organizational Problems at a
    Community Nonprofit
    Organization, 138–141
Organizations
    cases discussing structures of,
        120–133, 133–134, 207–210,
        217–220, 228–234, 248–251
    changing imperatives for
        participants in, 85–86
    explanation of, 2
    middleless, 84–85
Organizing and Communicating:
    Changing Processes, 245–257
Overload or Innovation, 224–228

Parker, David, 38
Paulson, John, 164
Pearlman, Lea, 169–173
Perkins, Jane, 141–147
Personal advantage perspective, 86–87
Personnel decisions, cases discussing,
    135–136, 214–216
Peters, Tom, 196
Peytons, Roger, 9–11
Posa, Ernest, 80
Power, cases discussing, 100–101,
    176–179

Power of Empowerment: A Case
History of Organizational
Communications, The, 120–133
Principles leaders, 83–84
Proactive change, 57
Project management, cases discussing,
108–109, 109–113
Public administration, cases
discussing, 9–11, 93–96
Public figures, cases discussing,
136–137, 157–158, 173–176
Public relations, cases discussing,
21–31
Public Utilities of Akron, Virginia, 207
Putnam, L. L., 4–6

Quasi-causality, as assumption of
mechanistic approach, 4

The R & D Lab: Teams Making "Go"
or "No Go" Decisions,
108–109
Rames, Fred, 108, 109
Reams, Jean, 35
Reasoner, Harry, 23, 25, 26, 28
Reductionism, 4
Reengineering—A New Organization
for Hockaday, 228–234
Rees, Richard, 142–144, 146, 148
Rehm, Bob, 66, 75–78, 80, 235–239,
241
Reinfield, Deanna, 207–209
Reinsmith, Steven, 78
Remnick, David, 47, 48
Revolution at Intex, The, 158–159
Reynolds, Leon, 34, 36
Reynolds, Nikki, 101–102
Reynolds Toy Company, 34–36
Rhodes, Karen, 98–100
Rims, Margaret, 93–96
Rivers, Jack, 109, 112
Roberts, Hal, 218, 219
Ron Arnold's Job Crisis, 97–98
Roth Corbridge Advertising, 220–221
Rowe, Howard, 24–25
Russia
cases discussing, 46–49, 234–241
conversations discussing, 65–75,
75–80
impact of changes in, 196

Schiller, Jerry, 205
Science Is Not All That Objective: The
Mitchell Laboratories Case,
214–216
Scott, W. G., 86
Sculley, John, 41
Self-leaders
leading others to become, 84
need to become, 86
Sellers, Tom, 105–107
Severance Pay, 157–158
Shephard, Eddie, 158
Shockley-Zalabak, Pamela, 54–55,
66–74, 80
Simco, Martha, 138–141
Simmons, Mary, 214, 215
Simpson, Alice, 155, 156
Simpson, Mark, 158, 159
Sims, H., 84
Singapore
competition related to, 196
conversation discussing, 63–65
Singapore: Impressions of Cultural
Climate in a Distance Learning
Program, 63–65
Singer, Helen, 108, 109
Smith, Alan, 219
Smith, Zalda, 95
Soviet Union, former. *See* Russia
Spain, 196
Standard, John, 165–167
Stein, Don, 155, 156
Sterligov, German, 46–47
Strategic planning, cases discussing,
105–107, 113–120
Styles, cases discussing, 89–93,
98–100, 100–101, 101–103,
148–150
Sullivan, Evelyn Hernandez, 191–193
Sutters, David, 170
Svinarenko, Igor, 48
Synchronous innovation, 198–199
Systems Computers, Inc., 45–46
Systems-interaction approach, 5–6

Taiwan, 196
Tandem Industries: Managing by
Electronic Adhocracy,
203–205
Tarasov, Artyom, 48

Technology
  cases discussing, 203–205, 205–207,
    207–210, 210–214, 214–216,
    247–248, 251–253
  risk involved in innovative,
    199–200
Telecommunications
  educational edge and, 256–258
  industrial edge and, 255–256
Thatcher, Margaret, 148–149
There Is Life After Management,
    187–189
Through Their Eyes: Russian
    Reflections on the U.S.
    Organizational Development
    Community, 75–80
To Manage, Value, or Do What with
    Diversity?, 42–45
Toffler, Alvin, 196, 199, 200, 248
"Too Little, Too Late" Case, The,
    163–165
Training
  cases discussing, 31–34, 42–45,
    160–163, 228–234
  future trends in, 200–201
Transitivity of communication
    functions, as assumption of
    mechanistic approach, 4
Tribal Issue Management (TIM)
    Forums, 114–120
Turner, Neva, 173–175

Uniresource, Inc., 221–222
U.S. Senator Williams and the Austin
    Manpower Administration,
    173–176
U.S. West Communications, 45

Video literacy
  cases discussing, 210–214, 247–248
  conversation discussing, 256–258
Vision, 83

Waite, Mark, 135–136
Walker, Kim B., 21–22
Wallace, Dick, 169–173
Wallace, Jim, 109, 111
Wallenstein, G., 198
Walsh, Joyce, 164, 165
Walsh, Ralph, 93–94
Walsh, Ruth, 93–94, 96
Watson, Thomas J., Sr., 41
Weinstein, Shelley, 256
Weisbord, Marvin, 80
Weiser, Mark, 245
"We Intended No Harm" Case, The,
    181–182
"What Do You Mean We Have to
    Retrain?" Case, The, 160–163
Wilcox, Lola, 80
Williams, Jim, 173–175
Williams, Joan, 109–113
Williams, Mary, 173–175
Willis, Chet, 38, 39
Wilson, Jim, 176–178
Winograd, Gaynelle, 65–75, 80, 234
Wisdom of "The People," The,
    113–120
Wright, Debra, 157
Wright, Morris, 173, 174

Yakovlev, Vladimir, 48
YERS, 93–96

Zaleznik, A., 82–83